a Yachting Monthly pilot

East Coast Rivers

From Southwold to the Swale

JACK H. COOTE

First edition, 1956; Second edition, 1957; Third edition 1961;
Fourth edition (revised), 1965; Fifth edition (revised), 1967;
Sixth edition (revised), 1970; Reprinted, 1971;
Seventh edition (revised), 1974; Reprinted, 1974;
Eighth edition (IALA revision), 1977; Ninth edition, 1979;
Tenth edition (revised), 1981; Eleventh edition (new charts), 1983;
Twelfth edition (revised), 1985; Thirteenth edition (Navaid Review), 1988;
Thirteenth edition (revised), 1989

Published by

YACHTING
MONTHLY

IPC Magazines Ltd, King's Reach Tower,
Stamford Street, London SE1 9LS. 1989
ISBN 85037-609-2

Cover
Main picture: Sunrise at Maldon.
Aerial picture: the Tide Mill, Woodbridge.

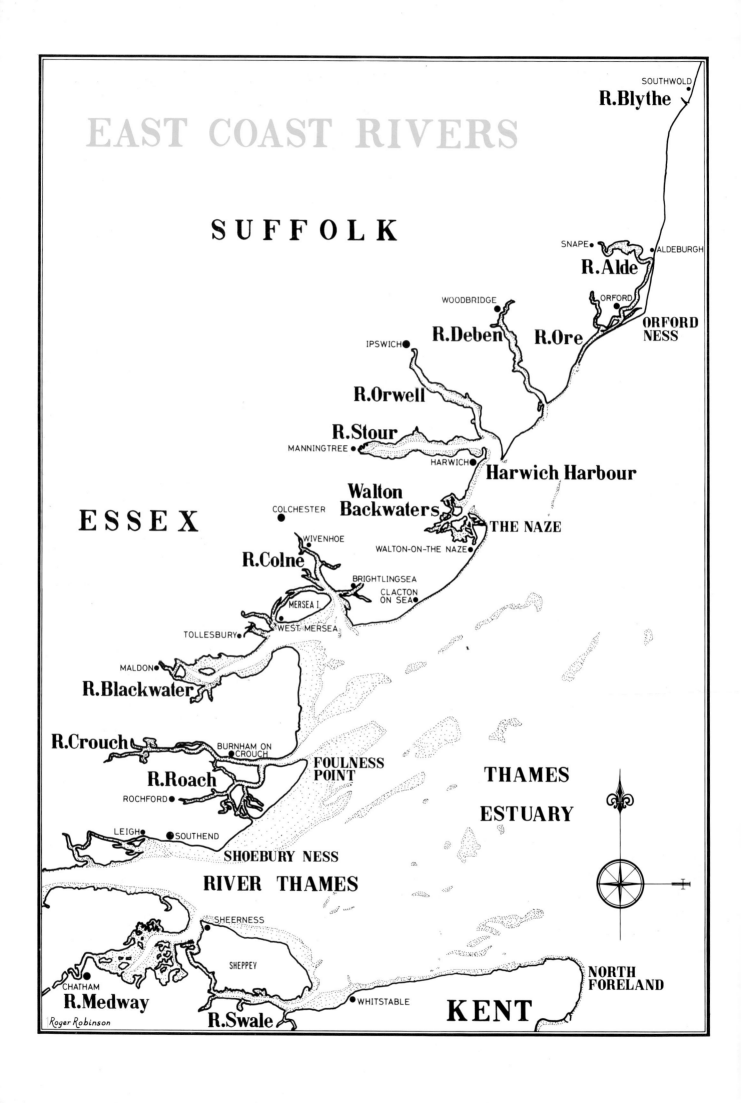

EAST COAST RIVERS
CORRECTIONS to 30 April 2002

page   *port/area and correction*

10   ORFORDNESS to LOWESTOFT Chart
    Aldeburgh Ridge buoy is lit *Q.R*
    NE Whiting buoy is lit *Q(3)10s*
    SW Whiting buoy is lit *Q(6)+L.Fl.15s*
    N Shipwash buoy is lit *Q*

17   SOUTHWOLD
    LH Col, para 6 – Maxine Awles took over in 2001 from Ken Howells as Southwold harbourmaster.
    Email address for the boatyard, Harbour Marine Services, is now info@harbourmarine.uk.com
    During summer months EC Wed does not happen in Southwold.

18   R BLYTH Chart
    Southwold light range is now *16/12M*

21   R ORE Chart
    Orford Haven buoy is lit *L.Fl.10s*

22   ORFORD
    LH Col, line 11 – Alde & Ore Association Guidelines no longer available by post from Hill House, Snape. Now distributed by the chart agents, Small Craft Deliveries, 12 Quay Street, Woodbridge Telephone 01394 382655. Email sales@scd-charts.co.uk Or www.scd-charts.co.uk

26   R ALDE Chart
    Orford Ness light range is *13m 17/12M*

31   R DEBEN Chart
    Woodbridge Haven Entrance in May 2002 has slightly less water than shown.
    A sketch chart based on 2002 survey carried out by Harbourmaster John White is available from Small Craft Deliveries, Woodbridge – details as above. Or contact John White or his assistant Duncan Read, see p.31 for Tel No, for up to date information.
    Woodbridge Haven buoy is lit *Mo(A) 15s*

37   WOODBRIDGE Tide Mill Yacht Harbour
    LH column line 13, high water at Woodbridge varies between 30 and 50 minutes later than Felixstowe Ferry. Data on the sill should read as follows: The yacht harbour has a sill over which there is 1.6m at MHWN and 2.5m at MHWS.

38   THE WALLET and Harwich aproaches Chart
    Orford Haven buoy is lit *L.Fl.10s*
    Woodbridge Haven buoy is lit *Mo(A)15s*
    Cutler buoy is lit *Q.G*
    Wadgate Ledge beacon is lit *Fl(4)G*
    Pye End buoy is lit *L.Fl.10s*
    Cork Sand beacon is lit *VQ.2M*
    Roughs Shoal buoy is lit *Q(9)15s*
    Roughs Tower buoy is lit *Q(3)10s*
    S Cork buoy is lit *Q(6)+L.Fl.15s*
    Medusa buoy is lit *Fl.G.5s*
    NE Gunfleet buoy is lit *Q(3)10s*
    Wallet No2 buoy is lit *Fl.R.5s*
    Wallet No4 buoy is lit *Fl(4)R.10s*
    Gunfleet Spit is lit *Q(6)+L.Fl.15s*
    N Eagle buoy is lit *Q*
    Eagle buoy is lit *Q.G*
    Knoll buoy is lit *Q*
    W Sunk buoy is lit Q(9)15s
    Black Deep No1 buoy is lit *Fl.G.5s*
    Wallet Spitway buoy is lit *L.Fl.10s Bell*
    Swin Spitway buoy is lit *Iso.10s Bell*
    Barrow Deep No 3 is lit *Q(3)10s Bell*
    Barrow Deep No 2 buoy is lit *Fl(2)R5s.*

40   HARWICH HARBOUR Chart
    Shotley Spit buoy is lit *Q(6)+L.Fl.15s*
    Fort buoy is lit *Fl(4)G.15s*
    NW Beach buoy is lit *Fl(3)G.10s*
    No7 buoy is lit *Fl(3)Y.7s*

41   Port Guide
    Water taxi service now operated by David Baines Tel: 07970 115382 (mobile).
    Harwich Haven Authority email: harbour.house@hha.co.uk www.hha.co.uk

44	R ORWELL Chart

44   R ORWELL Chart
        Delete yellow buoy in R Stour between Parkeston and Bristol buoys

52   R ORWELL Ipswich Port Guide
        VHF Ipswich Port Radio now Ch 68 and Neptune Marine call on VHF Ch 80 or 37.

55   R STOUR Chart
        Top chart   delete Yellow buoy just W of No 1 buoy
                         Pepys buoy is lit *Fl(4)R.15s*
        Bottom chart   Ballast Hill buoy amend the light characteristic to *Q* and the flash colour to white
                         Delete yellow buoy just W of No 6 buoy
                         Delete yellow buoy just W of The Horse buoy

57   WALTON BACKWATERS Chart
                 Pye End buoy is lit *L.Fl.10s*
                 Crab Knoll buoy is lit *Fl(2)G.10s*
                 East Coast Sails buoy is lit *Fl.G.5s*
                 Stone Creek buoy is lit *Fl.G.5s*

62   WALTON BACKWATERS Oakley Creek
        Text line 3 should read: ...spit off the west side of the entrance is marked by an E cardinal buoy.

63   R COLNE Chart
        No 12 buoy is lit *QR*
        Colne Point No 1 buoy is lit *Fl.G.3s*

72   R BLACKWATER Chart
        Thirslet Spit buoy *Fl(3)G.10s* should have a green conical topmark

76   R BLACKWATER Chart contd
        Hilly Pool buoy is lit *Fl(2)R.5s*

82   RAY SAND AND SPITWAY CHANNELS Chart
        Colne Pt No 1 buoy is lit *Fl.G.3s*
        Bench Head buoy is lit *Fl(3)G.10s*
        N Eagle buoy is lit *Q*

100   R THAMES SEA REACH Chart
        Delete Chain Rk buoy (LH edge)
        Garrison Pt light beacon characteristic should read *2 F.R (vert) Horn (3)30s*

106   R THAMES, Haven to Crayford Ness Chart
        Delete Green, white and red light symbol due S of Broadness light
        Delete red light symbol due S of Lower Hope buoy
        W Blyth buoy – amend the light characteristic to *Fl(4)R15s* and the flash colour to red

106   R THAMES, Crayford Ness to London Bridge Chart
        Amend Crayford Ness light characteristic to *Fl.5s.14M & F.3M*

118   R MEDWAY, Sheerness to Folly Pt Chart
        Port hand marker buoy due N of Swale Ness is lit *QR*

122   R MEDWAY, Folly Pt to Rochester Bridge Chart
        No 29 buoy is lit *Fl(3)G.10s*
        No 27 buoy is lit *Q.G*

120   MEDWAY Queenborough Port Guide
        VHF Call Ch for Harbourmaster and Trot boat is Ch 8. Not 74 as stated.
        Owing to staff shortages (May 2002) weekend trot boat only operating until 5pm.

126   MEDWAY Chatham and Rochester Port Guide
        No longer possible to land at Sun Pier.
        Chandler has closed down.
        Fuel barge no longer exists.
        Landing may be possible at port authority floating pier to W of Chatham YC, leave dinghies clear of pontoon front.

132   THE SWALE Chart
        Whitstable Street buoy is lit *Q*

133   SWALE Conyer Creek
        Add note: On E bank of creek a little upstream of Butterfly Wharf lie the remains of two spritsail barges (hulked 1948). Beware, as the sides have collapsed down side of creek bank, with ironwork projecting.

136   THAMES ESTUARY Routes Chart
        Little Sunk Beacon disappeared sometime during early summer of 2001. Not known whether it will be replaced.
        (bottom edge) Hook Spit buoy is lit *QG*
        S Margate buoy is lit *Fl.G.2·5s*

East Coast Rivers

The following short extract from the earliest sailing directions for the coasts of England, written in the time of Edward IV, shows that the inshore passage along the Essex coast remains much the same after five hundred years:

'From Orfordness to Orwell wanes (shallows) the course is south-west, and it (the tide) floweth south-south-east, and in Orwell Haven within the weirs south and north; and if ye go out of Orwell wanes to the Naze ye must go south-west. From the Naze to the marks of the Spits (Spitway) your course is west-south-west, and it (the tide) floweth south and by east. Bring your marks together that the parish steeple be out (clear) by east the abbey of St Osyth, then go your course on the Spits south till ye come to 10 fathoms or 12, then go your course with the Horseshoe (Shoe Spit).'

Contents

The East Coast Rivers

THE rivers and creeks, channels, guts and swatchways of the Kent, Essex and Suffolk coasts have an ancient charm and character quite unlike anywhere else. The labyrinth of offshore banks so menacing to the eyes of deep water sailors are a shelter to those who know them and the wandering creeks offer an endless choice of anchorage.

The revised edition of *East Coast Rivers* with its corrected charts and up-to-date photographs, some aerial, also includes a four language glossary of pilotage terms and a tidal atlas and constants. An annual correction service to help keep this pilot book up-to-date is offered, between editions.

The Author: Jack Coote began his sailing career on the Regent's Park lake and proceeded via the Norfolk Broads to a lifetime of cruising and exploration on the Southeast Coast. His first boat, a Broads sloop with a lifting cabin top, soon taught him that the steep seas of wind-against-current in the Thames Estuary demanded something more seaworthy and this led to *Iwunda* a 34ft centreboarder. With his wife and two daughters, both now married and one of them, Janet, a trained photographer like himself, his cruising inspired a series of articles in *Yachting Monthly* which were to be the nucleus of *East Coast Rivers*.

Other boats followed and the constant task of revising the book and gathering information from his network of helpers has never ceased.

Amendment service

Like charts, pilot books need revision at intervals. During the life of an edition therefore the author will provide correction data on request. Issued annually on or after the 1st of May following the publication of this current edition data sheet(s) may be obtained by writing to: J. H. Coote, The Towans, Hall Road, Rochford, Essex, enclosing a cheque or PO for £1.00 and a large self-addressed and stamped return envelope.

Introduction

Revised Thirteenth Edition

It might have been expected that the many changes brought about by the 1987 Navaid Review would have sufficed for a few years but, in the relatively short period during which the 13th edition of *East Coast Rivers* was in print, a significant number of further changes took place in the rivers and creeks of the Thames Estuary.

The principal changes will be found in the River Crouch, which is now marked by no less than twenty-four light buoys; and in the entrance to the Thames, where Trinity House has dispensed with a further six buoys. Many other more minor alterations have been made to both text and charts to keep the book as up to date as possible.

Jack H Coote   October 1989

Navaid Review

It is particularly fortunate that the need for this new edition should come at this time because in August, 1987, Trinity House published the *Navaid Review* by which they announced their intention to change or remove many of the buoys and other aids to navigation around the coasts of England and Wales.

The fifty or so proposed changes in the Thames Estuary and its approaches were scheduled to be made during the month of April, 1988, and thus it was possible to alter the text and charts accordingly before this edition was published.

In addition to the changes within the areas for which they will remain responsible, Trinity House wish to shed their responsibility for buoying and marking many harbours and rivers — handing those responsibilities over to various local authorities. This in turn could result in changes or reductions in the numbers of inshore marks maintained in future.

Cross Estuary Routes

For the past several editions I have included some suggestions for routes by which the Thames Estuary might be crossed between Essex and Kent. I was, and still am, keenly aware of the danger of seeming to encourage insufficiently experienced yachtsmen to set off across the shoals of the Thames delta without fully understanding the risks involved. It seems to me that as time goes by, yachtsmen will have to become increasingly self-dependent in matters of navigation, as organisations like Trinity House and the Port of London Authority (which surveys the Thames Estuary) are forced to reduce the scale of their activities (the *Navaid Review* is one example) by eliminating any marks and surveys that are not commercially necessary.

All of this means that even when equipped with the latest charts, a yachtsman must recognise that the soundings shown in a particular swatchway may well have changed since the time of the last survey. Therefore fair weather, a reliable echo-sounder, and a rising tide are more than ever essential for a safe crossing of the Estuary.

Waypoints

Increasing use of the Decca Navigator system makes it opportune to include some useful waypoints in this edition. The new information is at the head of each section, together with numbers of recommended charts.

Acknowledgements

As the editions go by I become indebted to more and more people who take an interest in *East Coast Rivers* and are willing to help me and their fellow yachtsmen by providing up-to-date local information. By now they are so numerous that I cannot refer to them all by name, but I am grateful to every one of them.

However, there are a few people who I feel I must mention. Derek Weston of Hoo regularly keeps me up-to-date with happenings on the Medway, while Graeme Wright tells me what is new in the Walton Backwaters. Ralph Rogers, in his barge yacht *Nancy Grey,* helped me by covering the Medway for the very first edition of *East Coast Rivers* and now has helped me again by reporting on a cruise he made last summer in *Pylstaart,* his 27ft Pintail.

Norman Wynn, a shipmate of mine from the days of *Iwunda,* frequently uses his fast boat *White Dolphin* to get me anywhere I need to take photographs or soundings. Furthermore, for this edition, Norman undertook to revise and rearrange the tidal data on page 97, a job that I have shied at doing for several years.

Jack H Coote, 1988

Important Notes

Buoyage

The IALA Buoyage System 'A' was established in the areas covered by this book in 1977.

'System "A" retains simplified *Lateral* marks to define the limits of channels inshore, but provides *Cardinal* marks to augment, if necessary, the Lateral marks; and to obviate the use of middle ground and secondary channel marks.

It should be noted that the general direction of Lateral buoyage in the area west of a line between Orford Ness and North Foreland is considered to be towards the south-west — in other words in the same direction as the flooding tide.

Lateral Marks

Lateral marks are used for well defined channels and they indicate the port and starboard hands of the route to be followed.

A *port hand* mark is coloured *red* and its basic shape is *can* for either buoy or topmark or both.

A *starboard hand* mark is normally coloured *green* and its basic shape is *conical* for either buoy or topmark (point-up) or both. (Sometimes it will be permissible to use black instead of green to enhance visibility.) By night a *port hand* buoy is identifiable by its *red light* and a *starboard hand* by its *green* light.

(The West Swin channel, for example, is now marked

by a series of red can (port hand) and green conical (starboard hand) buoys.)

Cardinal Marks

Cardinal marks are used in conjunction with the compass to indicate where there is best water. A cardinal mark is placed in one of the quadrants — N, E, S and W — and takes its name from the quadrant in which it is placed. It is safe to pass north of a N cardinal mark, east of an E cardinal mark, south of a S cardinal mark and west of a W cardinal mark.

The shape of a cardinal mark is not significant although in the case of a buoy it will be a pillar or a spar; but its *black double-cone topmark* is the most important feature.

The cone topmarks should be remembered:

North . . Points up
South . . Points down
East . . Points outwards
West . . Points inwards (wineglass)

Cardinal marks are used to indicate the safe side on which to pass a danger or to draw attention to a feature in a channel such as a bend or junction or the end of a shoal.

(The Sunken Buxey shoal in the entrance to the river Crouch is marked with a N cardinal buoy.)

Cardinal marks are coloured *black and yellow* and when lit, display a series of *quick* or *very quick white flashes*.

Other Types of Mark

There are three other categories of marks that can be used in System 'A'. They are: Isolated Danger Marks, Safe Water Marks and Special Marks.

A *black double sphere* topmark is the most important feature of an *isolated danger mark* which will have *red and black horizontal stripes* and can be erected on or moored on or above an isolated danger of limited extent such as a shoal or a rock well offshore. (The Whitaker beacon is an example.)

A *Safe Water mark* will be painted with *red and white vertical stripes* and have a *single red spherical topmark*. It can be used to indicate mid-channel or as a landfall buoy. The Medway No. 1 buoy is an example.

Finally, there is sometimes the need for Special marks to indicate traffic separation, spoilground, a lightship watch buoy as well as cable or pipeline marks including outfalls. A Special mark will be *yellow* and will usually have a single *yellow cross* (X) as a topmark. Sea Reach No. 1 buoy (Spher. Y) marking the entrance to the Yantlet dredged channel is a Special mark. Whenever a light is shown from a Special buoy it is *yellow*.

Chart datum
Lowest Astronomical Tide (LAT)

Although it has the effect of indicating that some creeks, swatchways and anchorages sometimes dry out, when many of us have never seen them without water, adoption of the lowest astronomically predicted tides (LAT) as the datum for this book has been deemed necessary in order to be in accord with Admiralty charts.

Abbreviations

The abbreviations employed for indication of the shape, colour and light characteristics of buoys and marks are as follows:

Can	. .	can shaped
Con	. .	conical shaped
Sph	. .	spherical shaped
R	. .	red
G	. .	green
Y	. .	yellow
B	. .	black
R W	. .	red and white
B Y	. .	black and yellow
B R	. .	black and red
V S	. .	vertical stripes
H S	. .	horizontal stripes
Lt (or L)	. .	light — white unless otherwise qualified (eg, Lt R — red light
F R	. .	fixed red light
F G	. .	fixed green light
Fl R	. .	flashing red light
Fl G	. .	flashing green light
Fl Y	. .	flashing yellow light
Oc R	. .	red light occulting
Oc G	. .	green light occulting
Fl (number)	. .	light showing given number of flashes as a group
Q	. .	light showing group of quick flashes (50−60 per min)
V Q	. .	light showing group of very quick flashes (100−120 per min)
L Fl	. .	light showing long flash of not less than 2 sec
s	. .	replaces abbreviation 'sec'
Iso	. .	light showing equal light and dark phases

Charts

All the charts have been specially drawn in the belief that a good deal of useful information and anticipatory pleasure can be obtained from the study of them before the commencement of a passage or a cruise.

Wherever Admiralty charts are available to cover the area required, it is strongly recommended that up-dated copies of these should be used in conjunction with the charts in this book.

Bearings

The bearings given throughout the book are magnetic and the variation in the area of the Thames Estuary is approximately 5 degrees W (1988), decreasing by about 8 minutes annually.

Tides

Although there are times when tides, as Para Handy said, 'is chust a mystery', they do follow patterns that are useful to know.

Spring tides occur a day or so after both new and full moon — hence the term High Water Full and Change (H W F C).

Neap tides occur midway between each spring tide.

Remember there is always more water at low water neaps than at low water springs.

The time of High Water at any given place is approximately 50 minutes later each day.

All tidal information is approximate, so allow a safety margin whenever possible. Watch the barometric pressure — a change of one inch in pressure can make a difference of a foot in the level of water.

The level of water does not rise and fall at a constant rate during the flood or ebb tide. The amount by which a tide will rise or fall in a given time from Low or High Water can be estimated approximately by the 'Twelfths' rule, which can be simply indicated as follows:

Rise or fall during 1st hour ....1/12 of range
,, ,, ,, ,, 2nd ,, ...2/12 ,, ,,
,, ,, ,, ,, 3rd ,, ...3/12 ,, ,,
,, ,, ,, ,, 4th ,, ...3/12 ,, ,,
,, ,, ,, ,, 5th ,, ...2/12 ,, ,,
,, ,, ,, ,, 6th ,, ...1/12 ,, ,,

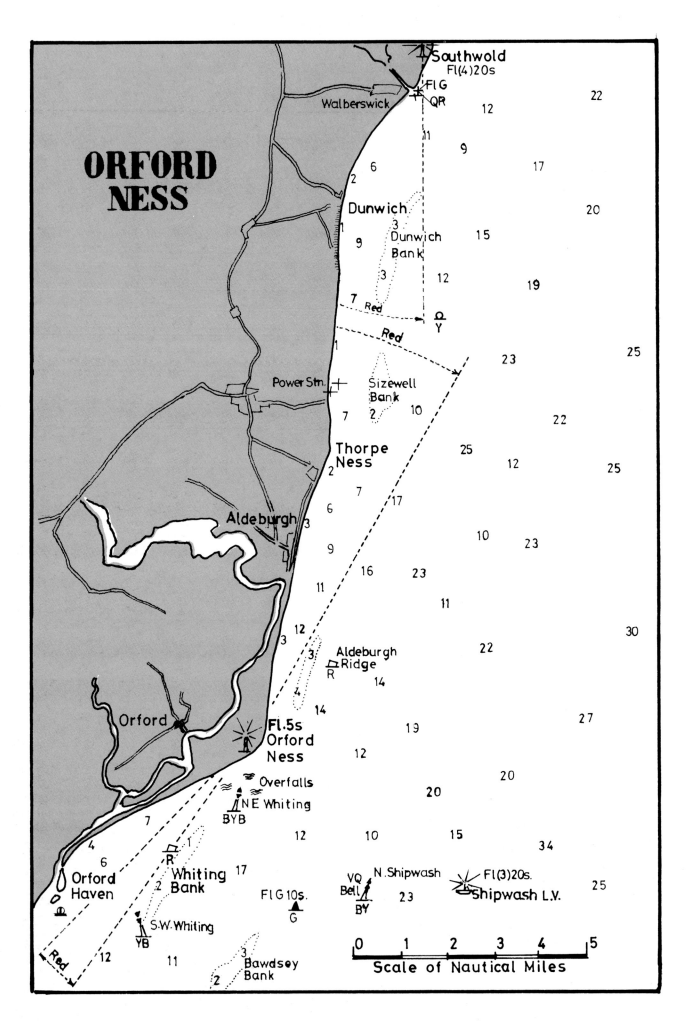

ORFORD NESS

Southwold
Fl(4)20s

Walberswick

FlG
QR

12   22

11

9

6   17

2

Dunwich   20

3   15

9   Dunwich
Bank

3   19

12

7   Red

Red   Ω
Y   25

1   23

Power Stn.   Sizewell
Bank

7   2   10   22

Thorpe   25   25
Ness   12

7   17

6   10   23

Aldeburgh   9

3   16   23

11   11

12   22   30

3   12

3   Aldeburgh
Ridge

4   R   14

14

Orford   19   27

Fl.5s
Orford   12
Ness

20

Overfalls   20

NE Whiting   15
BYB

7   12   10   15   34

4   R   VQ   N.Shipwash   Fl(3)20s.
Bell   Shipwash L.V.
6   Whiting   17   BY   25
Bank   23
2

FlG 10s.

S.W. Whiting
YB   G

Orford
Haven

Red   12   11   3   Bawdsey
Bank
2

0	1	2	3	4	5

Scale of Nautical Miles

1
Southwold

Tides

HW Dover — 1.05 Range: MHWS 2.6m MHWN 2.1m

Charts

Admiralty 1543
Stanford No. 3
Imray C28

Waypoint

Orford Ness Lighthouse 52.05.00N 1.34.55.E.

Hazards

Entrance. Not to be attempted in strong onshore winds.

ROWLAND PARKER, in his book *Men of Dunwich*, tells how — 'On the Night after New Year's Day' in 1286, 'through the Vehemence of the Winds and Violence of the Sea' the river Blyth found its way directly out to sea between Walberswick and Southwold rather than through the port of Dunwich. The men of Dunwich did in fact manage to stop up the gap for a few years after, but on the afternoon of 14th January 1328, a NE'ly gale again coincided with the high tides of the month and the town of Dunwich was devastated; this time beyond any hope of recovery. From that time Southwold has been a port; at first for trading and fishing but in recent years simply as a pleasant haven for cruising yachts from both sides of the southern North Sea. More than a thousand yachts called in during 1987.

Southwold harbour is about as far north of Orfordness, as Landguard Point is south of it — roughly 15 miles. There are several shoals lying a mile or so offshore between Orford Haven and Southwold. The largest of them, the Whiting Bank, is guarded at its northern end by an E Cardinal buoy and at its southern end by a S Cardinal buoy, while the red can, Whiting Hook buoy, marks the western edge of the shoal. All three buoys are unlit.

A solitary unlit red can buoy marks the eastern side of the Aldeburgh Ridge which lies about a mile offshore but has six to eight metres on its western side, very close to the shingle shore of the Ness itself. The only snag when taking this inshore course round Orfordness is that overfalls occur on the ebb.

There is one other shallow patch, the Sizewell Bank, about a mile offshore opposite the atomic power station, but this unmarked patch has some three metres over it at LWS.

It should be noted that the direction of buoyage changes to the N of Orfordness.

There is a lighthouse — Fl (4) WR — situated in the town of Southwold about a mile to the north of the harbour.

Since entry to Southwold harbour should be made on the flood (the ebb runs out at anything up to 6 knots), it will often pay when coming from the south, to use the north-going ebb and then wait off the harbour entrance for a while, either by heaving-to or lying to an anchor about a quarter of a mile S of the pierheads if the wind is light and offshore.

The best time to go in is during the second half of the flood, but whenever there is a strong wind from any direction between NE and SE, the entrance can be dangerous and certainly *must not be attempted if a red flag is flying by day or three vertical flashing red lights are shown by night.*

A flashing green light is shown from the N pier and a flashing red from the S pier.

The harbour master, Tony Chambers, is concerned that Southwold has a bad reputation with yachtsmen because of its difficult entrance. He is anxious to dispel this impression, and offers to provide up-to-date information by telephone — 0502 724712 (office), 724772 (home) — or on VHF Ch12. He is also willing to come out in his launch, — *Northern Lights* — to guide yachts in if necessary.

Generally, during the summer months, the harbour master reckons that the best way in is in line with the piers from about 300 metres off.

Once inside the pierheads, steer for a pile structure at the inshore end of the north pier. This staging is known as the 'Knuckle' and is marked by a beacon bearing two vertical green lights. When abreast of the Knuckle,

Visitors' berths alongside stagings will be found on the N bank of the river above the lifeboat slip and close to the 'Harbour Inn' *Janet Harber*

change course immediately to pass close along the dock wall, to avoid a shoal patch extending from the south bank. At the end of the wall, move to the centre of the channel again and continue midway between the stagings on both sides.

A wooden staging is reserved for visiting yachtsmen, and this will be found about a quarter of a mile beyond the ferry, on the north bank, just by the *Harbour Inn*.

The harbourmaster's office is on the caravan park, although it will eventually be relocated next to the Lifeboat shed.

Facilities at Southwold	
Water	Near visitors' berth.
Stores	Basic requirements from chandler, otherwise from Southwold (½ mile) EC Wed
Repairs	No repair services but slip and 10 ton crane available.
Fuel	Petrol and diesel from chandlery near lifeboat house.
Transport	Railway station at Halesworth, reached by taxi or bus from Southwold, or Darsham, by taxi from Walberswick. Bus to Lowestoft.
Telephone	At chandlers and near N pier.
Club	Southwold Sailing Club.

VHF Ch. 12, for the Harbour Master or Pilot.

In the summer a ferryman still plies between the Walberswick and Southwold shores
Janet Harber

Walberswick

Although most yachtsmen land on the N side of the harbour and visit Southwold, Walberswick too is a charming little place, that has attracted artists ever since the days of Charles Keene and Wilson Steer at the end of the last century.

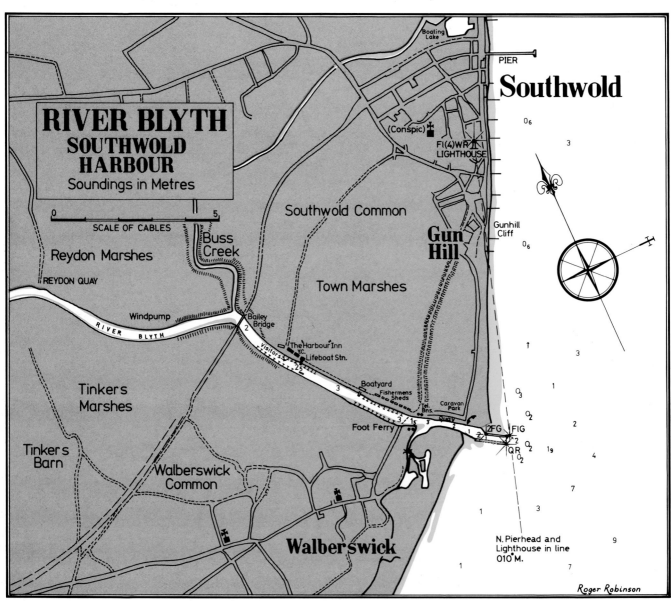

2
Orford River

Tides (at entrance)

HW Dover +0.10 Range: Springs 3.0m Neaps 2.7m

Charts

Admiralty 2693
Stanford No. 6
Imray C28

Waypoint

Orford Haven Buoy (1988) 52.01.70.N. 1.27.65.E

Hazards

Shoals and strong tides in entrance (Seek up-to-date information from Aldeburgh YC). Shoal just inside entrance.

THERE is a graphic description of his crossing the bar into the Orford river by Hilaire Belloc in his book *On Sailing the Sea*; but on second thoughts it might be better to defer reading it until after one's first entry.

Although given the dual names, the Ore and the Alde are merely different parts of a single river; the Ore being that part between the entrance (Orford Haven) and Randalls Point (between Orford and Slaughden Quay) while the Alde is the river thereon up to its navigable limit at Snape Bridge, a distance of about 16 miles.

As with the River Deben, the Ore reaches the sea through a narrow shingle banked outlet, and as a result there is a shingle bar and several drying and shifting shingle banks or 'knolls' in the entrance. The bar and the knolls, and the fact that the tides run in and out of the river very strongly indeed, combine to make Orford Haven rather more difficult to enter than the Deben, because there is no pilot on hand and only one leading mark compared with the two metes at Felixstowe Ferry.

The beacon (orange and white post with orange diamond shaped topmark) was erected by Trinity House in 1975 and has not been moved since, even though the shoal off N Wier Point has extended to the SW.

Their reasons for establishing a single beacon in a fixed position, to be used in conjunction with a buoy that will be moved to indicate the seaward end of a leading line, have been given by Trinity House. They say: *'without any local shore support or assistance, there is little more we can do in relation to any second beacon to provide a variable transit situation, which would, if not dealt with positively and responsibly, be a contributory cause of disaster to the small craft user.'*

Orford Haven

Orford Haven lies at the southern end of Hollesley Bay, some four or five miles N of the entrance to the Deben, but it is not easy to locate the actual entrance.

The only helpful landmarks are a Martello Tower about a mile SW of the entrance proper and a few houses in two small rows just N of the tower.

The offing buoy ('Orford Haven' Sph RWVS) is in about 6m of water at LWS and situated approximately half a mile E of the cottages at Shingle Street.

When attempting an entry unaided, it is important to stay well offshore until this safewater offing buoy is found. It must also be realised that the knolls and therefore the way in frequently change and it must not be assumed that it is safe to follow a direct course between the offing buoy and the beacon. Local knowledge should be sought if a winter has passed since the previous visit.

Any intending visitor should get hold of a copy of the annual sketch chart of the entrance that is prepared by the Aldeburgh YC in April or May.

This aerial photograph, taken at LWS during April 1988, shows why entry to the River Ore must never be attempted at low tide

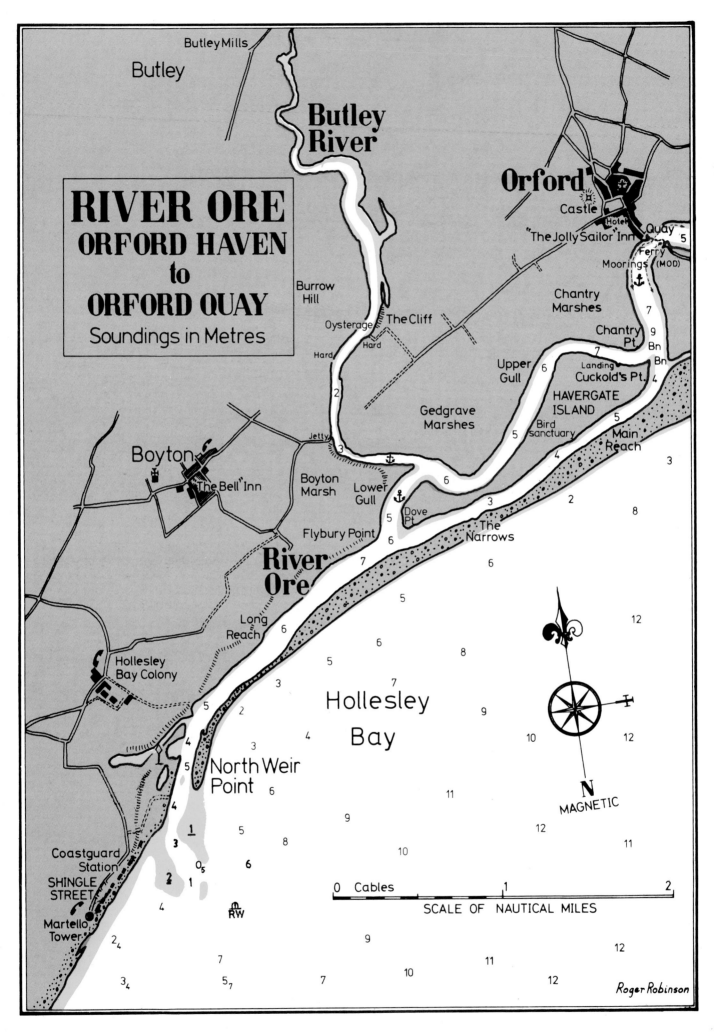

RIVER ORE
ORFORD HAVEN
to
ORFORD QUAY
Soundings in Metres

Roger Robinson

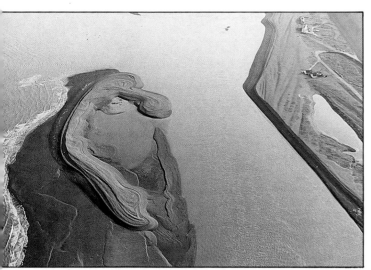

Remarkable shingle knolls often form in the entrance to the Ore. This one, off the end of north Weir point, existed in 1988

Trinity House move this offing buoy from time to time, so it is important to check its latest position

Janet Harber

The suggested directions provided by the AYC in the spring of 1989 were:

From a position some 2½ cables SW of the present location of the buoy (which is 52.01.08N; 1.28.00E) proceed on a course with the beacon in line with a chimney that is grey with a black top, bearing 002° T and about a mile N of the beacon. When the flagstaff and radio mast near the coastguard cottage bear about 285° T, alter course NW towards a bungalow and, when about 100 metres off the shingle bank abreast the bungalow, alter course to the NNE and into the river.

When abreast N Weir Point, keep over to the E side to avoid a drying patch in mid-river. When a cable beyond the notice board on N Weir Point, return to mid-channel.

(NB: These directions may not prove reliable in 1990.)

The River Ore

Within the entrance the tidal streams run very strongly indeed; probably up to 4 knots on the flood and as much as 6 knots during the latter half of a spring ebb. Because of this, entry against the ebb is virtually impossible, while departure on the ebb is certainly inadvisable.

Probably the best time to enter the river is about 2hrs to 2½hrs after LW, when there should be more than 2 metres over the bar and the worst of the shingle banks will still be uncovered.

While waiting for the flood a safe anchorage may be found inshore just S of the Martello Tower at Shingle Street, provided the wind is somewhere between SW and N.

Given sufficient power (not less than 5 knots), it is safest to leave the river on the early flood, when the tide outside will assist any boat bound south.

Both the flood stream and the ebb continue to run into and out of the river for an hour after the change in Hollesley Bay.

The Entrance

At LW there is little more than 100m between North Wier Point and the west side of the entrance, which makes it difficult to distinguish the way in from any distance off. But when entering on the flood, a boat will tend to be caught by the strong tidal stream and be carried into the river.

Long Reach

From the entrance to Dove Point, two miles to the NE, the river is little more than 100m wide and runs between a featureless steep-to shingle bank to the SE and a somewhat shallow shingle and mud shore backed by a sea wall to the NW. This part of the Ore is known as Long Reach, and there is an average of 6m all along it, although because the tides are so fierce and the holding in shingly mud is not very good, it is not advisable, except in emergency, to bring up below Dove Point.

At Dove Point the river divides around Havergate Island, one part running along the south and the other along the north side of this narrow island. There is a fairly extensive mud spit running out from Dove Point, but a middle ground buoy is usually located on the western end of it.

Havergate Island

Havergate is now an important and well-known bird sanctuary under the control of the Royal Society for the Protection of Birds, and landing is prohibited unless permission has been obtained from the Society.

Main Reach

The most direct route up river to Orford Quay is through Main Reach, which passes between the E side of Havergate Island and the attenuated shingle bank that stretches from Orfordness down to North Weir Point. The southern half of Main Reach is known as the Narrows, and here the river is hardly more than half a cable wide, and the tides, particularly the ebb, still run very strongly. At the top of Main Reach the river turns northerly towards Orford, about a mile away, and it is then possible to find good holding ground out of the main tidal stream.

A red spherical buoy is sometimes located in Main Reach at the point where the other arm of the river emerges from the W side of Havergate Island. This other arm first of all turns northerly round Flybury Point, and for about half a mile the reach is known as the Lower Gull; one of the best anchorages for a boat waiting to leave the river. The tides still run strongly in Lower Gull, but the holding is better than anywhere in Long Reach.

At the top of Lower Gull a fairly large creek known as the Butley River branches off in a north-westerly direction. The main stream at this point turns south-easterly for about half a mile and then again turns to the NE into Upper Gull. At the northern end of the Upper

Orford Sailing Club is based just above the Town Quay. Orford Church can be seen in the background   *Janet Harber*

Gull the channel turns easterly once more and continues for nearly a mile before uniting with Main Reach between Chantry and Cuckold Points.

On the average there is a greater depth of water through Lower Gull and Upper Gull than through Main Reach. There is, for instance, 10m in the Lower Gull, while the best depth in Main Reach is 5 or 6m towards its northern end.

The Orford Town Trust marks out most of the mud spits with withies — which sometimes have black flags.

The Butley River

This river or large creek leaves Lower Gull and at first follows a westerly direction for a quarter of a mile before turning north past Boyton Dock and Butley Ferry. The entrance to the creek is marked by a port-hand withy, and there is a good anchorage just inside with about 2m at LWS. Shallow draught boats can sometimes lie afloat as far up as Gedgrave Cliff amid pleasant surroundings.

There is an active oysterage in the upper reaches of the river near the Cliff. The beds or trays may not be marked by withies, but there are courteous notice boards indicating the extent of the layings, so visiting yachtsmen should respond by taking care.

Landing is possible towards HW, either at Boyton Dock (or jetty) or at the Butley Ferry hard. From Gedgrave beach on the E bank it is about two miles to Orford — the nearest source of supplies.

Orford Quay

Above Chantry Point the river widens and deepens a little, having between 8 and 10m up to Orford Quay. Extending from the E bank just below the moorings at Orford there is a mud bank that diverts the channel towards the opposite shore for a short distance. The drying edge of the mud is marked by a perch.

The keep of Orford Castle (80ft) is a conspicuous landmark from anywhere in the river S of Orford, and

will have been clearly visible from Lower Gull or Main Reach.

It was in 1165 that Henry II decided to build a castle at Orford and it was then that the original quays were constructed for unloading the building materials. The castle was completed in 1173, just in time to be used in Henry's conflict with his Barons. Orford became a flourishing port, sending wool to the Continent at first and later handling coastal trade in coal and grain until 1914.

The view from the top of the keep well repays the climb, as does the equally impressive panorama from the tower of St Bartholomew's church, which was built around the same time as the castle and where there are some excellent brasses and a pair of stocks.

There are moorings on both sides of the channel for a little way above and below Orford Quay, but a secure anchorage in about six metres with a mud bottom can be found just S of the quay. Landing at the quay itself or on the shingle next to it is possible at all states of the tide. Landing on the opposite shore, that is on the Orfordness side, is prohibited by the Ministry of Defence. It is as well to remember that the yacht moorings at Orford and at Slaughden Quay are laid with their ground chains *athwart* the stream.

The Harbour Master at Orford is Ralph Brinkley whose telephone number is (0394) 450481.

Facilities at Orford	
Water	Stand-pipe on the quay.
Stores	Shops in market square. EC Wed.
Petrol	Garage in town (¾ mile).
Diesel	From chandlers on quay.
Crane	On quay (may be hired). Tel: 450481.
Scrubbing	Near quay (inquire at chandlery).
Transport	Buses from market square to Ipswich and Woodbridge.
Club	Orford Sailing Club.
Telephone	In car park.
PO	In square.

3
The River Alde

Tides

HW Slaughden Quay approx 1.35mins after HW at entrance
HW Snape Bridge approx 30mins after Slaughden

Charts

Admiralty 2693
Stanford No. 6
Imray C28

Hazards

Because of winding gutway, make passage between
Slaughden and Snape only on rising tide.

ABOVE Orford the river turns easterly for a short way and then, abreast Raydon Point, the direction becomes north-easterly along Pigpail Reach. At Raydon Point a water pipe crosses the river to connect with the lighthouse at Orfordness, and the position of the pipe is marked by notice boards. North of Pigpail Reach, the river becomes the Alde, and turns more northerly with deeper water towards the W bank, although all through Blackstakes Reach and Home Reach up to Slaughden Quay, best water will be found roughly midway between the banks. Several racing marks (spar buoys) are located in midstream along these upper reaches of the Alde. Between Orford and Slaughden the depths vary between 5 and 7m at LW, and the width of the LW channel remains about 200m.

Slaughden Quay

Abreast the conspicuous Martello Tower, about a quarter of a mile below Slaughden, the river narrows and shallows for a short distance before deepening again and changing direction abruptly off the quay itself. At this point, the river Alde is separated from the sea only by the sea wall and shingle beach — not much more than 100m in all.

Moorings are laid athwart the stream, on both sides of the channel at Slaughden Quay and although boats are moored fore and aft, they are so closely packed that it is a problem nowadays for a visitor to find an anchorage near the clubhouse. There is a visitor's mooring just to the S of the clubhouse, but it must not be used for more than 24 hours. An alternative is to bring up between the Martello Tower and the clubhouse on the E side of the river.

There are two clubs at Aldeburgh; the Slaughden Quay SC and the Aldeburgh YC. The AYC has a visitors' mooring just off the clubhouse seen on the right of the photograph   *Janet Harber*

Facilities at Slaughden Quay (Aldeburgh)	
Water	At yacht club or stand-pipe quite near quay.
Stores	Shops in Aldeburgh (1 mile). EC Wed.
Fuel	Diesel from yard. Petrol and gas from chandler or in town.
Repairs	Derrick on quay. Yards and chandler nearby.
Transport	Buses from Aldeburgh to Saxmundham (8 miles). Trains from Saxmundham to Ipswich and London.
Club	Aldeburgh Yacht Club. Slaughden Sailing Club.

There is a useful derrick on the quay at Slaughden

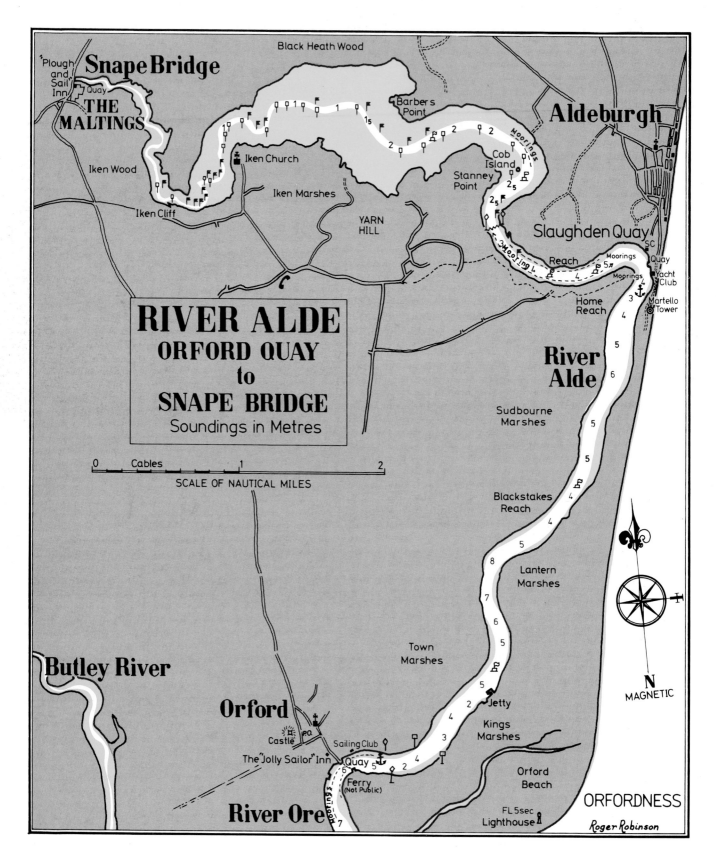

RIVER ALDE
ORFORD QUAY
to
SNAPE BRIDGE
Soundings in Metres

SCALE OF NAUTICAL MILES

This particular Tower, known as 'CC', was the northernmost of the chain that stretched round from the south coast and it is completely different from all the others being quadrafoil in shape.

Before leaving a boat, the best plan is to seek the advice of the Cruising Association boatman (Russel Upson), who is usually on hand. When you have either anchored or moored, there is clean landing at the quay, on the shingle next to it, or on the slip at the yacht club.

There is a boatyard with laying-up facilities and a chandler about a quarter of a mile from the quay.

Above Slaughden the river changes direction and, after all but breaking through to the sea, turns inland in a general westerly direction for the five or six miles to Snape Bridge. The character of the river now begins to change, and while the banks become farther apart, the LW channel becomes narrower. From here on the river is frequently marked by beacons to port and to starboard.

The marks are necessarily very numerous — there are more than forty in all (maintained by Aldeburgh YC, to whom we owe thanks) — and as they are not very

A ketch rigged Dutch barge is often berthed alongside the old quay at Snape Bridge, where Thames barges once brought grain for the Maltings

conspicuous in certain conditions of light, a very careful look-out must be kept to see that none is missed. It is of course helpful to commence a trip to Iken Cliff or Snape Bridge early on the tide so that the tortuous channel can be seen and the marks understood.

Through Westrow Reach and Short Reach there is about 5m in the channel at LW, and a starboard hand beacon marks the edge of mud extending from the N bank. In Short Reach a power cable crosses the river and is marked by the usual triangular topped beacons. At the top of Short Reach the channel turns north-easterly past two starboard hand beacons and a port hand beacon to Stanney Point. A racing buoy is usually located off Stanney Point but in any case Cob Island, a tiny circular clump of saltings, will serve to identify this point in the river. A derelict brick dock and some moorings will be seen over on the E shore, and here the channel turns back to the NW, round a series of three port hand beacons into Colliers Reach. Three beacons to starboard and three beacons to port mark the channel round Barber's Point and into Long Reach. By this time, the LW channel is but a cable wide, with depths of about 2m.

Past Barber's Point, the river, towards HW, widens to nearly a mile between its banks, and while marshland lies to the south, Black Heath Woods reach down to a sandy beach on the north shore at a spot known locally as 'Little Japan'. At the western end of Long Reach a series of four port hand beacons follow the course of the channel to where it turns sharply to the south towards Sandy Point. Then the channel turns north-westerly into Short Reach and south-westerly again into Church Reach — so named because Iken Church stands on a wooded promontory less than a quarter of a mile away. After this the channel turns westerly into Lower Troublesome Reach and S again into Upper Troublesome Reach. All these abrupt twists and turns of the channel are adequately marked, but care must be

taken to ensure that the beacons are passed in the correct order and that none of them is missed.

Above the two Troublesome Reaches, the channel closely approaches the shore near a sandy beach above which a group of oak trees grows. This spot, known as 'The Oaks', is very pleasant, and offers good landing between half-flood and half-ebb. Then comes Cliff Reach, leading up to Iken Cliff itself, where the LW channel again comes to within 20 yards of a sand and shingle shore.

Iken Cliff

There is not much more than 1.5 metres of water at best in the channel abreast Iken Cliff, or The Oaks as it is often called, but the bottom is mud and the spot provides one of the most attractive anchorages on the Alde. There are a few small boat moorings off the Cliff, but no stores are available near here.

From Iken Cliff to Snape Bridge is just over a mile, and the channel, which becomes little more than a gutway, winds between mudbanks and virtually dries out at LW. However, it is possible for craft drawing up to 2m to reach the quay alongside the Maltings at Snape Bridge, and there to take the mud. This last mile or so up to Snape is irregularly marked by some port hand cans and starboard perches.

The Maltings concert hall was built in 1967 as a centre for the Aldeburgh Festival, but now it is used throughout the year for many other purposes, including jazz sessions and television recording.

Yachtsmen have been known to visit the Music Festival by water, changing into evening dress aboard their boat alongside the quay.

There is food at the *Plough and Sail,* at the Concert Hall restaurant and at the Granary Tea Shop but the nearest source of supplies is at Snape, about half a mile away.

4
The River Deben

Tides

HW Dover +0.25 Range: Springs 3.5m Neaps 2.9m
(HW Woodbridge approx 1.00 after HW in entrance)

Charts

Admiralty 2693
Stanford No. 6
Imray Y16

Waypoint

Woodbridge Haven Buoy (1988) 51.58.36.N   1.24.17.E

Hazards

Strong tide and shoals in entrance (Observe leading marks strictly)
'Horse' shoal just above Felixstowe Ferry.

INVITING a friend to stay with him aboard his schooner, the *Scandal*, Edward FitzGerald, translator of *The Rubáiyát of Omar Khahyyám*, wrote: '*I think you would like this Bawdsey, only about a dozen Fishermen's Houses, built where our River runs into the Sea over a foaming Bar, on one side of which is a good sand to Felixstowe and on the other an orange coloured crag Cliff towards Orford Haven; not a single respectable House or Inhabitants or Lodger; no white Cravats, an Inn with scarce a table and chair and only Bread and Cheese to eat. I often lie here with my Boat: I wish you would come and do so.*'

That was a hundred and twenty years ago, but the Ferry Boat Inn remains although you may now have more than bread and cheese to eat should you wish.

For today's yachtsman who keeps his boat in the Medway, the Crouch or the Blackwater, a visit to the Deben must usually be made during the summer holiday cruise. The Woodbridge river, as the Deben is sometimes called, is only about nine miles long, but it is very attractive and nowadays entirely free from commercial traffic.

Perhaps the thing that comes first to the East Coast yachtsman's mind when he thinks of the Deben is that there is a shifting shingle bar at the entrance to

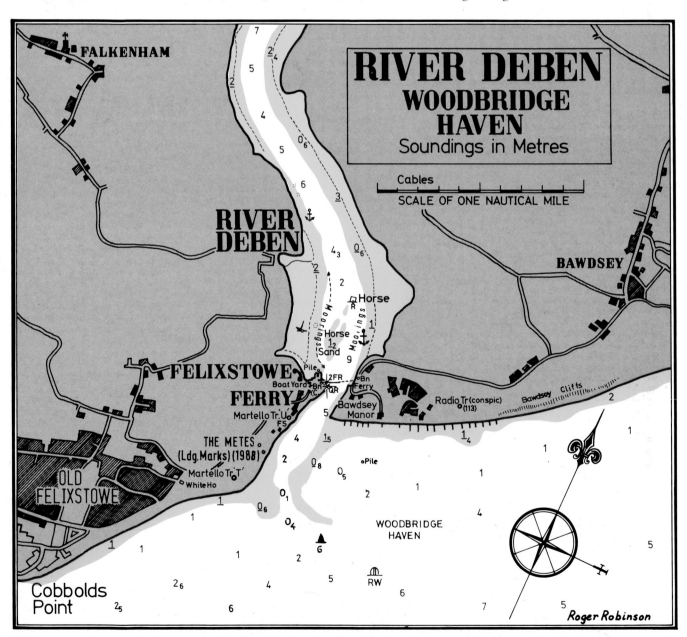

Right: Aldeburgh and the River Alde

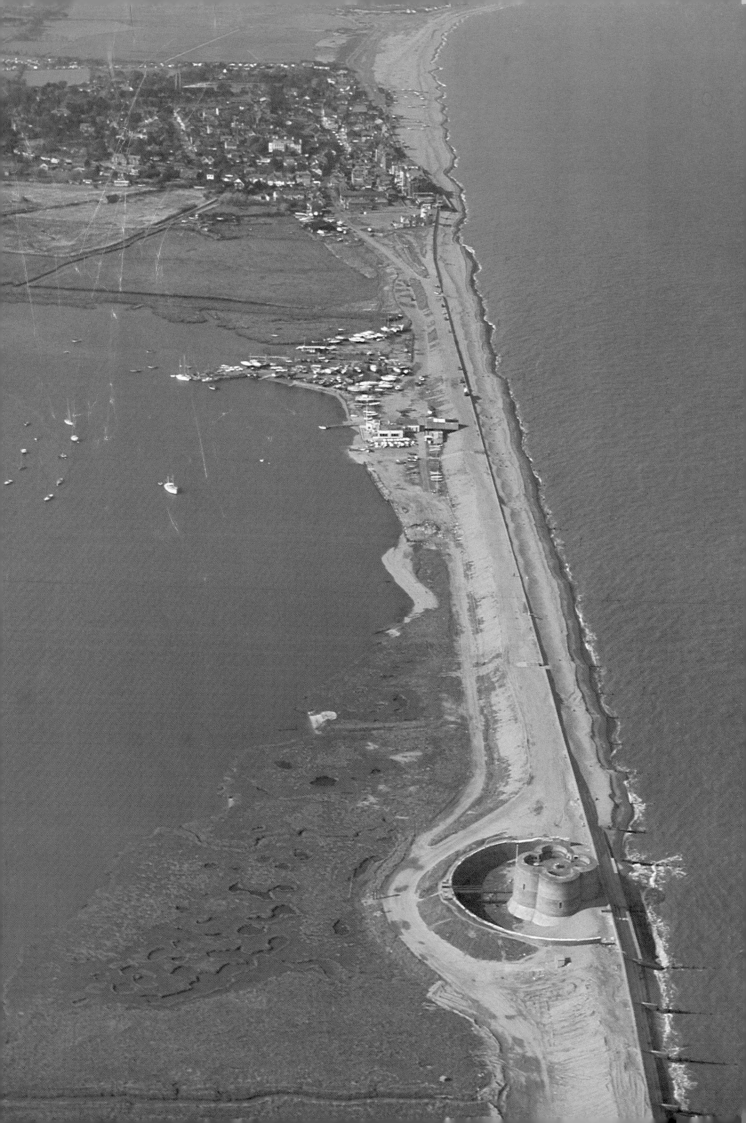

Above: Entrance River Ore with Shingle Street in the foreground

Below: There is clean landing on a shingle beach at Felixstowe Ferry

Above: Ramsholt Quay

Below: Entrance to the River Deben

Left: Woodbridge. Above: Levington Marina on the River Orwell

Below: Orwell Bridge with Ipswich in the background

Above: Walton Backwaters

Below: Goldhanger Creek. Right: There are scrubbing posts on the hard at Pin Mill

The 'metes' at the entrance to the River Deben should be held in line until quite close to the shingle on the west bank, before altering course to the north

Janet Harber

Woodbridge Haven. This bar ought not to worry anyone unduly because there is a pilot on hand at almost all times during the summer months.

Many more yachts enter and leave the river now than ever before and since most of them hail from Woodbridge, Waldringfield, Ramsholt or Felixstowe Ferry, their skippers usually have the benefit of local knowledge and so can often act as guide for a newcomer. Nevertheless, when there are no other yachts about and particularly for the first time 'over the bar', it is still a sound idea to take the pilot — Robert Brinkley — who will usually hear a call on VHF Channel 8 or come off by prior arrangement. His telephone number is Felixstowe 270853.

Approaches

Most yachts will approach Woodbridge Haven from the south — often from Harwich harbour, which is only 6 or 7 miles away. A good time to enter the river is about two hours after low water, when there will be a least depth of about 2m over the bar. With so little water to spare, an entrance should never be attempted where there is a bad sea running. But the appearance of the surrounding shoal-water would presumably be enough to scare anyone away on such occasions. A spring ebb can run out of the entrance at 6 knots and any attempt to enter at such times certainly cannot be recommended.

When the approach is from Harwich or from the Wallet, a course should be shaped to pass about half a mile off Felixstowe Pier, keeping a good look-out for floats marking lobster pots. When approaching the Deben entrance, most of the details along the low lying shore will be distinguishable — in particular the two Martello Towers (Tower 'T' and Tower 'U'); and the very conspicuous radar pylon just to the north of the entrance to Woodbridge Haven can be seen from many miles away on a clear day.

Woodbridge Haven buoy is maintained by Trinity House and is spherical with red and white vertical

stripes. It is unlit and must never be confused with the buoy on the bar which is much smaller.

When continuing without a pilot, the Bar buoy must be located before going in. This starboard hand green conical buoy is the only one now marking the bar. Neither is there a second starboard hand buoy inside the bar as there has been in recent years. It seems that Trinity House is only prepared to pay for laying one buoy. The precise course from the Bar buoy will depend upon the location of the leading marks or metes.

The 'metes' are both red rectangular boards, the front one bearing a white 'spade' or triangle.

As the shore is neared, the flood will tend to carry a boat in on a course parallel to the beach and about 20 or 30m from it, but there is little risk of approaching the shingle too closely as it is extremely steep-to.

Going in on the flood, the tide will now be pushing really hard, and the only obstacle then remaining is the Horse Shoal which occupies the centre of the river immediately above the Felixstowe-Bawdsey Ferry. The Horse Shoal is extensive, and dries out in parts to a height of about 1m. The main channel is to the eastward of the shoal, the channel to port being full of moored craft. It is safer therefore for a stranger to take the main or starboard channel where there is plenty of water until the 'Horse' buoy (red can) is reached at the N end of the shoal. Abreast this buoy there is very little water over what George Jones used to call an 'inner bar' and it certainly seems that many more boats go aground hereabouts than ever touch bottom in the entrance. Towards the northern end of the Horse Shoal it is necessary to approach the Bawdsey shore very close until the 'Horse' buoy is passed to port.

Anchorage

Because of the many moorings between the shoal and the Felixstowe shore, the safest place to bring up to an anchor is above these moorings on the western side of the river where it is easy enough to find good holding

This aerial shot of the entrance to the Deben was taken in the summer of 1988. It must not be assumed that the configuration of the shoals will be the same ever again!

ground in a fathom or two at low water. With this anchorage there is the problem of being nearly half a mile from the landing near the Ferry.

An alternative anchorage on the E side can sometimes be found just north of the telegraph cable that crosses the river just above the Ferry and which is marked by conspicuous red and white triangular topmarked beacons on either shore. The attraction of this spot is its close proximity to the convenient steep-to shingle beach on the Felixstowe shore, where one can land from a dinghy at all states of the tide. When bringing up hereabouts, special care must be taken to avoid the nearby moorings, which are laid athwart the stream. Also, it is essential to have ample scope of cable out because of the great strength of the tide — sometimes amounting to 5 knots. So take care when crossing to the other side by dinghy.

Facilities at Felixstowe Ferry	
Water	Standpipe near telegraph beacon.
Stores	Limited supplies from restaurant/shop.
Chandler	Near slipway.
Repairs	Boatyard and slipway.
Fuel	Diesel.
Transport	Good bus service to Felixstowe (3 miles).
Telephone	Box near Ferry.
Club	Felixstowe Ferry Sailing Club.

At Woodbridge Haven, springs range 3.5m and neaps 2.9m. HWF and C is at 1145hr.

While it is easier to leave Woodbridge Haven on the ebb tide, this results in any south-bound yacht having to face the remainder of the ebb after leaving the river. It is usually more convenient therefore to leave the Haven at about half-flood, depending upon auxiliary power to push a boat over the fast running tidal stream near Felixstowe Ferry. The force of this stream should never be under-estimated, and if an exit is to be made during springs, an auxiliary engine capable of driving the boat at 5 knots will be no more than sufficient unless some help can also be obtained from the sails.

For a mile or two above Felixstowe Ferry the Deben looks very much like a river in Essex rather than Suffolk — with low-lying mudbanks and saltings bordered by a sea wall. The channel, which in its centre has no less than 6m at low water, runs rather closer to the west bank up as far as Ramsholt Reach, where a somewhat abrupt change of scenery occurs.

On the east bank the land rises sharply to form a modest cliff topped by pleasant groups of pine trees before the October '87 hurricane. Nestling under the cliff, close to the old barge quay, is an inn, the *Ramsholt Arms,* and there are few places more pleasant than this on any of the East Coast rivers.

Ramsholt

In recent years the moorings at Ramsholt, like everywhere else, have multiplied, but fortunately there is usually room to anchor in mid-channel if there is no vacant buoy.

Facilities at Ramsholt	
Water	Tap in wall near gate of *Ramsholt Arms.*
Stores	None, but can be ordered from *Ramsholt Arms* for delivery from Alderton, 3 miles away.
Transport	None.
Telephone	Box near *Ramsholt Arms.*

Continuing up-river from Kirton Creek, the channel closely approaches the west bank for a while and then crosses to the east side abreast Shottisham Woods. There is a very pleasant landing here beneath the trees on a sandy beach known locally as 'The Rocks', so called because the remains of a hard can still be found at low water. There are no roads nearby, but on a fine day there is sometimes a 'traffic jam' of yachts!

At the top of the Rocks Reach, opposite Shottisham Sluice, is the first of the up-river marks, which continue as buoys or beacons all the way up to Woodbridge. The first two can buoys, 2 and 2a, and all subsequent port hand buoys are numbered evenly, while those on the starboard hand are odd-numbered.

The next two red cans (4 and 6) mark the mud that

stretches out from the west bank at this bend of the river. Just above these buoys there is a patch of shallow water over a 'horse', carrying as little as 1m at LWS. Above No 6 buoy the channel turns NW.

A conical green buoy (No 1) is the first to be left to starboard and it marks the downstream end of an extensive tidal island lying between Waldringfield and Stonner Point. At or near high water there is about 1.5m of water between the east bank and the island, but any boat using this route should proceed cautiously and take frequent soundings past Stonner Point. The two ends of this shallow short cut are marked by beacons with lattice-work truncated cone topmarks.

The main channel runs to the west of the island between two long lines of moorings off Waldringfield. There is a permanent gap left in the moorings opposite the beach, so that a limited number of visiting yachts can anchor there. But when this space is taken up and the fairway opposite the beach is likely to become congested, or racing is in progress, it will be better to move either up or down-river to anchor with more space, preferably on the west side of the channel.

Clean landing from a dinghy is possible along the shingle foreshore at almost any time.

Continuing up-river from Waldringfield the channel becomes narrower and the mud flats proportionately wider, so that special care must be taken between half-flood and half-ebb, when the mud is only just covered.

No 3 buoy, conical green, marks the northern end of the tidal island, and having left this mark to starboard after passing Waldringfield, the next two red can buoys (Nos 8 and 10) mark an extensive spot off the W bank.

Under Ham Woods there is a low cliff and sandy beach which just invites a picnic — but beware! At high water the beach is hard and sandy, but this hard bottom only extends for a limited distance, after which it abruptly changes to soft mud about a metre deep. If a landing is to be made at 'The Tips', one should return to the dinghy before the mud is uncovered; which happens quickly, for the shore is quite flat hereabouts.

The sandy shore at 'The Tips' resulted from an attempt at the end of the last century by Robert Cobbold to reclaim 150 acres of land from the river. The attempt was stopped by Trinity House, who felt that the scheme would alter the course of the river and interfere with its navigation.

After leaving No 8 and No 10 buoys to port, a green buoy (No 5) is left to starboard below Methersgate Quay. Then follows No 12, a red buoy, which is to be left to port opposite the quay, where there are few moorings. Another green buoy (No 7) marks a sweep of the channel towards the west shore, where moorings begin. A single red port hand buoy (No 14) marks the mud spit that extends from the west shore at the entrance to Troublesome Reach. Two starboard hand spherical green buoys (Nos 9 and 11) mark the bend past the entrance to Martlesham Creek and round Kyson Quay.

There are drying moorings and pontoons with water and power at the boatyard on the S side of Martlesham Creek.

Facilities at Waldringfield	
Water	On quay and at *Maybush Inn*.
Stores	General store, including PO. (EC Thurs but open Sun.
Petrol and oil	Garage on Woodbridge Road (1 mile). Diesel oil at boatyard.
Repairs and Chandlery	At boatyard with slip and 40-ton crane.
Scrubbing posts	Near YC.
Transport	Buses to Ipswich.
Telephone	Box near Inn.
Club	Waldringfield Sailing Club.

There is clean landing around high water at Kyson Quay, just above the entrance to Martlesham Creek.   *Graham Jones*

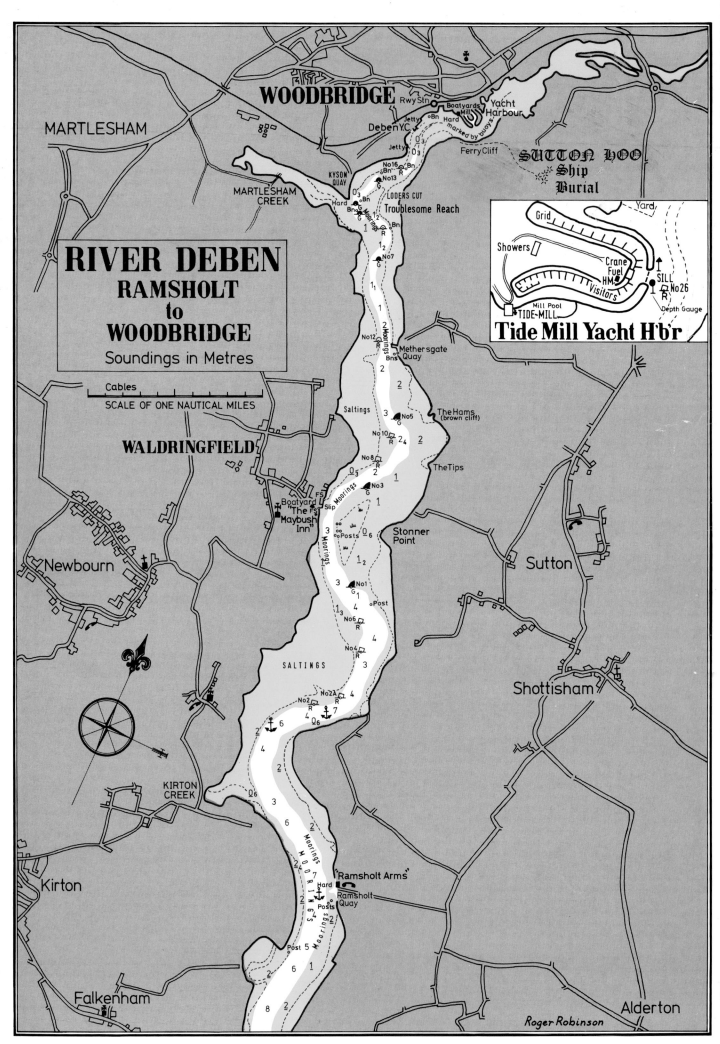

MARTLESHAM

WOODBRIDGE

Rwy Stn
Boatyards Mill
Yacht Harbour
Deben Y.C.
Hard
marked by buoys
Jetty
Ferry Cliff

SUTTON HOO
Ship
Burial

KYSON QUAY
MARTLESHAM CREEK
Hard
Bng
LODERS CUT
Troublesome Reach

No16 R
No13 G
O 3
Bn
Bn
Moorings
1
R
1₂
No7 G

RIVER DEBEN
RAMSHOLT
to
WOODBRIDGE
Soundings in Metres

Cables
SCALE OF ONE NAUTICAL MILES

WALDRINGFIELD

Newbourn

No12
Moorings
Bns
Methersgate Quay
2
2
Saltings
3 No5 G
The Hams (brown cliff)
No10 R 2 4
2
No8 R
O 3
The Tips
Moorings
No3 G
1
Slip
FS
Boatyard
"The Maybush Inn"
Moorings
Posts O 6
Stonner Point
1 2
3
No1 G
1
Post
1 3
No6 R
4
No4 R
3
SALTINGS
No2A R 4
No2 R
7
O 6
6
4
2
2
KIRTON CREEK
O 6
3
6
2

Sutton

Shottisham

Kirton

Moorings
MOORINGS
"Ramsholt Arms"
Hard
Ramsholt Quay
Posts
Moorings
2
Post 5
6 1
Falkenham
8 2
Alderton

Roger Robinson

Tide Mill Yacht H'br
Grid
Yard
Showers
Crane
Fuel
HM
SILL
No26 R
Visitors
Mill Pool
TIDE-MILL
Depth Gauge

20

The 12th-century tide-mill at Woodbridge has been restored and can sometimes be seen working during the summer months

One more spherical green (No 13) and one more red (No 16) buoy mark the way to the line of moorings extending down-river from Woodbridge.

Four more port hand (red can) buoys (Nos 18 to 24) mark the channel between Eversons shed and the entrance to the Tide Mill Yacht Harbour, and are helpful because deeper water changes from side to side of the river hereabouts.

Loders Cut

Towards the end of the last century a channel was cut to avoid the bend past Kyson Quay. The purpose of Loders Cut, as the channel is called, was to revive Woodbridge's failing maritime trade. The plan was not very successful, although the cut remains and can be safely used by light draught boats for about 1½ to 2 hours either side of high water. The port hand side of the cut is marked with stakes.

Woodbridge

There are moorings on both sides of the channel at Woodbridge, but most of the boats take the ground at low water. A few deeper draught craft are located in 'holes' where there is more water; one of these being in midstream abreast of Everson's building shed, quite close to the little bandstand on the sea wall promenade.

But generally, a visiting yacht must expect to come and go on a tide or else be prepared to ground for a while at low water. It is high water at Woodbridge 50 minutes later than at Felixstowe Ferry.

When staying at Woodbridge for a few hours in order to see the town and obtain stores the best place to bring up is between the moorings just above the clubhouse of the Deben Yacht Club, which was established in 1838. From here, it is easy to land at Everson's wooden jetty, or a cable further up, at Ferry Quay.

The old ferry dock is fitted out as a yacht harbour. Although it dries out at LW, there are stagings to lie to and the mud is soft.

Farther upstream the old tide mill pool has been excavated to form a horseshoe-shaped yacht basin, where yachts can lie afloat at all states of the tide.

The marina has a sill over which boats drawing 2m can pass at HW neaps and those drawing as much as 3m

at the top of a good spring tide. However, craft drawing more than 1.5m (5ft) should not attempt entry *after* HW on a neap tide.

There has been a tide mill where the present Woodbridge Mill stands since 1170 and, thanks to an energetic Preservation Society, we can still visit this last remaining tide mill on the East Coast.

Facilities at Woodbridge	
There are comprehensive facilities at the Tide Mill Yacht Harbour. Showers, toilets, water, fuel, etc.	
Water	Tap on Ferry Quay.
Stores	Many shops in town. EC Wed.
Petrol and oil	Petrol from garages in town. Diesel and gas from all yards.
Chandlery	On quay.
Repairs	Shipwrights near quay. Several slipways and cranes. Sailmaker near Yacht Harbour.
Telephone	Box in station yard.
Transport	Diesel train service to Ipswich, then to London. Buses to Ipswich.
Clubs	Deben Yacht Club Woodbridge Cruising Club.

When visiting Woodbridge by dinghy for stores, the only reasonable landing place at or around low water is the hard near Whisstock's boatyard.

Above the Tide Mill there are three more boatyards, one of them, the Granary Yacht Harbour, with a 12-ton crane and a chandlery. The yard nearest to Melton Bridge is mainly used for laying-up and has a 9-ton crane.

For those who like exploring in a dinghy it is possible to take the tide for another mile or so above Woodbridge to Wilford Bridge. Such an excursion can be well worth while if it includes a walk from Wilford Bridge to see the site of the Saxon burial ship at Sutton Hoo, the discovery of which, in 1939, has been described as 'the most marvellous find in the archaeological annals of England'. Replicas of the finds can be seen in Ipswich Museum, but the treasures are in the care of the British Museum.

5

Harwich Harbour

Tides

HW Dover +0.40 Range: Springs 4.0m Neaps 3.4m

Charts

Admiralty 1491
Stanford No 6
Imray Y16

Waypoints

Pitching Ground Buoy 51.55.38.N   1.21.16.E
Landguard Buoy 51.55.35.N   1.18.98.E
Cliff Foot Buoy 51.55.68.N   1.18.67.E
S Shelf Buoy 51.56.26.N.   1.18.76.E
Guard Buoy 51.57.04.N   1.17.88.E
Shotley Spit Beacon 51.57.26.N   1.17.68.E

Hazards

Shipping entering and leaving (Keep clear of dredged channel).

THE earliest indirect reference to a harbour at Harwich is to be found in the *Anglo-Saxon Chronicle* for the year 885:

'The same year sent King Alfred a fleet from Kent into East Anglia. As soon as they came to Stourmouth there met them sixteen ships of the pirates and they fought with them, took all ships and slew the men. As they returned homeward with their booty they met a large fleet of pirates and fought with them the same day, but the Danes had the victory.'

Some people believe that Bloody Point off Shotley owes its name to the first of these two battles, fought more than a thousand years ago.

Nowhere else on the East Coast is there an expanse of protected deep water as extensive as that formed at the junction of the rivers Orwell and Stour, which emerge to the sea as one between Beacon Cliff and Landguard Point.

The Haven Ports, comprising Felixstowe, Harwich and Ipswich, between them now handle so much traffic that, on average, a ship passes Landguard Point every five minutes, day and night. With the deeper dredged channel now open, some of the world's largest container ships use it and small boat sailors must therefore stay well clear of the channel whenever possible.

The buoyage and marking of Harwich Harbour and the River Stour are the responsibility of the Harwich Harbour Board and are not therefore affected by the Trinity House *Navaid Review*.

Approaches

From the S or SE the harbour can be approached in small craft by two routes, both avoiding the many shoals and banks that lie off the entrance. The course from the S, through the Medusa Channel, is described under 'Approaches to Walton Backwaters' and the same directions will serve until the Landguard Buoy (BY N Card Q) is in sight.

Another way into Harwich Harbour from the SE is through a channel known as the Gullet, passing about midway between the Medusa (Con G Fl G 5s) and the S Cork (S Card) and leaving the unlit Stonebanks (Can R) to port.

From the E the main deep water channel is exceptionally well marked by pairs of buoys, starting from the Harwich Fairway buoy (RWVS Pillar Iso2s).

Because of the big ship traffic, a yacht should, whenever possible, steer clear of the well marked dredged channel.

When approaching Harwich Harbour from the Deben or the Alde, it is possible to follow a course close to (N of) the Beach End buoy and then continue along the steep-to western side of Landguard Point, close E of the NW Beach buoy. The deep water channel must then be crossed as quickly as possible to keep away from the berths at the Port of Felixstowe.

When approaching from the E it is best for yachts to keep to the S of the dredged channel, past the Cork

A constant stream of shipping uses the dredged channel into Harwich harbour and yachts must keep a sharp lookout   *Janet Harber*

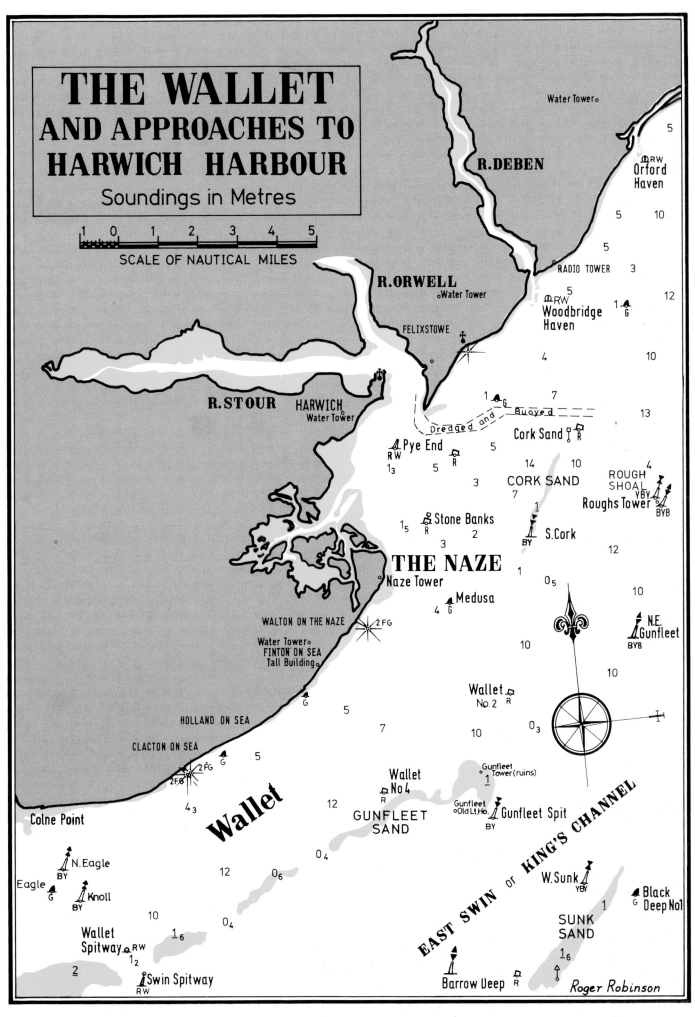

THE WALLET
AND APPROACHES TO
HARWICH HARBOUR
Soundings in Metres

SCALE OF NAUTICAL MILES

R.DEBEN

Water Tower

Orford Haven
RW

R.ORWELL
Water Tower

RADIO TOWER

Woodbridge Haven
RW

FELIXSTOWE

HARWICH
Water Tower

R.STOUR

Dredged and Buoyed

Cork Sand
R

Pye End
RW

CORK SAND

ROUGH SHOAL
YBY
Roughs Tower
BYB

Stone Banks
R

S.Cork
BY

THE NAZE
Naze Tower

Medusa
G

N.E. Gunfleet
BYB

WALTON ON THE NAZE
2 FG

Water Tower
FINTON ON SEA
Tall Building

Wallet No.2
R

HOLLAND ON SEA
G

Wallet No4
R

Gunfleet Tower (ruins)

Gunfleet Old Lt.Ho.
Gunfleet Spit
BY

CLACTON ON SEA
G
2 FG
2 FG

Wallet

GUNFLEET SAND

Colne Point

N.Eagle
BY

Eagle
G

Knoll
BY

Wallet Spitway
RW

Swin Spitway
RW

EAST SWIN or KING'S CHANNEL

W.Sunk
YBV

Black Deep No1
G

SUNK SAND

Barrow Deep
R

Roger Robinson

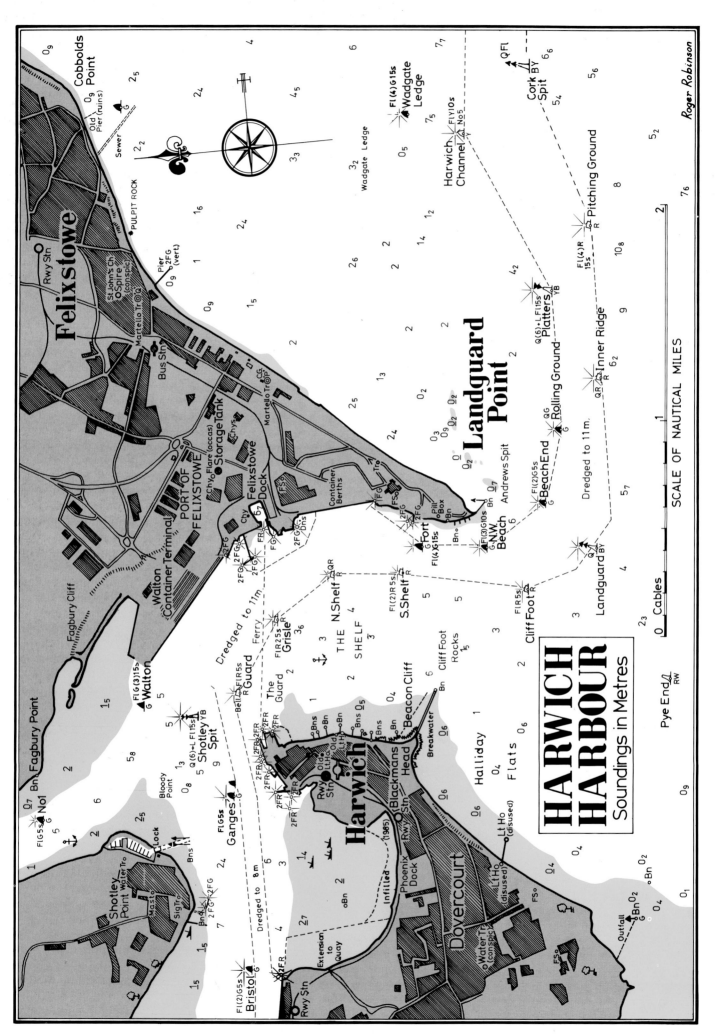

HARWICH HARBOUR
Soundings in Metres

Cobbolds Point

Felixstowe

Fagbury Point
Fagbury Cliff

Walton Container Terminal

PORT OF FELIXSTOWE

Felixstowe Dock

Container Berths

Landguard Point

Andrews Spit

NW Beach

Shotley Point

Walton

Ganges

Shotley Spit

Bloody Point

Lock

THE SHELF

The Guard

N. Shelf

S. Shelf

Grisle

Cliff Foot Rocks

Cliff Foot

Beacon Cliff

Blackmans Head

Breakwater

Harwich

Dovercourt

Halliday Flats

Bristol

Pye End

Rolling Ground

Beach End

Inner Ridge

Pitching Ground

Platters

Wadgate Ledge

Harwich Channel

Cork Spit

Landguard

Roger Robinson

SCALE OF NAUTICAL MILES

Cables

24

The Spritsail barge 'Ethel Ada' was the first craft to enter Shotley Spit Marina after it had been officially opened by Admiral-of-the-Fleet, Lord Lewin in 1988.

Sand, Cork Ledge, Cork Spit and Pitching Ground buoys, before turning to the N, leaving the Landguard and Cliff Foot buoys to starboard.

The old disused leading light towers on the Harwich shore, built in the time of Charles II and still standing, no longer serve as aids to navigation, but the lower one now houses a maritime museum.

The Harbour is entered between Beacon Cliff breakwater to the W and Landguard Point to the E. The width of the entrance is rather less than a mile including the water over the Cliff Foot Rocks, located 1½-3 cables off the end of the breakwater. These rocks have as little as 2m over them at LWS and, when entering the Harbour from Dovercourt Bay, they can be avoided by passing within a cable of the beacon on the end of the breakwater. Whenever the latter course is taken it is important to continue in a north-easterly direction over towards the Felixstowe shore after clearing the breakwater. Any temptation to turn to the N across the Guard shoal must be resisted until a position has been reached about midway between the Harwich and Felixstowe shores. The Guard shoal has no more than a metre over it in patches at LWS.

There are no shoals on the E or Felixstowe shore, which is now entirely given over to quays and jetties that are in constant use. It is therefore prudent to keep a very sharp look-out for movement of ships or ferries berthing or leaving the port.

Listening to Harwich Radio on VHF (Ch 71) will often provide immediately useful information about movements in or near the harbour. To talk to the Harbour Control Launch, use Ch 11.

Anchorages

There are several areas within which anchoring is always prohibited because of the necessity to maintain a clear passage for the heavy traffic to and from Ipswich, Parkeston Quay, Harwich and Felixstowe. The principal areas prohibited are:
(1) Anywhere in the fairway or within 200ft thereof between Parkeston Quay and the Rolling Ground buoy.
(2) Between the western edge of the dredged channel and a line joining the Guard and N Shelf buoys.
(3) Anywhere in the vicinity of the Harwich-Zeebrugge Train Ferry jetty.

If pausing only to visit the town of Harwich to collect stores a convenient spot in which to anchor when the

wind is SW can usually be found on the northern edge of the Guard shoal just S of the Guard buoy, but safely outside the main channel and the prohibited anchoring area bounded by a line between the Guard and N Shelf buoys. Hereabouts there are depths of about 4m within a reasonably short distance of the beach or the Pound. Take care not to get too near the container quay that now extends from the Navy Yard Wharf.

Facilities at Harwich	
Water	Town pier or from Trinity House Buoy Yard, by courtesy of Trinity House.
Stores	Shops in town nearby. EC Wed.
Petrol and oil	From garages in town.
Repairs	Two yards both near the quay. Sailmaker in town.
Transport	Good train service to London. Buses from quayside to Colchester, Manningtree, Walton-on-the-Naze. Coach service to London. Passenger ferry service between Harwich and Felixstowe Dock.
Clubs	Harwich and Dovercourt Sailing Club. Harwich Town Sailing Club.
Harbour Office	Harbour House, Angel Gate. (The harbourmaster will give yachtsmen all possible help.)

VHF Channel 71 (Harbour Operations Channel.)

Harwich Harbour operating frequency, Channel 71, is extremely busy at all times and yachtsmen are asked not to use it. However, it is useful for them to monitor that frequency in order to anticipate the movements of shipping.

Shotley

On the north shore at Shotley there is good anchorage except in strong southerly or westerly winds. Probably the best spot to choose is inside the trot of moorings situated about two cables SE of Shotley Pier. Three or four metres with a mud bottom is easy to find here, within a short distance from both the hard and the pier.

The Ganges training base is no more. Only the flagstaff remains to remind us that once a year some brave cadet would stand proudly atop its cap.

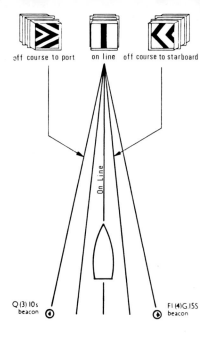

off course to port   on line   off course to starboard

On Line

Q (3) 10s beacon   Fl (4) G 15s beacon

An INOGON leading-line indicator is located on the east side of the lock into Shotley Point Marina

Shotley Point Marina

Instead, we now have the Shotley Point Marina with its water, power, fuel and chandler as well as its adjacent yacht club and restaurant. To reach the marina from Shotley Spit S Cardinal buoy, a yacht should proceed parallel to the deep water channel into the River Stour, passing close N of the conical green Ganges buoy to the beacons marking the outer end of the dredged channel leading to the marina lock-gates. The beacons are lit; Q (3) 10s to Port and Fl (4) G 15s to Starboard.

A special form of indicating signal has been installed at the Shotley marina to facilitate keeping to the dredged channel leading to the lock. The INOGON system, as it is called, depends upon the 'passive interaction between the helmsman's line of vision and a mosaic pattern produced by the leading mark.' The practical result is that when a yacht is on the correct bearing, a vertical black line will be seen down the middle of the screen, while any deviation from the correct course will cause the moiré pattern to form arrows indicating whether course should be changed to port or to starboard. The density of the arrow pattern will indicate how great the correction should be. There are waiting pontoons just outside the lock.

Judith Jones

Shotley Spit is now marked by a S Cardinal light buoy

Facilities at Shotley	
Water	From Sailing Club.
Stores	Limited supplies.
Petrol and oil	Garage nearby.
Transport	Bus service to Ipswich via Chelmondiston (Pin Mill). Ferry service: Shotley to Harwich (Thurs., Fri., Sat., Sun.).
Club	Shotley SC (with limited number of visitors' moorings).

Felixstowe Dock

When, in 1886, Col Tomline dug out a dock at the end of his private railway, he could never have dreamt of the port of Felixstowe as it is today.

Felixstowe Dock is no longer suitable for yachts, even as a temporary berth, and anchoring in the vicinity is strictly prohibited. (Gone are the days of *Goblin* in *We Didn't Mean to Go to Sea*.)

Harwich Pound

It is possible for small yachts, drawing no more than a metre or so, to lie afloat for a while around the high water period, tied up within the Pound, together with the local fishing craft. Conditions are sometimes rather dirty here, and there is usually much coming and going. The berths alongside the E pier are used by ferry boats, while berths alongside the railway or W pier will usually be occupied by Trinity House servicing ships. There are landing steps at both corners of the Pound. From early June until the end of September there is a passenger ferry service between Harwich Pier and Felixstowe Dock.

Landing is possible at most states of the tide at a quay to the S of Train Ferry Pier, in Gas House Creek. This is where some of the local fishing boats berth.

Much of the large expanse of drying mud known as Bathside Bay, to the W of Harwich and N of Dovercourt, is being filled in in preparation for the extension of Parkestone Quay. This project, together with a dredging programme to increase LW depths in the channel, foretells not only that there will soon be more ships in the entrance to the Stour, but that some of them will be larger than we have seen up to now.

The River Orwell

Tides

HW Dover +0.50 Range: Springs 4.1m Neaps 3.4m
HW Pin Mill approx 20mins after Harwich

Charts

Admiralty 2693
Stanford No 6
Imray Y16

Waypoints

Walton Buoy 51.57.48.N   1.17.68.E
Orwell No. 1 Buoy 51.57.93.N   1.16.91.E
Marsh Buoy 51.58.25.N   1.16.77.E

Hazard

Large ships in narrow dredged channel

IN his book *Orwell Estuary,* W G Arnott comments on the unchanging nature of much of the river: *'One wonders that the river and its surroundings remain so unspoilt and have suffered so little from the overspill of Ipswich. For this we have largely to thank the much maligned landowners of the estates along its banks. These estates represented a system for which some will say there is little moral justification, but . . . in the case of the Orwell (it) has saved its banks from spoilation.'*

The Orwell extends for about nine miles in a general north-westerly direction from the northern side of Harwich Harbour up to the docks at Ipswich. A considerable commercial traffic uses the river, and some of it is surprisingly large. For the benefit of these big ships a dredged and well-buoyed channel is provided by the Ipswich Port Authority which, since the last edition, has added four new buoys and made a number of amendments to the existing buoys and lights. This channel does, however, become very narrow above Pin Mill, and the buoys must be carefully observed unless a good tide covers the mud flats on either side.

On leaving Harwich Harbour, the entrance to the Orwell lies between Shotley Point to the W, and the northern extension of Felixstowe's deep-water quays to the E. The two channel marks indicating the entrance are Shotley Spit Bn (S Card YB Q (6)+L Fl 15s) and the Walton buoy (Con G Fl (3) G 10s). To the NE of these buoys is the conspicuous Fagborough Cliff, with a height of 60ft. There is an average depth of 7.5 metres in the main channel, for a width of about two cables, although at HW, with the mud all covered, the width from bank to bank is almost a mile.

When entering the Orwell from the Stour it is not necessary to round Shotley Spit beacon, which can be safely left a cable or so to starboard.

East Shotley Anchorage

There is a useful anchorage just inside the river and on the W shore, roughly NE of E Shotley Martello Tower (now topped by a large green water tank). This spot is known as Stone Heaps, and there is something of a hard on which to land, and a footpath that can be followed via the sea wall and past the marina into the village at Shotley Gate.

Even today a barge or two may be brought up, waiting a tide at Stone Heaps. The holding in mud is good, but care must be taken to anchor out of the channel and yet in enough water to remain afloat. This is not always as easy as it seems, as the edge of the channel is quite steep-to. A riding light is essential.

The next channel buoy (Con G Fl G 2.5s) marked No 1, is off Fagbury Point opposite Stone Heaps. A telegraph cable crosses the river between Fagbury Point and the Shotley shore, its precise position being indicated by red and white beacons with diamond-shaped topmarks. Other cables cross the river farther up, and all are marked in the same way, with a beacon on each shore.

Above Fagbury Point the river follows a northerly direction through Lower Reach to Collimer Point. There is low, marshy ground on either side of Lower Reach, but behind the marshes there are hills which close in on the river abreast Collimer Point. A little below the Point is a pair of buoys marking the width of the channel that is dredged to 6m all the way up to Ipswich. The starboard hand green conical buoy of the pair is called 'Trimley' and it flashes green every 2.5 seconds. Abreast Collimer Point itself there is a second pair of buoys — both of them lit. There is also a tide gauge on the Point, and inshore of that are the remains of another of the hards that once were in regular use

The entrance to the Suffolk Yacht Harbour is via a dredged channel, marked on either hand by beacons

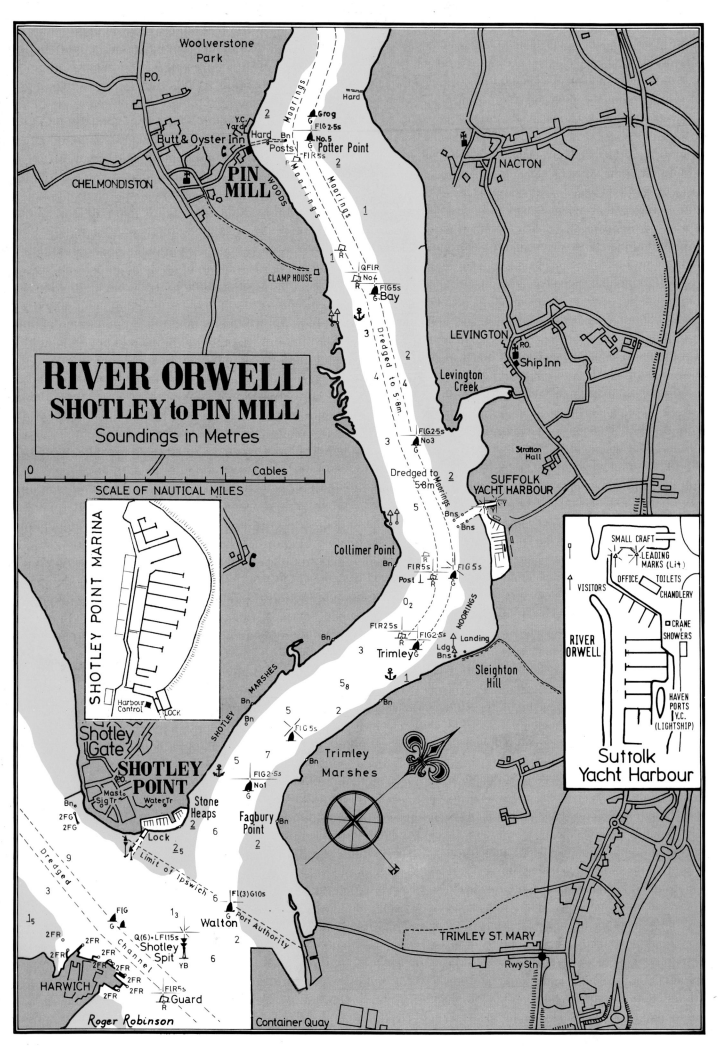

RIVER ORWELL
SHOTLEY to PIN MILL
Soundings in Metres

Woolverstone Park

P.O.

Hard

CHELMONDISTON

Butt & Oyster Inn

Y.C. Yard

Hard

Posts

Bn

PIN MILL

Woods

Moorings

Moorings

Moorings

Grog
G FIG 2·5s
No.5
G FIR5s
Potter Point

2

NACTON

1

CLAMP HOUSE

1
R
QFIR
No4
R
FIG5s
G Bay

2

LEVINGTON

P.O.
Ship Inn

Levington Creek

3

Dredged to 5·8m

2

4   4

Stratton Hall

5

FIG2·5s
No3
G

3

Dredged to 5·8m

2

Moorings

SUFFOLK YACHT HARBOUR

5

Bns
Bns

SCALE OF NAUTICAL MILES

0   1   Cables

Collimer Point

Bn

FIR5s
Post
R
R
FIG5s
G

O·2

Bn

FIR2·5s
R

FIG2·5s
G

Trimley G

Ldg
Bns

Landing

Moorings

SHOTLEY POINT MARINA

Harbour Control   LOCK

Shotley Gate

SHOTLEY POINT

P.O.

Bn

Mast
Sig Tr
Water Tr

Bn

Bn

SHOTLEY

MARSHES

FIG5s

5   7

Bn

3

5·8   1

Sleighton Hill

Bn

Trimley Marshes

2

RIVER ORWELL

SMALL CRAFT
LEADING MARKS (Lit)
OFFICE   TOILETS
VISITORS   CHANDLERY
CRANE
SHOWERS
HAVEN PORTS Y.C. (LIGHTSHIP)

Suffolk Yacht Harbour

2 FG
2 FG

Bn

5   7

Stone Heaps   2

FIG2·5s
No1
G

Fagbury Point   Bn

2

Lock

2·5

Limit of Ipswich Port Authority

Dredged

9

3

6

Fl(3)G10s
G
Walton

1·5   2FR

2FR   2FR

FIG
G   1·3

2

2FR   2FR

2FR

Q(6)+LFl15s
Shotley Spit
YB

6

TRIMLEY ST. MARY

Rwy Stn

HARWICH

2FR   2FR

FIR5s
R
Guard

Roger Robinson   Container Quay

28

One of the first marinas to be established on the East Coast, Suffolk Yacht Harbour at Levington remains popular because of its friendly atmosphere and attractive setting

along both banks of the river. On the opposite shore it is also possible to land fairly conveniently just S of a small area of saltings below Sleighton Hill. There are a few small boat moorings nearby.

After rounding Collimer Point and entering Long Reach, the direction of the river becomes north-westerly, and the true character of the Orwell is revealed.

Just above Collimer Point, on the N side of the river, is the Suffolk Yacht Harbour at Stratton Hall, near Levington Creek. The entrance to the harbour is a dredged channel about 30m wide, holding some 1.5m of water at LW neaps.

The entrance channel to the marina is marked at its outer end by a spherical orange buoy and then by port and starboard poles with topmarks. There are leading lights at night. (Outer Iso Y 1s and Inner Oc Y 3s + 1s).

Visitors should, if there is space, temporarily leave their yachts at a pontoon just inside and opposite the entrance, while reporting to the harbourmaster for instructions. There are berths for some 350 craft and the harbour is still being extended.

Deep draught boats, unsure of the entrance, can sometimes find a mooring free immediately up-river of the entrance buoy.

Facilities at Suffolk Yacht Harbour	
Water	Near entrance. All pontoons.
Fuel	Diesel oil from pumps near entrance.
Stores	From shop on site.
Repairs	Shipwrights and engineers on site. Slipway and scrubbing posts.
Chandlery	Store on site.
Telephone	Available.
Transport	Buses Felixstowe and Ipswich (1 mile walk).
Club	Haven Ports YC (In LV87).

VHF Ch 37 (Daylight hours).	

Suffolk Yacht Harbour is a long way from public transport or any shops, so these telephone numbers could be important: Local taxis . . . dial 382. Fresh groceries (delivered) . . . dial 231.

Levington Creek

The next buoy, No 3 (Con G Fl G 2.5s), and a few yacht moorings lie off the entrance to Levington Creek marked by withies. This little drying gutway was once regularly used by trading barges, and it is still possible to sound a way up to the old wharf at the head of the creek. From the wharf it is only a short walk to the hamlet of Levington, with its general store, Post Office and *Ship Inn*.

Between Levington and Potter Point there is another pair of lit buoys — 'The Bay' is conical green with a flashing green 5s light while its opposite — a red can buoy No 4 — has a quick flashing red light.

There is the possibility of anchoring on the S side, just below No 4 buoy and opposite Clamp House, where there will be shelter from the SW and landing is possible.

For the East Coast cruising man, the Orwell means Pin Mill and it is this unique hamlet, with its waterside inn and the prospect of a collection of spritties on the hard, that brings us back time and time again.

If it is at all possible it is preferable to find a mooring rather than drop an anchor at Pin Mill. Quite often there are one or two moorings available for visitors, just above the hard. The harbourmaster will usually know when a mooring is free.

If an anchorage has to be found, it is better to be below the moorings and well clear of the dredged channel, because ships approach the Pin Mill moorings very closely as they round No 5 buoy at Potter Point. The holding, in mud, is good, while protection is almost complete. Only in the case of strong north-westerly winds will a boat be disturbed, except by the sometimes considerable wash from passing freighters or tankers.

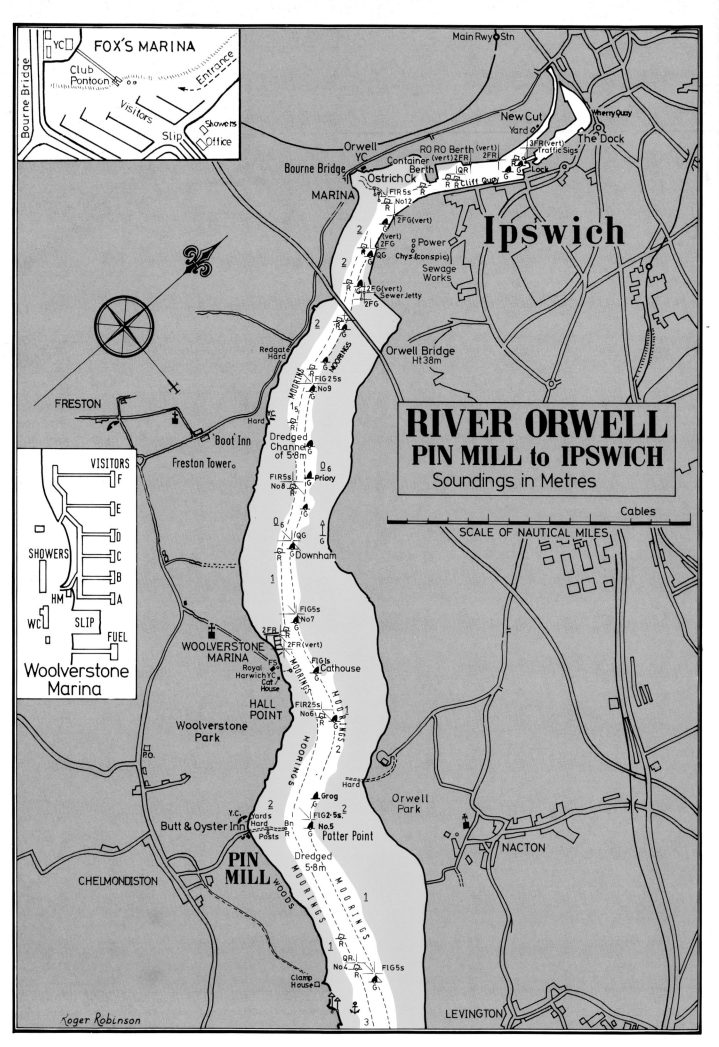

FOX'S MARINA

Bourne Bridge

YC
Club Pontoon
Visitors
Slip
Entrance
Showers
Office

VISITORS
F
E
D
C
B
A
SHOWERS
HM
WC
SLIP
FUEL

Woolverstone Marina

Main Rwy Stn
New Cut
Yard
Wherry Quay
The Dock
3FR(vert)
Traffic Sigs
RO RO Berth (vert) 2FR
Container (vert) 2FR 2FG
Berth
QR
R R Cliff Quay G Lock
Orwell YC
Bourne Bridge
Ostrich Ck
MARINA
Fl R 5s
No12
2FG(vert)
(vert)
2FG
QG
2FG(vert)
Sewer Jetty
2FG

Ipswich
Power
Chys (conspic)
Sewage Works

MOORINGS

Redgate Hard
Orwell Bridge
Ht 38m

FRESTON
Hard
YC
Boot Inn
Freston Tower

Fl G 2 5s
No9
Dredged Channel of 5·8m

1·5

Fl R 5s
No8

RIVER ORWELL
PIN MILL to IPSWICH
Soundings in Metres

Cables

SCALE OF NAUTICAL MILES

0·6
Priory
IG
0·6
IQG
G
G Downham

1

Fl G 5s
No7
G

2FR
WOOLVERSTONE MARINA
2FR(vert)
FS
Royal Harwich YC
Cat House
Fl G 1s
Cathouse

HALL POINT
Fl R 2 5s
No6
G
1
MOORINGS
2

Woolverstone Park

P.O.

Hard

Orwell Park

NACTON

Grog
Fl G 2·5s
2
No.5
Potter Point

Y.C.
Butt & Oyster Inn
Yard's Hard
Posts
Bn
R
PIN MILL
CHELMONDISTON
WOODS
MOORINGS

Dredged 5·8m

1

1
QR
R
No4
Fl G 5s

Clamp House

LEVINGTON

3

Roger Robinson

Pin Mill, with its famous 'Butt & Oyster' at the foot of a lane that every East Coast yachtsman will tread sooner or later

The very long hard at Pin Mill is not long enough to provide landing at low water springs. You may have to wait an hour or more to avoid the mud. When the tide is rising it is as well to haul the dinghy well up the gulley formed by the stream running down the side of the hard.

At the top of the hard is the *Butt and Oyster* Inn, itself awash at HW springs. The hard continues, almost imperceptibly, straight into a lane that leads up the valley to Chelmondiston.

The upper hard at Pin Mill is no half-hearted affair, but a fine expanse of firm shingle on which there are usually several barges undergoing repair. Scrubbing, too, is made easy by reason of the several stout posts that are available.

The village of Chelmondiston is about three-quarters of a mile from the hard at Pin Mill, and the walk up the lane seems to belong to Devon rather than Suffolk.

Facilities at Pin Mill	
Water	Tap alongside clubhouse of Pin Mill SC. At chandler, near hard.
Stores	Shops at Chelmondiston. EC Wed.
Fuel	Petrol, diesel and gas at top of hard.
Repairs	Boatyard and chandler.
Scrubbing post	On hard. (For use, consult HM.)
Transport	Bus service to Ipswich and Shotley from Chelmondiston.
Club	Pin Mill Sailing Club.
Telephone	In car park.

Chelmondiston

There are grocery stores, a butcher's shop and a PO at Chelmondiston — 'Chelmo' for short — which has become a busy little village.

Above Pin Mill the channel turns more northerly into Potter Reach, and about two cables beyond the buoy marking Potter Point, on the eastern shore, is a hard that can be used at most states of the tide to land in Orwell Park. No 6 buoy (R can Fl R 2.5s) marks the mud off Hall Point, while a green conical buoy (Fl G 5s) on the other side of the channel is located in Park Bight, together with a continuous line of moorings used by craft based on Woolverstone Marina.

Woolverstone

The dredged channel now approaches the W bank of the river to within a cable, abreast the 'Cat House' buoy (Con G Fl G 1s). On the S bank there is a short pier and a concrete landing place known as Cat House Hard which belongs to the Woolverstone Marina and is used by their customers as well as members of the Royal Harwich Yacht Club, whose premises and dinghy landing are nearby.

The Royal Harwich YC was formed in 1845 and by 1848 was holding its first 'Eastern Coast Regatta' in Harwich Harbour, where the headquarters of the club remained for the next hundred years. In 1946 the club moved up-river to Woolverstone, where they at first occupied buildings remaining from a small naval base. Then, in 1969, a fine new clubhouse was opened by Robin Knox-Johnston.

Legend has it that in the heyday of smuggling, a china cat would be placed in a lighted window of the house at this point, to indicate that the 'coast is clear'.

The RHYC is always happy to allow visiting yachtsmen to use its facilities, which, during the season, consist of showers, light meals and a bar. The club has no moorings of its own, as these all belong to the Woolverstone Marina, apart from seven private mooring buoys just upstream of the hard in Potters Reach.

There is no room to lie to an anchor. *Under no circumstances should a boat anchor inside the buoyed channel,* as vessels up to 9,000 tons use the river regularly.

There is a pontoon marina taking 200 boats immediately upstream of the pier, just S of the dredged channel, so that the berths are accessible at all times. Visitors are welcome and can usually be accommodated for a short stay. The visitors' berths are on pontoon 'F', the last one upstream. A boatman is on duty during the summer months on Friday evenings and all day on Saturdays and Sundays (Tel: 0473 84206).

Facilities at Woolverstone Marina

Water	From end of pier.
Diesel fuel	From end of pier.
Petrol, paraffin and Calor Gas	From Marina.
Repairs	Yard equipped for all services. Slipway. 25-ton mobile crane.
Showers and toilet	Near pontoons.
Chandlery	Nearby.
Stores	From Pantry at Marina (Off Licence).
Club	Royal Harwich Yacht Club.
Telephone	Kiosk on hard.

No 7 buoy (Con G Fl G 5s) together with a red can (Fl R 5s) mark the commencement of Downham Reach and now the dredged channel becomes less than a cable wide so that the buoys must be strictly observed unless it is near HW. Another unlit green conical buoy marks the eastern edge of the channel through Downham Reach; the western edge is indicated first by a lit red can (Fl R 5s) and then by No 8, a red can light buoy (Fl R 5s), abreast the prominent tower in Freston Park. Just above No 8 buoy there is a green conical buoy (Fl G 5s) called the Priory, on the east side of the channel. The next pair of lit buoys are the Hill (Fl R 5s) and No 9 (Fl G 2.5s).

Along here there are a number of small boat moorings just outside the channel. They belong to the Stoke SC whose clubhouse is just below Freston Tower. From Freston hard it is a short walk up the road to the *Boot Inn*, where water may be obtained and where buses stop on the Shotley-Ipswich route.

By now the Orwell bridge will dominate the view ahead, but since it provides a clearance of 125ft (38m) and the width between the only navigable span is 300ft (92m) it should inconvenience yachtsmen very little. No ship can hit any of the eight piers that rise from the river bed because their bases are all protected by artificial 'islands'.

However, the bridge crosses the navigable channel at an angle so that the pilot of any commercial vessel about to pass under it will have his attention fully occupied without having to worry about any nearby yacht. Common sense therefore dictates that whenever possible the yachtsman should avoid being in the vicinity of the bridge if a commercial vessel is passing through.

There is an unlit port hand buoy, No 10, opposite the green conical No 11 buoy very near the bridge where the dredged channel is only about half a cable wide.

A green conical buoy, the E Fen (QG), marks the east side of the channel above the bridge while No 12 Cliff Reach Buoy (Can R Fl R 5s) on the west side also serves to indicate the entrance to Ostrich Creek through which a small stream, Belstead Brook, enters the river after passing under Bourne Bridge. The last buoy with a light is the red can Factory buoy (QR) off the CAST container terminal, although there are several more unlit buoys leading right up to the entrance to the Wet Dock.

Ostrich Creek

The Orwell YC has both drying and deep water moorings on the W side of the river up to the West Bank Container Dock. There is a visitor's mooring near No 12 channel buoy and a floating pontoon accessible at all times.

There is a small pool just to the E of the pontoon, with three posts to which visitors may moor overnight — given permission from the Orwell YC.

For day to day requirements, it is not really necessary to go farther afield than the vicinity of the clubhouse and Bourne Bridge.

Having passed under the Orwell Bridge, *'Viola'* is bound down the river, through Harwich Harbour and out to sea

Fox's Marina

This 100-berth marina and boatyard is situated next to Bourne Bridge (abreast No 12 buoy) and opposite the conspicuous power station. Entrance is through a dredged gutway marked on both sides by beacons. Facilities include a 25-ton travelift, and a very large chandler.

The Orwell Yacht Club and the *Ostrich Inn* and restaurant are both nearby.

Facilities at Wherstead	
Water	From clubhouse or pontoon.
Stores	Shops nearby.
Petrol and oil	Garage adjacent to clubhouse.
Gas	From Marina.
Repairs	Boatyard nearby with travelift.
Transport	Buses into Ipswich (1½ miles). Good train service from Ipswich to London.
Telephone	From club or box nearby and at marina.
Club	Orwell Yacht Club. Fox's Marina YC.

The lock and bridge at the entrance to Ipswich Wet Dock will be opened on request from one hour before until HW

Ipswich Dock

When it was opened in 1850 the Wet Dock at Ipswich was the largest in Europe and right up to the 1930s it was being used by square rigged grain ships. Until recently the basin was not available to yachts but now there are two small marinas within the dock: Oyster Marine at the Wherry Quay and Neptune Marina at the Neptune Quay.

When planning to enter the Dock a yacht should contact Ipswich Port Radio (Ch 16 or 14) when at No 9 buoy, to check the time of opening the lock gates. Neptune Marina's telephone number is (0473) 34578. There is a pontoon against which a boat can lie outside the lock while awaiting its opening.

The Dock is approached along a closely buoyed channel past the Ro-Ro terminal opposite Cliff Quay.

The lock gates and swing bridge open from about an hour before HW until just after that. Red and green traffic control lights are located above the Orwell Navigation Service building on the E side of the lock.

Yachts should not berth alongside any of the commercial quays without first obtaining permission from the Port Authority.

VHF Channel 16 then 14 or 12.

Above the lock and to port is New Cut and a yard where boats dry out against stagings and where there are some facilities, including water and diesel fuel, repairs and a 20-ton crane. Stores can be easily obtained from shops nearby. EC Wed.

Fox's Marina at Ipswich is located opposite the Power Station and the entrance channel, marked by port and starboard beacons, commences near No 12 buoy

Tides (Wrabness)

HW Dover +1.05 Range: Springs 4.1m Neaps 3.4m

Charts

Admiralty 2693
Stanford No 6
Imray Y16

Waypoints

Ganges Buoy 51.57.07.N   1.17.11.E
Stour No. 12 Buoy 51.56.92.N   1.06.10.E

Hazards

Ferries turning off Parkeston Quay.

THE river Stour has never been as popular with yachtsmen as the Orwell and this is probably due to a number of reasons; Parkeston Quay with its attendant movements of large ferries, the absence of any waterside hamlet to compare with Pin Mill and the difficulty of lying afloat out of the fairway anywhere above Wrabness.

Yet the Stour is quieter and more spacious than the Orwell and, moreover, its twin towns — Mistley and Manningtree — have been called 'two of the best-looking places in Essex'.

There is really not much reason to worry about the ferries off Parkeston Quay, since even at low water the channel is almost half a mile wide. However, it is true that beyond Wrabness the width of the low-tide channel narrows rather abruptly. Although well buoyed, it does involve a risk of grounding, particularly when a first passage is attempted while the wide mud flats are covered. But this objection is not peculiar to the Stour, since much the same conditions are found in the upper tidal reaches of almost all the rivers of the Thames Estuary.

Channel Widths

The navigable channel extends from Harwich to Manningtree, some nine miles. The Stour separates the counties of Essex and Suffolk, and its general direction is westerly throughout the eight miles or so to Mistley. At high tide the river appears to be a mile or more wide throughout the whole of its length. In fact its width at LW, while nearly half a mile abreast Shotley Pier and much the same from there to Harkstead Point, diminishes rapidly thereafter to about two cables off Wrabness Point and up as far as Stutton Ness. Then, along the mile or so of Straight Reach, the channel again narrows to less than a cable just below Ballast Hill. The final reaches between Ballast Hill and Mistley Quay become narrower still, until abreast the quays the channel at LW is less than 50 metres wide.

The most useful anchorage in the entrance to the Stour is over on the north bank of the river close to Shotley Pier. Anchorage is prohibited in the vicinity of Parkeston Quay, since the continental ferry traffic is considerable. The first useful small boat anchorage above Harwich Harbour is off Erwarton Ness, about a mile and a half W of Parkeston.

There are two starboard hand marks between Parkeston Quay and Harkstead Point; first a S. Cardinal beacon (Q (6)+LFl(2)15s) and then a green conical buoy (QG). But in daytime when visibility allows, there is a

There are a few yacht moorings as well as the light-vessel moorings off Shotley and across the Stour is the container and ferry port at Parkeston Quay

conspicuous factory chimney to be seen straight up the river, at Cattawade, some eight or nine miles from Harwich. It is useful to remember that with this chimney dead ahead a course of 280°M will lead through the best water as far up the river as Harkstead Point. The depth of the water in the channel is never less than 5m, until about a mile below Harkstead Point, when the mid-river water shallows gradually from about 5m to 3.5m abreast the Point.

Erwarton Ness

With any north in the wind there is good anchorage off Erwarton Ness about a cable from the derelict quay in line with the S cardinal beacon (Q Fl(6) LFl 15s). There is good holding in mud, but no protection from either easterly or westerly winds. Landing is possible near the ruined staithe between half-flood and half-ebb. Erwarton village is about a mile away, although the inn, the *Queen's Head*, is a little nearer. Water and a few supplies can be obtained in the village.

Holbrook Bay

Continuing up-river from Erwarton Ness, Harkstead Point is the next low headland on the north shore, while on the south bank, Wrabness Point is notable for its height (40ft) in East Coast waters. Once clear of Harkstead Point and the S cardinal Holbrook beacon (Q Fl(6) LFl 15s), the scene to the north will open out to disclose the extensive buildings and conspicuous central spire of the Royal Hospital School on the high ground at Holbrook. When the tide has no more than half flooded, the extensive mud flats of Holbrook Bay cover an area roughly two miles long and a mile deep. Two or three ill-defined creeks lead across these flats, the more important of them being Gallister Creek and Holbrook Creek.

Gallister Creek

There is enough water and just enough space to lie quietly to an anchor a cable or so inside Gallister Creek, but for landing it is probably better to use Holbrook Creek.

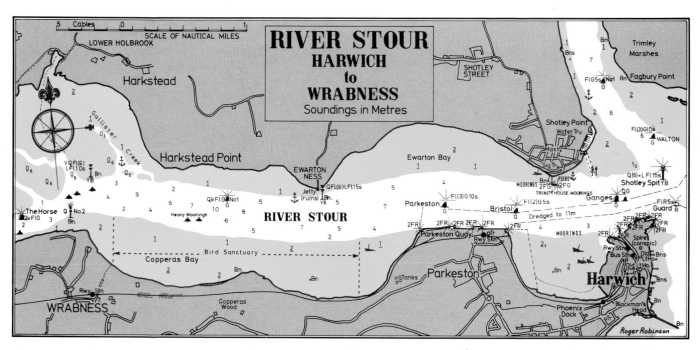

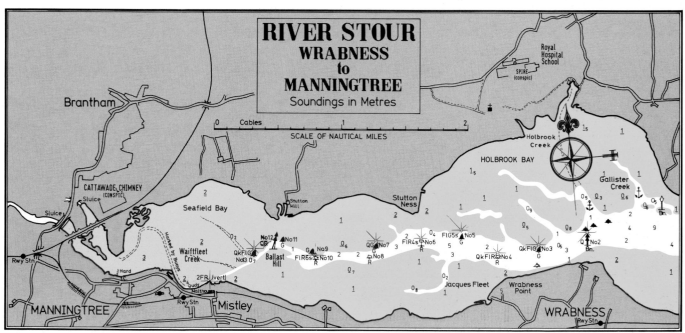

Although it dries out for most of each tide, Holbrook Creek holds moorings for quite a few small cruising boats

Holbrook Creek

This creek is marked by withies along its western edge and there is enough depth and space to allow anchoring for a quarter of a mile inside. Any exploring farther up the creek should be done just before the mud banks are covered and while the gutway can be followed.

Clean landing is possible at the head of Holbrook Creek near HW, and Holbrook village and stores are about a mile away.

Wrabness Point

There used to be a horse in mid-stream off Wrabness, but following extensive dredging for shingle this now seems to have merged with the flats on Holbrook Bay so that the only channel now runs close to the point, past a port hand N cardinal beacon (Q) and a conical green (QG) starboard hand buoy. Because of the constant dredging for shingle, the holding ground in the channel off Wrabness is no longer as safe as it used to be and if there is no vacant mooring, it will usually pay to move a bit further upstream towards the next port hand buoy. *In any case beware of anchoring in mid-channel because of the commercial shipping using Mistley Quay. If stopping overnight, a riding light is essential.*

The village of Wrabness is reached by climbing a pathway up the cliff and following the lane past the church towards the railway station. The church is one of the two in this district which have their bells in a wooden cage-like belfry in the churchyard.

A television mast on the south side of the river provides a conspicuous mark by day and by night.

Facilities at Wrabness	
Water	From stand-pipe at top of cliff.
Stores	Obtainable in village. EC Wed.
Transport	Train service to London.

When continuing up-river from Wrabness a stranger to the Stour will do well to set off before the mud flats are covered and while the course of the channel is visible as well as the buoys which mark it. In these narrow upper reaches the buoys must be given a wide berth whenever it appears that they are being swept by the tide over the banks they are intended to mark.

From the anchorage off Wrabness the channel turns a little N of W for about a mile, past a port hand buoy (Q R) and a conical green buoy (Fl G 5s) to starboard. Jacques Fleet and the bay of the same name are to the south. A gravel dredger and a few barges may sometimes be lying here.

The next mark is No 6 Beacon (Fl R 4s) with a tide gauge, marking Smith Shoal; it is located about three cables south of Stutton Ness, and the best water here is no more than two cables from the Suffolk shore.

West of Stutton Ness the channel continues for a mile along Straight Reach, becoming narrower and shallower. There are three conical green buoys to be left to starboard and three red cans to be left to port along this reach. Then comes a bottleneck at Ballast Hill, where for a short distance there is a depth of only 1m and a width of less than a cable at LW. The port hand at Ballast Hill is the N cardinal No 12 (QR).

Use of the sounder or sounding pole offers the best

chance of getting through here early on the tide. Once past the shingle patch that forms Ballast Hill, there is an isolated widening and deepening of the channel in Cross Reach. This hole provides the only spot in which a boat drawing 1.5m of water can remain afloat within reasonable distance of Mistley.

After Cross Reach the channel turns south-westerly along Waiftfleet Reach and Miller Reach, and from hereabouts the warehouses and maltings and the twin towers of the ruined Adam church at Mistley will all come into view.

The buoyage and marking of the winding channel of the river between Wrabness and Mistley Quay have been changed considerably several times in the last few years and this has made it very difficult to provide information that will remain reliable throughout the life of an edition.

Westwards from Baltic Wharf the best water will be found within twenty or thirty metres of the quayside. The depths here at LW are nowhere more than about 1m, and one of the few holes having this much water should be sought opposite a small dock or basin about half-way along the quays.

There is good holding in the channel at Mistley, but the tide runs very hard during the first half of the ebb, when the rate can be as high as 4 knots. At Mistley it is HW 50 minutes later than at Harwich.

Landing at the quayside by means of one of the several vertical ladders is not very easy, except at high water, but it is worthwhile going ashore at Mistley to walk to the top of Furze Hill and enjoy the fine view of the river from there and to see the famous twin towers that remain from the church that Robert Adam designed in 1776.

Facilities at Mistley	
Water	From the quay.
Stores	Several shops in main street near quay. EC Wed.
Petrol and oil	From garage.
Transport	Train service to London.

Above Mistley

Manningtree can be reached in craft drawing as much as 2m, provided the buoys are carefully observed, and the ship is prepared to take the ground soon after arrival at Manningtree. In a shallower draught boat, drawing no more than 1m, it is also possible, just before HW, to take the North or Second channel across Seafield Bay direct from Ballast Hill to the bend in the channel known as the Hook. But if you are sailing across the flats off Mistley, look out for the wreck that lies there.

The local centreboard classes belonging to the members of the Stour Sailing Club race around a course which takes them right across Seafield Bay to within a cable or so of the Suffolk shore.

The quay at Manningtree is not so extensive as at Mistley, and there is no water at all at low tide.

It is only a ten or 15 minute walk to Manningtree from Mistley along a pleasant riverside road.

Facilities at Manningtree	
Water	From quayside.
Stores	Shops in town. EC Wed.
Petrol and oil	Garages nearby.
Transport	Direct train service to London.
Club	Stour Sailing Club.

Swans are still walking on the 'horse' off Mistley Quay, but the freighter has turned in deep water before departing

8
The Walton Backwaters

Tides (Stone Point)

HW Dover +0.40 Range: Springs 4.1m Neaps 3.3m

Charts

Admiralty 2692
Stanford No 6
Imray Y16

Waypoints

Stone Banks Buoy 51.53.16.N   1.19.34.E
Pye-End Buoy 51.55.00.N   1.18.00.E

Hazards

Lines of lobster pots off Walton-on-the-Naze.

THE map that Arthur Ransome's Swallows and Amazons drew of their 'secret waters' would still serve quite well for navigating the Walton Backwaters for little has changed, except the number of boats.

All the creeks give good protection in almost any weather, and the Backwaters are an excellent base from which to make a number of modest cruises to the Stour, the Orwell or the Deben.

Approaches

The entrance to the Backwaters is located about half a mile off the Dovercourt foreshore, and half a mile or so south of the mouth of Harwich Harbour. Whether approaching from the north or the south, it is necessary

to find Pye-End buoy, marking the northern extremity of an area of hard sand known as Pye Sand and the Sunken Pye.

When approaching Harwich from the south through the Wallet and the Medusa channel the most prominent landmark is the Naze Tower, erected by Trinity House in 1720, and standing 160ft above the cliffs just north of Walton-on-the-Naze. The Medusa buoy (Con G Fl G 5s) lies just over two miles E of Walton pier and, from a position midway between the pier and the Medusa, the Naze Tower will bear approximately NW while the next mark, the Stone Banks buoy (Can R can topmark), will lie about three miles away to the NNE. Any less than a mile offshore around the Naze will probably have

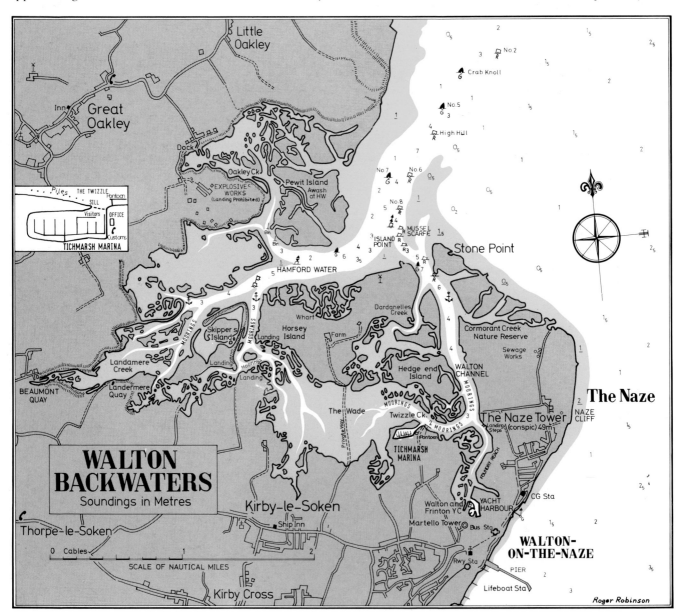

The Pye End buoy is larger now but it no longer has a topmark

you bumping the bottom. There is considerable erosion of the cliffs, and as a result a shoal patch seems to be spreading out beneath the tower.

Another problem hereabouts is the multitude of lobster pots that are set by inshore fishermen. However hard one tries it is difficult to avoid them in poor visibility and practically impossible at night So, if you find your progress seems slower than usual, see whether you have a line and pot caught by your rudder or prop.

In good visibility such landmarks as the tall spire of St Nicholas Church at Harwich and the large cranes at the Port of Felixstowe will be seen before the Stone Banks buoy comes up. This buoy, as its name suggests, marks a number of isolated clumps of stones and rocks with no more than 2m over them at LWS. A course only slight W of N from the Stone Banks buoy will bring Harwich breakwater (awash at HW) in view ahead. When about a mile from the breakwater and the entrance to Harwich Harbour it should be possible in conditions of reasonable visibility to spot the Pye-End buoy (Spher. RWVS) which is located approximately 1 mile due S (mag) from the end of the breakwater and is now the responsibility of the Harwich Harbour Board.

The buildings along the shore of Dovercourt Bay provide a background which makes it rather difficult to locate Pye-End buoy from the SE, but one of the largest

houses has white walls and an extension at each end with gables facing seaward. Fortunately for us, Trinity House, who own the property, keep the white walls freshly painted so that they serve well as a landmark and when this twin-gabled building comes into line with Dovercourt lowlight, it is safe to set a course along this line until the Pye-End buoy comes into sight.

The shallowest part of the approach to the Backwaters is the area known as the Halliday Rock Flats where there is less than 2m in places during LWS. This shoal water will prevent many craft from attempting the entrance before two or three hours of flood. It is HWFC hereabouts at approximately midday and midnight. Springs rise 4m and neaps 3m.

When approaching the Backwaters from the north, the well-buoyed big-ship channels should be crossed as quickly as possible and then followed, outside it, as far as the Landguard buoy (N Card YB Q) from which a course of approximately 245°M will lead to the Pye-End Buoy less than a mile away. This same course, if continued, should find the No 2 red can buoy at the entrance to the channel into the Backwaters.

As there are no light buoys marking the entrance it is practically impossible for the stranger to enter Walton Backwaters safely after dark. Even in bright daylight the newcomer will look to the SW from abreast the Pye-End buoy and find it difficult to believe that any kind of deep water channel lies ahead. But after sailing in a generally south-westerly direction for a quarter of a mile or so, the next buoys — No 2, a red can buoy, and No 3 (Crab Knoll), a green buoy with iron strapping to form a conical top, will come into view. The Dovercourt shore shelves regularly, and is the safer side to work until this first pair of buoys have been reached, after which the channel becomes narrower and deeper, and the sand is steep-to on either hand.

The next green conical buoy, No 5, is about half a mile farther to the SW, and it marks the western edge of the channel where it narrows to a bottleneck, little more than a cable wide, at a point known as High Hill, marked by a red can bearing that name. There are eight or nine metres of water in the channel here, but since the sand on either side is quite steep-to, short boards are essential whenever it is necessary to turn to windward, and continuous use of the echo sounder, or very smart use of the lead, is the only sure guide to the limits of the channel, when the tide has covered the banks and there are no ripples. It is also as well to remember that spring tides run out of here at 2½ knots during the first part of the ebb.

From High Hill onwards, the channel widens to two or three cables and is marked on the W side by a green conical buoy (No 7) and on the E side by red cans (Nos 6 and 8). From hereabouts it is usually possible to see the Horsey Island Point buoy (N Card) at the junction of Hamford Water and the Walton Channel.

Entrance to Walton Channel
When bound for the Walton Channel there are three more unnumbered red can buoys to be left to port round Mussel Scarfe. This series of buoys *should not be passed too closely* because under certain conditions of tide and westerly wind they can be over the bank they mark. Neither should the Island Point buoy be approached too closely when entering or leaving the Walton Channel, as there is an extension of the mud bank to the E, just south of the buoy. A green conical buoy marks this hazard.

Stone Point, at the entrance to Walton Backwaters; with Dovercourt and Harwich beyond

The last two port-hand buoys mark the NW and W edge of Stone Point respectively. The outer (northernmost) of these two also indicates the SW end of a channel known as 'The Swatch', which is used (near HW), by local craft bound for the fishing grounds off the Naze.

Stone Point

The steep-to shingle bank at Stone Point provides a popular landing place at all states of the tide, while the anchorage nearby offers excellent protection. The holding ground in the channel is good, but the depths are considerable and, since the ebb runs hard in midstream, as much as 3 knots during springs, it is preferable to anchor close to the E bank, where there is a slight contra-flow eddy during the first part of the ebb.

On a fine day in summer, Walton Stone Point is a good spot for a bathe and picnic, but it is a privately owned bird sanctuary and nature reserve. Unfortunately some unthinking people light fires, leave rubbish and trample down the plants and grass that are so important to the wild life of the area. If this kind of thoughtless behaviour were to continue Stone Point might be prohibited to yachtsmen but fortunately the Point is under the control of the Walton and Frinton Yacht Club, whom we must certainly support.

The Walton Channel is not buoyed between Stone Point and the Twizzle, but the best water is to be found midway between the banks, except near the mouth of Stone Creek, where mud extends to the W, and the channel is nearer the Horsey Island shore. The depths in the channel decrease from 7m off Stone Point to rather less than 5m where the creek changes direction and name and becomes the Twizzle, at the entrance to which there is a shoal area.

There are many moorings in the Walton Channel below the junction with Foundry Reach, but even more craft are moored in the Twizzle, which carries a depth of nearly two metres for about a mile. Some very small craft are permanently moored in Foundry Reach, but as this dries out for most of its length it is only of use to larger craft towards HW when, on a good tide, they can berth alongside the clubhouse of the Walton and Frinton YC long enough to take on water or even to do some shopping in the town.

The landing at the clubhouse can be reached by dinghy for all but an hour on either side of LW. Visitors to the Backwaters are always welcome at the club, and the members of the WFYC are to be congratulated on their enterprise in buoying the way in from Pye-End.

If the tide does not suit, or the long trip to the clubhouse from the Twizzle is unattractive, it is possible to land from a dinghy at some concrete steps built on to the sea wall of the E bank of Foundry Creek, just above its junction with the Twizzle. From these steps or a nearby slip, it is a walk of about a mile into Walton, and even longer to the clubhouse, but by taking a footpath nearby, general stores and a telephone box near the Naze can be reached more easily than those at Walton.

Facilities at Walton-on-the-Naze	
Water	From alongside clubhouse.
Stores	Shops ¼ mile from clubhouse. EC Wed.
Petrol and oil	From garages in town. Diesel from yard near quay.
Repairs	Several shipwrights in Mill Lane, near club. Derrick available.
Transport	Trains to London via Colchester. Buses to Colchester, Clacton and Harwich.
Club	Walton and Frinton Yacht Club.
Telephone	At clubhouse.

The Walton-on-the-Naze Yacht Basin is adjacent to the Walton and Frinton Yacht Club in Mill Lane. This yacht basin has retaining gates that are opened around the time of high water (approximately 20 min after HW Harwich) when there is a depth of about 2m in the entrance at neap tides and about 2.5m at springs. (It is not always possible to open the gates on some neap tides and in any case they are opened only during working hours.)

The Twizzle

The Twizzle, which runs in a generally westerly direction, is really a continuation of Walton Channel, and it offers complete protection in an average depth of 2m at LW except near its entrance. Craft are moored on both sides of the Twizzle and anchoring is certainly not advisable because many of the ground chains are laid across the channel. After enquiry at the clubhouse or one of the local yards it is sometimes possible to borrow one of the moorings for a short period.

There is clean landing on shingle at Colonel's Hard about two cables inside the Twizzle, on the S shore of the creek. The Walton Lifeboat is sometimes moored off this hard, from which the town can be reached by walking along the sea wall.

Titchmarsh Marina

The Titchmarsh marina (400 boats) is on the S side of the Twizzle, a little to the W of Colonel's Hard. There is about 2m of water in the basin, but very little over the sill in the entrance at LW neaps and this means, as it does at several other east coast marinas, that no boats can leave or enter at LW springs. But in this case there is a line of dolphins and a pontoon in the Twizzle nearby and, as they belong to the marina, boats can lie there while they wait for water over the sill.

Facilities at the marina include: showers and toilets, water to the pontoons, a 30 ton travel-lift, chandlery and a telephone box from which to call a taxi — because it is a long way into Walton-on-the-Naze. There is a Customs Post above the harbourmaster's office.

The Twizzle is navigable at LW by craft drawing 1m as far as the western end of Hedge End Island — about a mile from the entrance of Foundry Creek. Farther W, the Twizzle becomes a narrow, winding gutway through the extensive mud and saltings of Horsey Mere. The gutway is marked by a confusion of withies that would require much acquaintance to understand. The creek finally peters out to the E of the rough roadway known as the Wade, which crosses Horsey Mere to join the mainland with the farm on Horsey Island.

There are oyster beds at the extreme W end of the Twizzle, so care must be taken not to ground in this area.

Those who have read Arthur Ransome's *Secret Water* will remember the exciting race the 'Explorers' had when they crossed the Wade during a rising tide.

It is possible to sail straight across Horsey Mere from the Twizzle to Kirby Creek, provided the boat does not draw more than about 1m and the trip is made about an hour before HW, on a day near to, but *before,* spring tides.

Hamford Water

Hamford Water is also known as the West Water. It runs in a generally south-westerly direction from the Island Point buoy moored off the mud spit extending from the north-eastern corner of Horsey Island, to the north-eastern end of Skipper's Island, where the channel divides. There is plenty of water in this main reach of Hamford Water — 7m near the entrance, and 5m about a mile inside. The width of the channel is nearly two cables at LW and the N side of it is marked by a green conical buoy. Both protection and holding are excellent, unless you are unlucky enough to drop your hook on top of one of the massive growths of 'pipe weed' that have infested these waters in recent years. When any kind of anchor lands on a patch of this stuff (which is really a worm called *sabella pavanina* and not a weed) its holding power becomes negligible. It is therefore a good idea to test (under power if necessary) that your anchor is holding before settling down for the night and certainly before leaving the boat.

Oakley Creek

Oakley Creek branches to the north, out of Hamford Water and between Bramble and Pewit Islands. The spit off the W side of the entrance is marked by a N cardinal buoy. There is enough water for light draught craft to lie afloat for nearly a mile within, but it is probably best to resist any temptation to anchor there because the creek is used once or twice a week by freighters which load at the wharf belonging to an explosives factory at Oakley, where landing is strictly prohibited. The movements of these ships can be by day or night, so it is doubly important not to be there after dark.

Landermere Creek

By continuing west along Hamford Water, a boat drawing up to 2m can safely reach the division of the channel where Landermere Creek turns towards Landermere Quay. There are some moorings just beyond here but usually enough space and depth to anchor clear of them. Landing from a dinghy is possible at the quay from about half-flood. Stores must be sought at Thorpe-le-Soken.

At around high water it is possible to take a dinghy beyond Landermere up to Beaumont Quay, where a plaque will inform you that the stones used for its construction came from the old London Bridge. An overhead power cable spans the cut and prevents boats with masts from reaching the quay. The quay is only a quarter of a mile from a main-road bus route to Thorpe-le-Soken, where there are shops from which most stores can be obtained.

Kirby Creek

This creek joins Hamford Water on its S side about a quarter mile beyond Oakley Creek, offering one of the most popular anchorages in the Backwaters.

The Naze Oyster Company has some of its layings in Kirby Creek and, like anywhere else that oysters are cultivated, a yachtsman is responsible if by anchoring or grounding he damages any of the stock. Notice boards to this effect will be seen at the entrance to the creek.

Fortunately, relations between the Oyster Company and the Walton and Frinton YC are good and, in order to avoid any conflict, a couple of small yellow buoys now mark the N and S limits of the layings that are being worked at any particular time. Yachts should never anchor between these marks.

If for some reason conditions in Hamford Water are uncomfortable, yachtsmen may be able to anchor just within Kirby Creek and above the layings, but then they must beware the treacherously long spit of mud that extends from the NE end of Skipper's Island. Alternatively, it may be possible to pick up a vacant

It is just possible to lie afloat at LW in a 'hole' off the SE end of Skippers Island, quite close to a landing place on the mainland shore

Graham Jones

mooring at the southern end of the creek, near the tiny islet off Horsey Island.

Skipper's Island is used by the Essex Naturalists' Society, and they have erected an observation tower from which they can watch the many species of birds that come to the Backwaters. For stores a landing can be made at a wooden staithe on the mainland opposite the SE corner of the Island. This is a good landing except at dead low water, but the walk along the sea wall to Kirby-le-Soken is about a mile and a half.

From abreast the wooden staithe Kirby Creek turns sharply to the E, to emerge into Horsey Mere, and then turns S again up to Kirby Quay. The quay can be reached by dinghy towards HW, and the tortuous gutway is plentifully marked by withies, which are no doubt understood by local sailors, but at first acquaintance are only likely to baffle the uninitiated.

The village of Kirby-le-Soken is no more than a quarter of a mile from the quay, and the village shops will satisfy a yachtsman's day-to-day needs.

There is an old quay and a shingle hard at Landermere, where a few small craft dry out for most of the tide

9
The River Colne

Tides (Brightlingsea)

HW Dover +0.55 Range: Springs 5.0m Neaps 3.8m (HW Colchester approx 20 mins after HW Brightlingsea)

Charts

Admiralty 3741
Stanford No 4
Imray Y17

Waypoints

Knoll Buoy 51.43.85.N   1.05.17.E
NW Knoll Buoy 51.44.18.N   1.02.50.E
Inner Bench Head Buoy 51.45.88.N   1.01.62.E

Hazards

Knoll, Colne Bar and Bench Head shoals near LW.

NOT since the days of the trading barges has the river Colne been so busy with commercial traffic as it is again now. Small freighters berth every day at Colchester or Wivenhoe and shortly may also call at Brightlingsea when a new quay is completed there.

But for many people the Colne is known for its oysters — still cultivated in Pyefleet Creek, as they were when the Romans were at Colchester.

The river Colne is smaller and more intimate than its close neighbour, the Blackwater. Both these rivers join the sea at the NW Knoll buoy, midway between Colne Point to the E and Sales Point to the W. The distance from the Knoll buoy to the Hythe at Colchester is about 11 miles, most of which lies in a north-north-westerly direction.

Approaches from Seaward

When approaching the Colne from the S through the Swin Spitway or from the N, up the Wallet, make for

the Knoll buoy (N Car Q) and then leave both the Eagle (Con G QG) and the Colne Bar (Con G Fl(2)G 5s) buoys close to starboard before shaping a course of 350°M into the entrance of the river. From a position near the Bar buoy a group of three more buoys will usually be seen in daylight — the Fishery buoy (Spher Y), the Colne Point buoy (Con G) and the Inner Bench Head (Can R Fl(2)R 5s). Only the last of these will of course be visible at night.

Shoal draught boats can, provided it is not too near the time of low water, cross Colne Bar north of the Eagle and as much as a mile inside the Bar buoy. When coming south a sudden increase in depths will indicate when the bar has been crossed.

From the Inner Bench Head light buoy inwards, the channel is buoyed on both sides — *even*-numbered red cans to port and *odd*-numbered green conical buoys to starboard. There is a depth of some 9m between the first

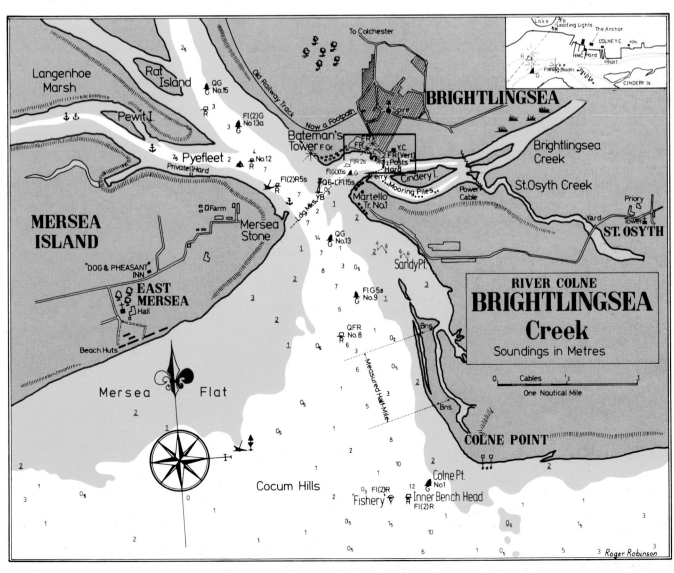

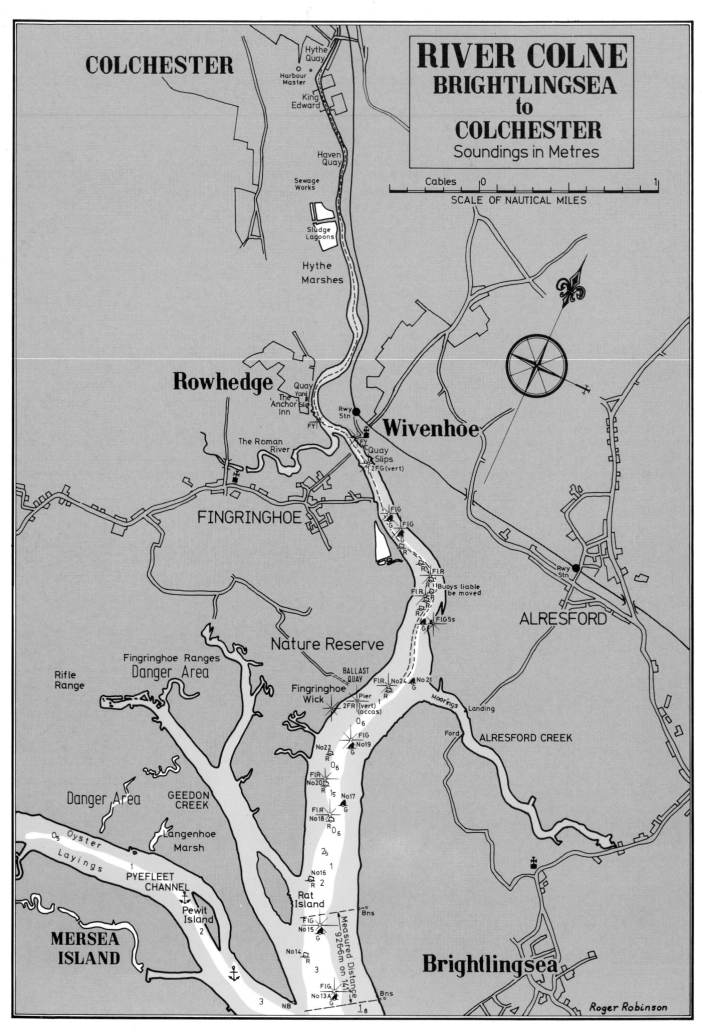

COLCHESTER

Hythe Quay
Harbour Master
King Edward
Haven Quay
Sewage Works
Sludge Lagoons
Hythe Marshes

RIVER COLNE
BRIGHTLINGSEA
to
COLCHESTER
Soundings in Metres

Cables 0 1
SCALE OF NAUTICAL MILES

Rowhedge
Quay Yard
The Anchor Inn
Quay Slip
FY
Rwy Stn
Wivenhoe
FY
Quay Slips
2FG(vert)

The Roman River

FINGRINGHOE

FlG
G FlG
G
R
R FlR
R
FlR Buys liable
R be moved
R
G FlG5s

Rwy Stn

ALRESFORD

Nature Reserve

Fingringhoe Ranges
Danger Area

Rifle Range

BALLAST QUAY
Fingringhoe Wick
Pier
2FR(vert)
(occas)
FlR No24 No21
R G

Moorings Landing
Ford ALRESFORD CREEK

0.6
FlG No19
G
No22
0.6
FlR
No20 R
1.5 No17
G
FlR
No18 R
0.6

Danger Area

GEEDON CREEK

Oyster
0.5 Layings
1
PYEFLEET CHANNEL
Pewit Island
2
Langenhoe Marsh

2.5
1
No16
2

Rat Island
Bns

FlG
No15
G

MERSEA ISLAND

No14
R
3

Brightlingsea

Measured Distance 926m on 141°

FlG
No13A
G
Bns
NB
3
1.8

Roger Robinson

44

This yacht is motoring into Brightlingsea Creek from the River Colne. A starboard hand light buoy now marks the spit that extends from the south side of the entrance

pair of channel buoys, and there is not much less than 6m anywhere within the channel until abreast the entrance to Brightlingsea Creek. However, carefully observe the buoys on both hands, since the water shoals quite rapidly, particularly to the W.

Approach from the Blackwater

When sailing to the Blackwater from the Colne it is safe, except near low water, for craft drawing 2m or less to cross from the deep water of the Colne on a course that has St Peters Chapel (near Sales Point) bearing 240°M. This will lead about midway between the Bench Head and Cocum Hills shoals.

In clear weather, from a position abreast the Inner Bench Head it is possible to see Brightlingsea Church tower on high ground, due N (mag), distant four miles. Another mark that will help the newcomer get his bearings is the very large building shed at Brightlingsea, which may be seen over the low-lying shore from several miles away.

Brightlingsea Creek

The buoy at the entrance to Brightlingsea Creek is a South Cardinal yellow and black buoy (QFl(6)LFl 15s). The entrance it marks is very shallow, with not much more than 1m best water at LWS. A conical green buoy (Fl(3)G 5s) inside the entrance is intended to keep you off the spit the extends from St Osyth Stone Point.

Batemans Tower, although condemned at one time, is now safe and lit with an orange sodium lamp, and this mark together with No 13 buoy (Con G Fl G) should make the entrance to Brightlingsea easier at night. The correct course into the creek itself is 42°M and by day this line is indicated by two leading marks (orange and white stripes) known locally as the 'cricket stumps' and set up on poles in the town. By night these marks bear two fixed red leading lights.

Most of the local yachts at Brightlingsea are moored fore and aft, rafted together (3 boats in each bay) between two lines of piles in the creek running S of Cindery Island. At low water there is only about 1.5m and even less on the E side of the posts.

The first bay of posts in both rows are reserved for visiting yachts, but if these three berths are already occupied, move along the W side of the lines until there is a space. But before assuming that you have found a vacant berth, check with the harbourmaster.

There is little water in the creek that runs to the N of Cindery Island, and on up to the head of the creek, where there is a jetty used by gravel barges. Because of this traffic, which can be at night, there are no moorings to the N of Cindery Island and a fairway must be maintained at all times.

Brightlingsea offers excellent facilities to the yachtsman. There is a fine hard on which almost any boat can stand upright against one of the several posts available. Arrangements for using the posts should be made with the Hard Master whose office is near the YC jetty; he is in attendance from Monday to Friday in the mornings only. (Tel: (0200630) 2200).

The Colne YC has a catwalk and pontoon by the clubhouse just E of the town causeway and meals can usually be obtained at the club.

Facilities at Brightlingsea	
Water	Tap at top of hard on CYC jetty by arrangement.
Stores	Shops in town (½ mile). EC Thurs.
Chandlers	Near town hard.
Petrol and oil	From chandlers.
Repairs	Advice from harbourmaster.
Sailmaker	Behind *Anchor Inn*.
Transport	Buses to Colchester, whence good service to London.
Clubs	Colne Yacht Club. Brightlingsea Sailing Club.
Telephone	At top of hard.

St Osyth Creek

Above Brightlingsea, there are two tidal islands — W and E Cindery Islands, dividing Brightlingsea Creek into two branches, abreast the junction with St Osyth Creek. This latter creek is no more than a mile long and is very narrow, particularly near the entrance where the best water (perhaps as much as 1.5m at LW) will be found between a tiny hummock of land known as Pincushion Island and the S bank. Shallow draught boats can safely reach the head of the creek for about an

The wharf at the head of St Osyth Creek is a favourite haunt of old Essex smacks

hour or so either side of HW. The creek is sparsely marked by withies.

St Osyth itself is worth visiting to see the remains of the twelfth-century Priory, although all signs of the tide-mill have now disappeared. There is a boatyard with a crane and slip and a chandler near the quay, which is wooden faced and has several ladders. This is a popular venue for owners of Essex smacks.

East Mersea Point

Opposite the entrance to Brightlingsea Creek is Mersea Point — the eastern extremity of Mersea Island. There is good landing on the shingle of Mersea Point, and one can walk to the *Dog and Pheasant,* about a mile away.

Good holding ground in 5m, well protected from all but south or south-easterly winds, can be found clear of the few moorings and between Mersea Point and the old wreck that dries out just below the entrance to Pyefleet Creek. This wreck, of a ship called *Lowlands,* is marked by a red can buoy (Fl(2)R 5s).

Since chartered sailing barges and coasters frequently bring up off the entrance to Brightlingsea Creek, it is essential to use a riding light when anchored over night.

Pyefleet Creek

A cable or two above the wreck on the W side of the river is the entrance to Pyefleet Creek — an important oyster preserve — which nevertheless provides an excellent anchorage with good protection. In fact, an anchorage in Pyefleet is usually more comfortable than a berth within Brightlingsea Creek, because of the swell that often enters that creek at the turn of the tide.

Pyefleet Creek is one of the most popular Saturday night anchorages on the whole of the East Coast. Perhaps this is because it provides that sense of remoteness for which so many of us feel a need. There are no landing places and no cars in sight and although there may be twenty or thirty craft at anchor, everyone (except the waterskiers) is there for the peace and quiet and acts accordingly.

The deep water in the entrance to Pyefleet is indicated by a line of mooring buoys, belonging to the Colchester Oyster Fisheries, who may charge for their use. There is plenty of room and plenty of water for a mile or more up the creek, and yachts may bring up either just within the entrance or anywhere up to or even above Pewit Island, which is easily recognised by its oyster packing sheds. Great care must be taken to avoid anchoring or grounding on any of the oyster layings in the Pyefleet. Craft drawing up to 2m can remain afloat as far up as Maydays Marsh, where the channel divides; the S branch leading to the Strood which joins Mersea Island to the mainland.

The only disadvantage of the Pyefleet anchorage is that no supplies are available nearer than Brightlingsea, which can seem a long way when a strong wind is blowing up or down the Colne. When anchoring higher up the creek — above Pewit Island, landing must be carried out with great caution as the area is used by the Army as a range.

Returning to the Colne river buoyage, red can buoys mark the mud spits formed by the small creeks which enter the river N and S of Rat Island. Above Rat Island the channel continues in a NNW'ly direction before turning NE'ly round Aldboro Point. Two red cans and a green conical buoy mark the course of the channel round this bend.

Alresford Creek

Fingringhoe Marshes, a nature reserve controlled by the Essex Naturalist Trust, are now on the port hand and a disused jetty will come into view on the same shore. The next buoy (green conical) will be found off the entrance to Alresford Creek. For a quarter of a mile inside the creek there are small boat moorings up to a ford at which landing can be made on either bank. From the ford up to Thorington Mill at the head of the creek is a little over a mile, but most of the creek dries out at LW. Out in the river there is enough water for large boats to lie afloat at LW out of the channel opposite Aldboro Point.

Above Alresford Creek the channel continues in a northerly direction and is well marked with both lit and

The attractive waterfront at Wivenhoe at HW. At low tide the channel practically dries out

unlit buoys round the sweeping bend known as Hyde (or High?) Park Corner. The mud flat extending from the Fingringhoe shore is extensive and the narrowing channel leads right over to within half a cable of the pleasantly wooded Alresford shore, before turning NW'ly again towards the other bank.

The last two channel buoys, located just below the ballast quay on the Fingringhoe shore, are numbered 27 and 29 and both are green conical with flashing green lights. Above this point there are no more buoys, and the best water lies roughly midway between the banks.

From abreast the quay at Fingringhoe, it will be easy to see the buildings at Wivenhoe — particularly the large building sheds S of the town. The river front at Wivenhoe has a pleasant and unusual atmosphere, especially at high water with the sun shining on the quayside houses. All the boats at Wivenhoe dry out at about half-ebb, when they settle in soft mud with their bows towards the quay.

Facilities at Wivenhoe	
Water	From quayside hose.
Fuel	Diesel from yard. Petrol from garage ¾ mile.
Stores	Local shops including PO. EC Thurs.
Repairs	By yard. Crane 3 tons.
Chandlery	At yard.
Transport	Train service to Colchester and London.
Club	Wivenhoe Sailing Club.

Across the river from Wivenhoe is the entrance to Fingringhoe Creek or the Roman River — a reminder that the Romans settled in these parts nineteen centuries ago.

Rowhedge

Up-river on the W bank is Rowhedge, another little riverside town that some yachtsmen will have heard of because it was here that Alain Gerbault's famous *Firecrest* was built in 1892. There is still an active yard at Rowhedge, building and maintaining lifeboats for the RNLI, as well as caring for yachts.

For a first-hand account of life in Rowhedge around the turn of the century, read Margaret Leather's charming book — *Saltwater Village*.

HW at Rowhedge and Wivenhoe is about the same as Burnham-on-Crouch. Access to the quay at Rowhedge is possible from about two hours before and 1½ hours after HW.

Facilities at Rowhedge	
Water	From quayside hose.
Diesel fuel	From hose.
Stores	Local shops including PO.
Chandlery	Nearby.

It is unwise, and above Fingringhoe quay it is prohibited, to anchor in the channel because of the commercial traffic to and from Colchester.

The remaining three miles of river between Rowhedge and the road bridge above the Hythe at Colchester should only be attempted after about four hours of flood. The best water, which will vary from 2m to 3m at the top of the tide, will generally be found midway between the banks. At night, during HW, one bank is lit by a continuous line of 'street' lamps.

Berths alongside the quays at the Hythe dry out entirely and the barges and coasters using the port take the mud while they are there. The Hythe is not a good place to lie overnight, as ships may leave or arrive on the tide and there is very little room for them to manoeuvre.

Colchester

While Colchester offers no special facilities for the yachtsman all kinds of supplies are available there, and the town (Camulodenum, one of the principal centres of Roman Britain) has much to show the visitor, especially the castle and its museum. EC day is Thursday.

Near HW, boats can lie alongside the wall of the 'Anchor' at Rowhedge, but a sharp lookout for shipping is necessary

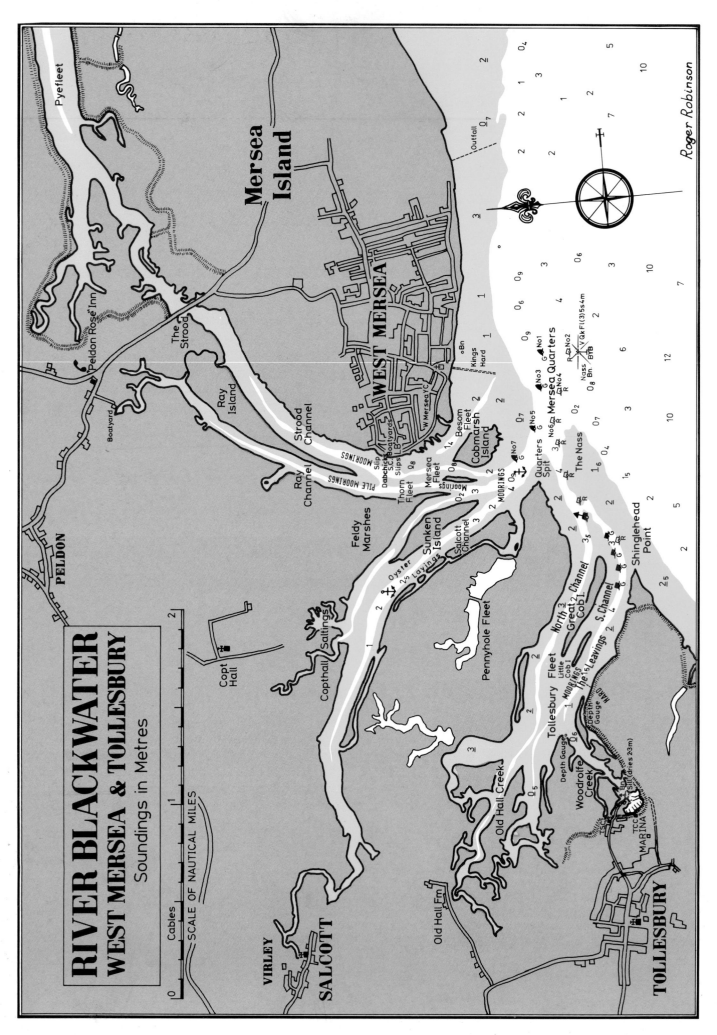

RIVER BLACKWATER
WEST MERSEA & TOLLESBURY
Soundings in Metres

SCALE OF NAUTICAL MILES

Cables

0   1   2

Pyefleet

Peldon Rose Inn

Boatyard

PELDON

Copt Hall

Copthall Saltings

VIRLEY

SALCOTT

Old Hall Fm

Old Hall Creek

Mersea Island

The Strood

Ray Island

Strood Channel

Ray Channel

Feldy Marshes

MOORINGS

PILE MOORINGS

Thorn Fleet

Mersea Fleet

Oyster Layings

Sunken Island

Salcott Channel

Pennyhole Fleet

WEST MERSEA

Slip
Dabchicks S.C.
Boatyards
W Mersea Y.C.
Kings Hard

Bn.

Besom Fleet

Cobmarsh Island

Quarters Spit

Moorings

The Nass

Quarters
G No5
No6 No7
R No4
R

Mersea Quarters

No3 G
R No2

No1

Nass. Bn. BYB
V.Qk.Fl(3)5s4m

Outfall

Shinglehead Point

North Channel

Great Channel

S. Channel

Cob I.

Little Cob I.

The Leavings

Tollesbury Fleet

MOORINGS

Depth Gauge

Depth Gauge

Woodrolfe Creek

NASS

Bn.
Silt (dries 2·3m)

TS

TCC MARINA

TOLLESBURY

Roger Robinson

48

Tides (Nass Beacon)

HW Dover +0.30 Range: Springs 5.1m Neaps 3.8m (HW Maldon approx 25 mins after HW West Mersea)

Charts

Admiralty 3741
Stanford No 4
Imray Y17

Waypoints

Bench Head Buoy 51.44.53.N 1.01.05.E
Nass Beacon 51.45.80.N 0.54.90.E

Hazard

Thirstlet Spit

IT is not widely known that Arnold Bennett owned a Dutch barge-yacht called *Velsa* which he kept in Walton Backwaters but also sailed to Holland and other Essex and Suffolk rivers, so that he could write (in the *Log of the Velsa*):

Time was when I agreed with the popular, and the guide book, verdict that the Orwell is the finest estuary in these parts; but now I know better. I unhesitatingly give the palm to the Blackwater. It is a noble stream, a true arm of the sea; its moods are more various, its banks wilder, and its atmospheric effects much grander. The season for cruising on the Blackwater is September, when the village regattas take place and the sunrises over leagues of marsh are made wonderful by strange mists.'

The entrance to both the Blackwater and the Colne is generally considered to be at the Bench Head buoy, some 15 miles down-river from Maldon. Coming up from the south, either from the Thames or from Kent, most yachts follow the example of the sailing barges and go through the Swin Spitway. There is rather less than a metre of water in this swatchway at low water springs these days.

The deepest water is in a line between the Swin Spitway buoy, a safewater pillar buoy with spherical topmark (Iso 10s Bell), to the SE of the swatch, and the Wallet Spitway buoy (Sph R W V S LFl 10s Bell), a mile away to the NNW. Quite often a yacht gets a fair wind through the spitway when entering the Blackwater, but if ever it is necessary to beat through, then very short boards and constant use of the lead are essential because the water shoals on to the Buxey Sands on the one hand and the Gunfleet Sands on the other.

From the Spitway, course is changed to bring the Knoll buoy (N Car B Y VQ) close to port after about two miles. Then, about a mile away is the Eagle (Con G Q G); to be passed close to starboard. With Eagle abeam, the red can of the NW Knoll light buoy (Can R Fl(2) R 5s) will usually be visible. The NW Knoll is passed close to port, and then without altering course appreciably the unlit conical green Bench Head buoy can be left to starboard at the entrance to the Blackwater.

With the Bench Head astern, a newcomer to these waters will find it difficult to identify anything along the low-lying stretch of coast, except the conspicuous Nuclear Power Station at Bradwell. Some four or five miles separate St Peters Flats to the SW and the shore of the river Colne away to the NE. But a course of 295°M from the Bench Head will lead to the Nass beacon. This course is in fairly deep water — for the East Coast at least — and when the tide is running up against a westerly wind it is easy to tell where the channel lies because of the rougher water. After a while St Peter's Chapel should become visible on Sales Point to the SW, and at about the same time the trees and higher ground at West Mersea will take shape. The safest course is roughly midway between these two shores.

The Nass Beacon, a yellow and black steel post without a topmark, is topped by a windmill generator and a quick flashing light, so that it is often easier to find by night than by day. There is little water near the Nass beacon — perhaps no more than 2m at LWS.

West Mersea

West Mersea is probably the most popular sailing centre on the River Blackwater and consequently it tends to be crowded. However, piles have been established in the Ray Channel and two boats can lie between each pair of posts; but beware of any submerged ropes. Furthermore, it is easier to negotiate the narrow channel now that boats do not lie awkwardly across the stream at the turn of the tide. Visitors can moor temporarily between piles 1 and 2, while seeking a more permanent

From the moorings in Thornfleet, the old oyster packing shed is nearby, while the power station at Bradwell can be seen some two or three miles away to the south

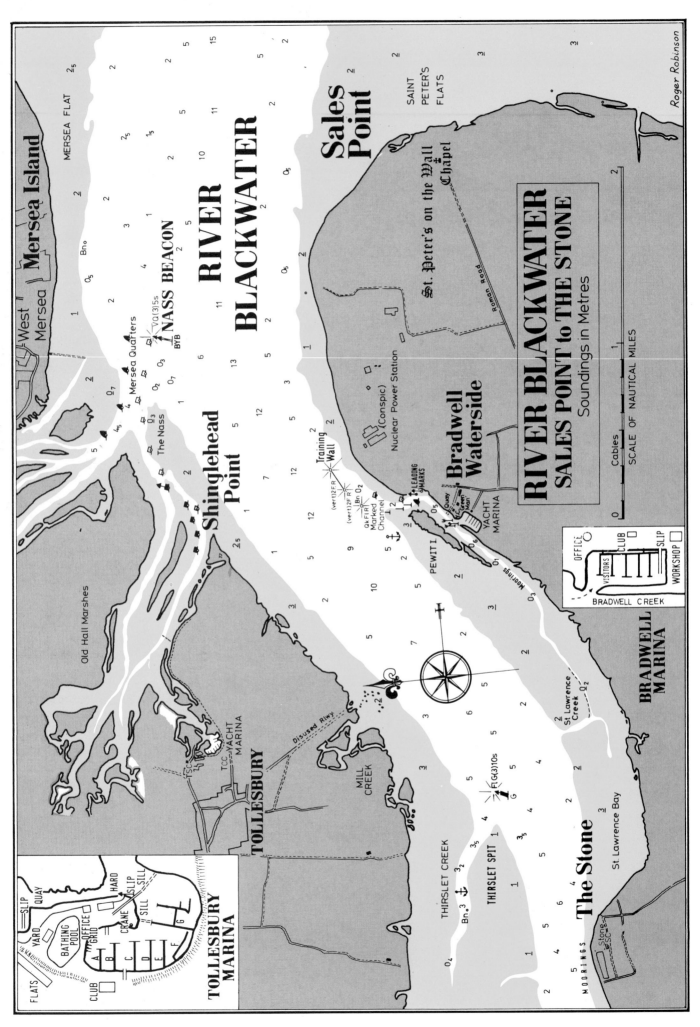

Mersea Island

West
Mersea

MERSEA FLAT

MERSEA FLAT

**RIVER
BLACKWATER**

Mersea Quarters

NASS BEACON
VQ(3)5s
BYB

The Nass

**Shinglehead
Point**

**Sales
Point**

SAINT
PETER'S
FLATS

St. Peter's on the Wall
Chapel ☩

Roman Road

(Conspic)
Nuclear Power Station

**Bradwell
Waterside**

LEADING
MARKS
Quay
Green Man
YACHT
MARINA

PEWIT I.

Moorings

**RIVER BLACKWATER
SALES POINT to THE STONE**
Soundings in Metres

Cables | SCALE OF NAUTICAL MILES

OFFICE ○
CLUB □
SLIP □
WORKSHOP □
VISITORS
BRADWELL CREEK

Training
Wall
(vert)2F.R
Bn O₂
QkFl.R
Marked
Channel
(vert)2F.R

**BRADWELL
MARINA**

St Lawrence
Creek

Old Hall Marshes

TOLLESBURY

TCC YACHT
MARINA
TSC

Disused Rlwy

MILL
CREEK

Fl(3)10s
G

THIRSLET CREEK

THIRSLET SPIT

Bn.

The Stone

St. Lawrence Bay

MOORINGS

Stone
SSC

**TOLLESBURY
MARINA**

FLATS
SLIP
QUAY
HARD
YARD
OFFICE
SLIP
SILL
CRANE
GRID
SILL
SILL
BATHING
POOL
A
B
C
D
E
F
G
CLUB □

Roger Robinson

50

berth. The deeper water is along the Mersea side of the piles.

It is risky to drop anchor anywhere but in the Quarters because of the many moorings farther in. In any case no yachtsman must anchor or go aground on any of the several oyster beds hereabouts. The principal oyster layings are in Mersea Fleet, running between Cob Marsh Island and Packing Marsh Island, and in the Salcott Channel leading out of the Quarters and up to the little villages of Salcott and Virley. In fact, space has become so scarce at Mersea that moorings have now been laid well inside Salcott Creek. There are other oyster beds in the creeks leading to Tollesbury.

When moored in the Quarters it is a long way in to the landing at West Mersea, but quite often the club boatman is around in his launch and he is always helpful.

Facilities at West Mersea

Water	Stand-pipe at top of pontoon jetty.
Stores	Shop at top of pontoon, and at West Mersea village ¾ mile walk. EC Wed.
Scrubbing posts	On foreshore (contact WMYC).
Sailmaker	Nearby.
Transport	Buses to Colchester (8 miles), whence trains to London.
Club	West Mersea Yacht Club. Dabchicks SC.
Telephone	Near *Victory* Inn.

Tollesbury

Tollesbury Creek leads directly out of Mersea Quarters, and soon divides into the South Channel, which holds the more water, and the North Channel, with the Cob Islands between.

A red can marked with a 'T' indicates the junction of the Creek with the Quarters and this is followed by three further red cans numbered 1, 2 and 3. Pass between No 3 and an E Cardinal buoy marking the spit extending from Great Cob Island and keep close to a series of green cans numbered 5, 6 and 7, until the line of moorings in South Channel shows the best water up to Woodrolfe Creek, the entrance to which is marked on the port hand by a withy.

On the W bank there is a tide gauge showing the depth of water over the sill at the yacht marina.

If not intending to enter the marina, the best place to remain afloat is off the entrance to the creek where there are one or two visitors' moorings belonging to the Tollesbury Yacht Harbour.

Tollesbury Marina

This marina can now accommodate some 200 yachts. The way up to and into the basin is marked, over the last quarter of a mile where the channel winds most, by a series of beacons bearing triangular topmarks — inverted red ones to port and black ones, the right way up, to starboard. Visitors should use the second pontoon to port after entering.

At HWS there is some 2m over the sill, but only about 1.5m at neaps. Access and exit are normally possible for about two hours either side of HW.

There is a hard just SE of the entrance to the creek and from there it is about a mile along the sea wall to the yacht harbour.

Although it has no topmark, the Nass beacon at the entrance to Mersea Quarters is an East Cardinal mark

Facilities at Tollesbury

Water	On hard.
Stores	At Tollesbury village (1 mile). E C Wed.
Fuel	At marina.
Repairs	At yard and marina. Both with slipways.
Chandlery	From two chandlers.
Transport	Buses from Tollesbury to Maldon and Kelvedon. Buses to Colchester.
Clubs	Tollesbury Cruising Club (marina). Tollesbury Sailing Club.

On leaving the Quarters and rounding the Nass into the deep water of the Blackwater, the course when proceeding up to Osea Island or Maldon is approximately 250°M. Frequently, quite large ships are laid up in the main channel between the Mersea and Bradwell shores.

Bradwell Creek

About a mile up-river from the Nass, on the south shore is Bradwell Creek. The entrance is difficult to see but is in fact only about a quarter of a mile SW of the Barrier wall off the Nuclear Power Station.

The entrance to Bradwell Creek is marked by a substantial beacon (Q R) bearing a notice warning that 'Moorings in Bradwell Creek are laid across the tide, that is, in a NW/SE direction'. There is very little water over the entrance 'bar' at LWS.

From the beacon a line of red can buoys indicates the port side of the gutway and a line of withies marks the other side. Two triangular topped orange painted leading marks are located near the NE end of the Pewit

The west side of the entrance to Bradwell Creek is marked at first by a series of withies, which should be followed until a pair of leading marks come into line on the opposite shore

Island, but they do not seem to be really necessary now that the channel is so well buoyed.

When the last of the can buoys has been left to port, the channel changes direction towards the SE, as indicated by two orange-painted triangular-topped leading marks that will be seen rather low down in the saltings under a concrete slabbed section of the sea wall. After steering on these beacons for about a cable, the last mark — a green conical buoy — should be left to starboard before continuing along the line of moored craft that extends past the quay and the entrance to Bradwell Marina, right to the SW end of Pewit Island.

At the quay itself, there are still a few of the gnarled old tree-trunk piles to remind us of the days when the creek was always busy with sailing barges, loading from the farms around. There are still two scrubbing posts in use. They were erected by the Bradwell Quay YC who are quite willing for visitors to use them provided they book a time and pay a small fee to the club.

The Essex County Council have based their Field Studies and Sailing Centre here at Bradwell Waterside, and there is usually a good deal of youthful activity as a result.

Bradwell Marina

This marina is entered from Bradwell Creek immediately above the quay. A pair of orange painted triangular leading marks are located in the SW corner of the basin to assist entry during daylight. At night, there is a pair of white lights to indicate the way in. There is a visitor's berth at the end of the first pontoon to port after entering. If staying temporarily, this is the place to be in order to remain afloat.

Facilities at Bradwell	
Water	In Marina or from Bradwell Quay YC. (Near top of Hard).
Stores	General Store and PO near Quay.
Fuel	Diesel from Marina.
Repairs	At Marina. Slip up to 35 tons.
Transport	Buses to Maldon.
Clubs	Bradwell Cruising Club (Marina). Bradwell Quay Yacht Club. (Visitors welcome.)

The village of Bradwell (Bradwell Juxta-Mare) is about a mile from the quay and the Chapel of St Peter,

The leading marks are seen against a white painted patch on the sea wall on the east side of Bradwell Creek

probably the oldest building in England from which Christianity was preached, is another mile away along a track towards the sea.

Thirstlet Creek

Out in the river again, the next thing to watch for is the green buoy (Fl(3)G 10s) marking a spit of hard sand which protrudes into the river on the north side at the entrance to Thirstlet Creek.

Until the buoy is located, there is nothing to indicate how far into the river the spit extends, and many yachts have sailed headlong on to the hard sand while heading, as they thought, straight up the middle of the river. When coming down-river, a safe course results from steering on Bradwell Power Station. Although the water is deepest along this northern shore, the sand is dangerously steep-to, and care must therefore be taken not to stand over too far. It is safer to keep well over to the south shore until abreast St Lawrence Bay.

A couple of miles above Thirstlet Creek, also amid the northern flats, is the entrance to Goldhanger Creek, marked by a conical green buoy. This also serves as a main river channel buoy and must, therefore, be left to port when entering the creek. The creek leads up to a hard near Goldhanger village, but this can really only be reached by dinghy since there is very little water at the head of the creek, even at HWS.

But for those who appreciate the quiet of remote anchorages, there is enough water in which to lie afloat overnight for half a mile or more within the entrances to both Thirstlet and Goldhanger Creek. There is a reasonably hard foreshore near the top of Goldhanger Creek and a path along the sea wall can be used to reach the village, a mile or so away.

Stone St Lawrence

Over on the south shore is Stone St Lawrence, easily located by the many boats moored in the bay and bungalows and caravans on shore. Landing from a dinghy is possible on the shingly beach at all states of the tide. Water can be obtained from the clubhouse of the Stone Sailing Club, and a few simple provisions may be found nearby.

Another club (Marconi SC) has its clubhouse half a mile farther up-river and at night a fixed yellow light is shown from a corner of the building. There is a visitor's mooring opposite the club and water from a stand-pipe at the top of the slip.

From St Lawrence Bay the little pier at Osea Island can be seen in daylight and its fixed green light at night. It is safe for any but deep draught boats to set a course direct to the end of the pier. Larger boats must watch out for a shallow patch known as the Barnacle just east of the pier.

Lawling Creek

Half a mile or so across the river from Osea lies Lawling Creek, the entrance to which is sometimes indefinitely marked by a red can (Fl 3s). Once over the shallow bar (1m LWS) the course of the channel is marked by a series of red and green spar buoys. It is also useful to know that those mooring buoys that are numbered together with a letter 'C' have been laid in the middle of the channel. A yacht can reach the yard for about half the tide, but in a dinghy it is possible at almost any time. As well as the many swinging moorings that extend throughout the length of the creek, the yard now has six floating pontoons and three slipways. All forms of repair and rigging can be undertaken and there is a launch service available. Contact can be made on Channel 37.

A great deal of dinghy racing goes on in Maylandsea Bay, and there are a number of racing marks that have little or nothing to do with the run of the channel.

Facilities at Maylandsea Bay	
Water	From boatyard pontoons at head of Lawling Creek.
Stores	Several shops about a quarter mile from yard.
Fuel	At yard.
Repairs	Boatbuilders with slipways and crane.
Chandlery	At yard.
Transport	Poor. Nearest buses from Mundon (2 miles).
Telephone	Near shops.
Clubs	Maylandsea Bay Yacht Club; Harlow Sailing Club.

It is a good thing for yachtsmen that the Maldon Corporation and the Maldon Harbour Commissioners buoy the Blackwater above Osea Island, because the channel follows a much less obvious course in the upper reaches of the river. Just above Osea pier a green conical buoy guards a mudbank known as the Doctor. Above the Doctor the channel turns to the NW, past a port hand red can buoy. If a boat draws four or five feet, this is about as far up-river as she can expect to reach and remain afloat at LW. Two more buoys — one a green conical (Fl G 3s) and the other a red can — known locally as the 'Doubles', and beyond them there is a single port hand red can called Clark's buoy.

By this time a rather long, low, white building should be seen about a mile ahead. This is the clubhouse of the Blackwater SC and it will serve as a mark on which to steer until the red can buoy marking Hilly Pool Point at the northern end of Northey Island is seen to port. A light (Iso G 5s) is shown from the roof of the Blackwater SC.

After rounding the Point and turning sharply southwards into Collier's Reach, the cluster of houses round Heybridge Lock will come into view about half a mile away. It is never very easy to tell whether the lock gates are open or shut until close to and in line with them, but provided it is clear to the Lockmaster that you wish to enter, he will usually hail you from the head of the lock or fly a green flag when he has room for you. If it is necessary to wait, there is good holding ground in the river outside the lock.

From an hour before to an hour after high water a boat drawing six or seven feet should have no great difficulty in getting into or out of Heybridge Lock. Because of the need to retain water in the canal during the summer months, the lock is worked for only one hour before HW during neap tides. At springs the lock will be worked over a longer period. Prior notification and confirmation is required if the lock is to be used at night.

The Chapel of St Peter-on-the-Wall, is a two mile walk from Bradwell Quay. The chapel is said to be the oldest religious building in England

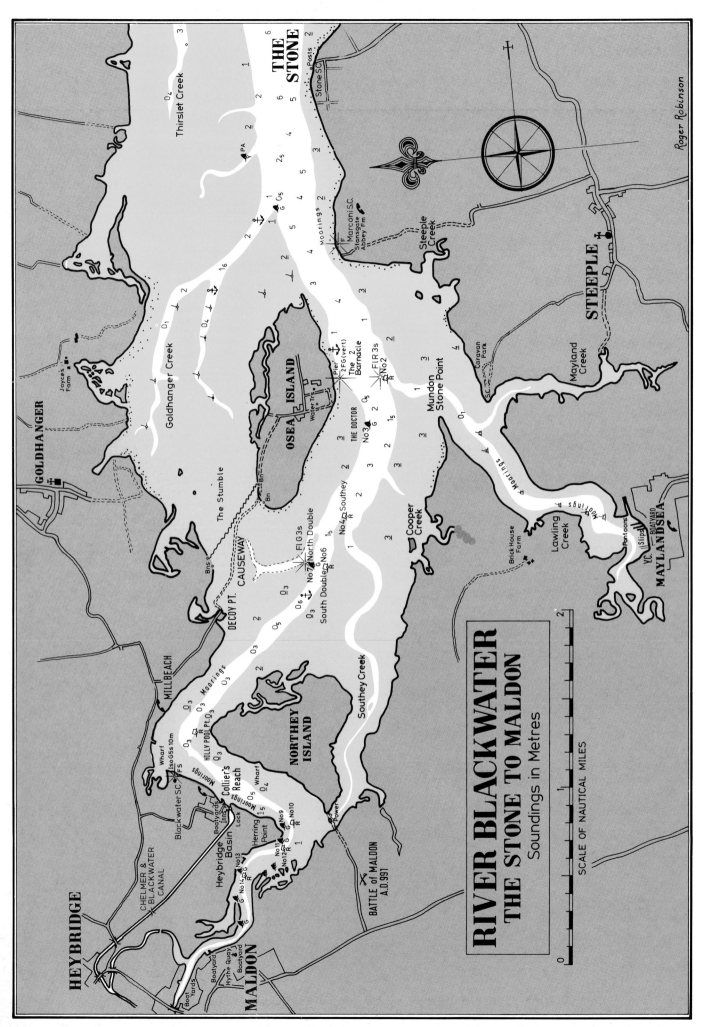

RIVER BLACKWATER
THE STONE TO MALDON
Soundings in Metres

SCALE OF NAUTICAL MILES

THE STONE

Thirslet Creek

Stone S.C.
Posts

Roger Robinson

Steeple Creek
Marconi S.C.
Stansgate
Abbey Fm

STEEPLE

Moorings

Mayland Creek

Caravan Park
S.C.

GOLDHANGER

Joyce's Farm

Goldhanger Creek

OSEA ISLAND

Water Trs

Pier
2 FG(vert)
The Barnacle
F.I.R 3s
No2

Mundon Stone Point

Brick House Farm

Lawling Creek

Y.C. BOATYARD
Pontoons
Slips
MAYLANDSEA

The Stumble

Bn

Bns

The Doctor
No3

Cooper Creek

Moorings

DECOY PT.

CAUSEWAY

F.I G3s
No7 North Double
South Double No6

No4 Southey
R

Southey Creek

MILLBEACH

Moorings

HILLY POOL Pt.

NORTHEY ISLAND

Wharf
Iso G5s 10m
FS

Wharf

BATTLE of MALDON
A.D. 991

Collier's Reach
Moorings

Herring Point

Moorings
No9
No10
R

Power

No11
No12 No13
R

HEYBRIDGE

CHELMER & BLACKWATER CANAL

Blackwater S.C.
Boatyards
Heybridge Basin
Lock

No14
G

Wharf

Boatyard

MALDON

Boatyard
Hythe Quay
Yards

The pontoons at Maylandsea near high water

Facilities at Heybridge Basin	
Water	Stand pipe near inner lock gates.
Stores	Limited supply from chandler.
Chandlery	From chandler.
Fuel	Near lock.
Transport	Infrequent buses to Maldon (whence good connections).
Telephone	100 yards from lock.
Repairs	Slip outside lock.
Club	Blackwater SC (Est 1899) quarter mile from lock.

up to Maldon the winding channel is well marked with conical green buoys on the starboard and red cans on the port hand. Apart from one or two holes, the river dries out completely at Maldon, and most of the boats take the mud, either near the Town Quay, or off the yard next to it where visiting yachts may berth alongside pontoons near the slip, either temporarily afloat or for longer periods if prepared to take the ground (mud).

As you pass the western end of Northey Island, give a thought to the heroic defence of Maldon by Brythnoth's men against the Danes a thousand years ago — because hereabouts was where it happened.

Heybridge Basin and the Chelmer and Blackwater Navigation Canal were constructed in 1797. The bridges and locks were designed by Rennie and the 14 miles of canal end in Chelmsford. A licence is necessary for boats navigating the canal.

Heybridge Basin is managed by the Chelmer and Blackwater Navigation Co (with offices at 10 Bradford Street, Braintree). Capt. Edmond, the lockmaster, is on the telephone at the lock cottage (Maldon 0621 853506).

From off the entrance to the rock, the river continues in a south-westerly direction for about a quarter of a mile before turning N round Herring Point. From here

Facilities at Maldon	
Water	At quayside and boatyards.
Stores	Many shops in town. EC Wed.
Fuel	From pumps at yard pontoon.
Repairs	Two yards with slipways.
Sailmaker	Near quayside.
Transport	Numerous bus routes from Maldon bus terminus.
Clubs	Maldon Yacht Club. Maldon Little Ship Club.

VHF The yard keeps a listening watch on Ch 37	

There are slipways at both of the yards at Maldon, where all the craft dry out at LW

Tides (Burnham on Crouch)

HW Dover +1.10 Range: Springs 5.2m Neaps 4.2m (HW at Whitaker Beacon approx 20 mins before HW at Burnham)

Charts

Admiralty 3750   Stanford No 4   Imray Y15

Hazard

Shoal water between Swin Spitway and Whitaker Beacon

Waypoints

Wallet Spitway Buoy 51.42.56.N   1.06.96.E
Swin Spitway Buoy 51.41.74.N   1.07.64.E
Whitaker Bell Buoy 51.41.45.N   1.10.40.E
Whitaker Beacon 51.39.37.N   1.06.17.E
Ridge Buoy 51.40.16.N   1.05.00.E
Sunken Buxey Buoy 51.39.48.N   1.00.75.E
Outer Crouch Buoy 51.38.20.N   1.58.12.E
Buxey Beacon 51.41.08.N   1.01.24.E

SOME people say Burnham's popularity as a sailing centre has declined recently, but if you arrive in the Crouch during Burnham Week, you'll be thankful the place is no more popular than it already is.

As a river, the Crouch can hardly be described as beautiful. Its higher reaches are certainly pleasanter than the five or six miles between Burnham and Shore Ends, where nothing much can be seen above the bordering sea walls except for a short while at high tide. Yet because of these unobstructed shores, the Crouch offers racing yachtsmen the best possible sport, and with the smaller river Roach entering at right angles, a variety of courses can be laid to suit all wind conditions.

The Crouch Harbour Act of 1974 established the Crouch Harbour Authority, which now has jurisdiction over the tidal waters of both the Crouch and the Roach out as far as Foulness Point.

In 1987 Trinity House announced its intention to hand over responsibility for the buoyage and marking of the River Crouch to the Crouch Harbour Authority. The principal commercial user of the river is the company importing and landing timber at Baltic Wharf near the Essex Marina, opposite Burnham. As of the early part of 1988 it seemed likely that the Harbour Authority would come to some arrangement with the commercial interests as to the number and type of buoys necessary to allow navigation of the river at any time. This has now happened and as a consequence *all* the buoys in the

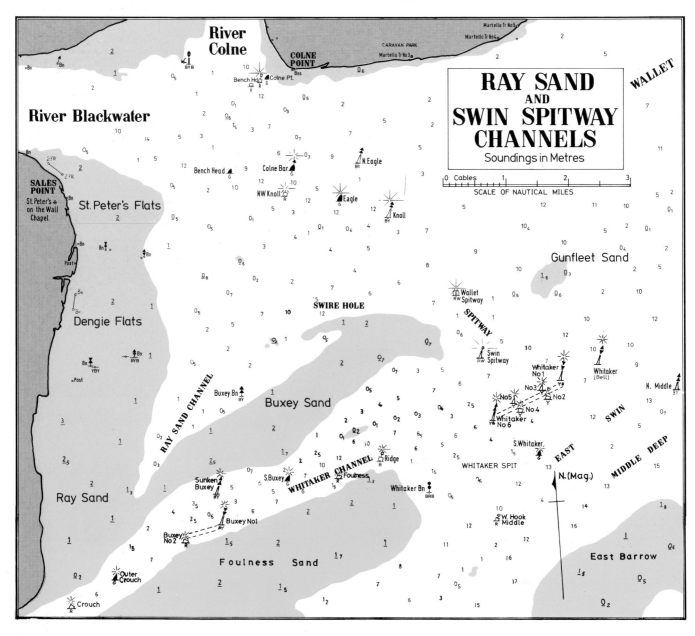

Crouch between the Whittaker and Wallasea are lit. Furthermore, the number of buoys has been increased. (All alterations are shown on the sketch charts on pages 56, 58 and 59.)

From Battlesbridge, the navigable limit of the river, down to Shore Ends where the Crouch clears the land, is approximately 15 miles. From Shore Ends out to the Whitaker bell buoy marking the extremity of the Whitaker Spit is another nine or ten miles.

Excluding the top-of-the-tide entrance through Havengore Creek and the river Roach, there are two approaches to the Crouch: through the Whitaker Channel from the Swin, and through the very shallow Ray Sand (Rays'n) Channel between Dengie Flats and the Buxey Sands. The deep water approach will be considered first.

There are very few landmarks to help a yachtsman into the entrance to the Crouch, but in good visibility it should be fairly easy to spot the group of buoys marking the dredged channel that begins about half a mile SW of the Whitaker Bell buoy (E Card, Q(3) 10s). The western end of the dredged channel is marked by Whitaker No 6 (N Card, QF1), and a course of 255°M should then lead close N of the Ridge buoy (Can R Fl R 10s) and the new Foulness buoy (Can R FlR 10s).

It is important to pass close to the Ridge buoy because a recent survey (*YM* July 1989) showed that a shoal with a drying patch has formed about three or four cables N of the buoy. This shoal seems to have reappeared, since it was well known 80 years ago, when it was called the 'Swallowtail'.

The North Cardinal Buxey Beacon marks the north-western edge of the Buxey Sand

When coming S through the Swin Spitway, shape a course of 170°M from the Spitway buoy until the Ridge buoy bears 255°M, before changing on to that bearing to pass just N of the Ridge buoy itself. From the Ridge buoy a course should be set to leave the S Buxey green conical buoy close to starboard and then the Sunken Buxey (N Card Q Fl) close to port.

Now that a channel has been dredged and buoyed to the S of the Sunken Buxey shoal, shipping will use that route; but it is expected that yachts will continue to pass to the N of the Sunken Buxey buoy — particularly when beating against a southwesterly.

In good visibility, the 'skyscrapers' at Southend will be seen from the Sunken Buxey and from just N of the buoy, a course of 240°M will lead close to the Outer Crouch buoy (Con Fl G 5s), about two miles away. In daylight this buoy is not easy to pick up because it is backed by the sea wall surrounding Foulness Point, but once it has been located, course should be shaped to leave it close to starboard and thence into the river.

The Raysand Channel

Shallow draught boats bound from the Blackwater to the Crouch can, at the right state of the tide, come through the Ray Sand or Rays'n Channel. There is little or no water in the southern end of the swatchway at LWS, in fact it is possible at low water extraordinary springs to walk virtually dry footed from the mainland to the Buxey Sands.

The time honoured Buxey Beacon still stands where it did when Maurice Griffiths wrote *The Magic of the Swatchways*, but no longer with its easily recognised sign-post topmark. Instead, a N Cardinal mark tops the beacon, which, like the Whitaker, now has a tripod base. Trinity House has now disowned this and several other beacons in the Thames Estuary, so we must hope that local authorities or yacht clubs will see that they are maintained in future.

The Dengie Flats were once used as a dive-bombing range and four derelict target craft still remain as a reminder. These wrecks are marked by unlit beacons; the two inshore having W Cardinal topmarks and the outer two with E Cardinal topmarks.

When bound from the Wallet past the Knoll buoy, the best course to hold into the Rays'n will be 235°M. The N Buxey buoy will no longer be there to guide you, but sudden changes in depth near the Swire Hole should serve to locate you on the chart. When the Buxey beacon bears 180°M, change course to 215°M to pass it about half a mile away to port.

Finally, when the conspicuous pylons on Foulness Island come to bear 210°M, change on to this course until the deeper water of the Crouch is found — about a mile to the W of the Sunken Buxey buoy, with its double cone (N Cardinal) topmark.

A small spherical yellow buoy is laid in the S entrance to the Rays'n by the Burnham yacht clubs and is intended to indicate the best water through the swatch. But do not expect to find any clear cut channel or gutway. Very shallow draught boats, using a rising tide, can often sneak through the Rays'n closer inshore by following a course approximately 185°M and about a mile to seaward of the outer pair of wrecked target vessels.

About three-quarters of a mile SW of the Outer Crouch buoy and just inside the river itself is the Crouch buoy (Can R Fl R 10s). After the Crouch buoy direction is changed to a westerly course, which can be

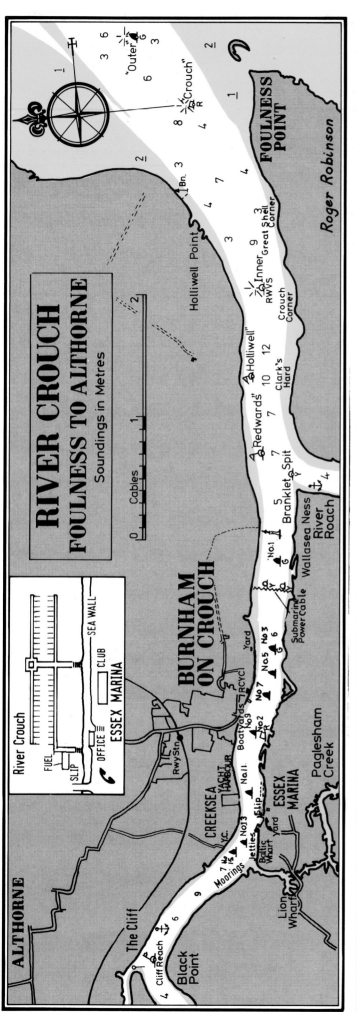

RIVER CROUCH
FOULNESS TO ALTHORNE
Soundings in Metres

Cables

"Outer"
"Crouch"
FOULNESS POINT
Roger Robinson
Holliwell Point
Bn.
Great Shell Corner
Inner
RWVS
Crouch Corner
"Holliwell"
Clark's Hard
"Redwards"
Branklet Spit
Wallasea Ness
River Roach
No.1
No.3
No.5
Submarine Power Cable
Yard
No.7
No.9
No.2
RCYC
BURNHAM ON CROUCH
Paglesham Creek
Boatyards
ESSEX MARINA
No.11
CREEKSEA Y.C.
No.13
Jetties
Baltic Wharf
Yard
Moorings
Lion Wharf
The Cliff
Cliff Reach
Black Point
Rwy Stn.

ESSEX MARINA
River Crouch
SEA WALL
CLUB
FUEL
SLIP
OFFICE

ALTHORNE

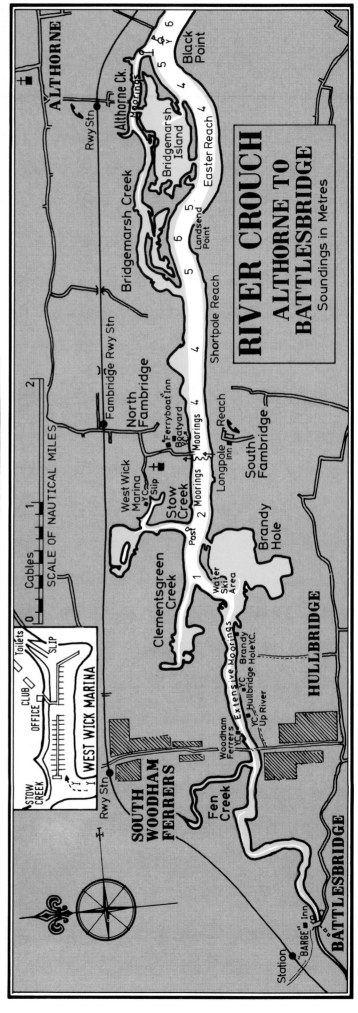

RIVER CROUCH
ALTHORNE TO BATTLESBRIDGE
Soundings in Metres

ALTHORNE
Rwy Stn
Althorne Ck.
Moorings
Black Point
Bridgemarsh Creek
Bridgemarsh Island
Easter Reach
Landsend Point
Shortpole Reach
Fambridge Rwy Stn
North Fambridge
Ferryboat Inn
Boatyard
West Wick Marina Y.C.
Slip
Stow Creek
Moorings
Longpole Reach
Longpole Inn
South Fambridge
Brandy Hole
Post
Moorings
Clementsgreen Creek
Water Ski Area
Extensive Moorings
Woodham Ferrers Y.C.
Brandy Hole Y.C.
Hullbridge Y.C.
Up River
HULLBRIDGE
Fen Creek
SOUTH WOODHAM FERRERS
Rwy Stn
Station
"BARGE" Inn
BATTLESBRIDGE

SCALE OF NAUTICAL MILES
Cables

WEST WICK MARINA
STOW CREEK
OFFICE
CLUB
Toilets
SLIP

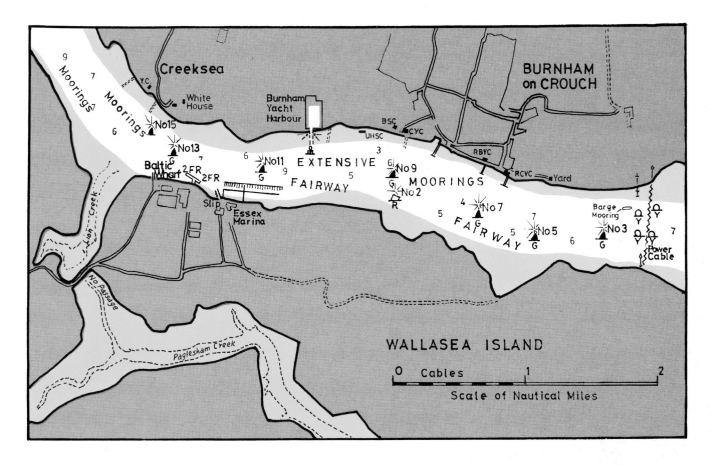

held up-river as far as the junction of the river Roach, about three miles away. Half-way between the Crouch buoy and the entrance to the Roach is the 'Inner Crouch' (Sph RW L Fl W 10s), which can be passed on either hand. Two racing buoys may be seen on the northern side of the channel, just below the entrance to the Roach, and these should be left to the north to be sure of missing the mud of Redward Flats. The Branklet Spit buoy (Spher Y) marks an arm of mud that extends north-easterly from Wallasea Ness. West of Branklet Spit deepest water is to be found near the N bank of the river; but because the south shore is steep-to, it is often the safer one to work.

A short channel has been dredged (to 4 metres) through the Horse shoal, just above the mouth of the Roach. The E end of the channel is marked by a N Cardinal buoy (QFl) and the other end by the Fairway No 1 (QG), which ships will leave to starboard.

The many yacht moorings off Burnham commence just above a group of four yellow spherical buoys marking submerged cables carrying 33,000 volts. The Burnham Fairway is on the S side of the river and although narrow, it is well marked by eight starboard-hand buoys (Q Fl G) and one port-hand can buoy (Q Fl R). There is at least 4m of water throughout the length of the Fairway and the south shore is steep-to. When it becomes necessary to beat up-river and boards on the port tack are extended in among the moored craft, a close watch should be kept on the effects of the tide, for the ebb at spring tides can run at 3 knots past Burnham.

Anchoring is obviously prohibited in the Fairway and the multitude of moorings makes it very difficult to bring up to an anchor anywhere in the area. The Royal Corinthian Yacht Club has a visitor's mooring sited directly off their conspicuous clubhouse, but if this is occupied, enquiries ashore will usually lead to the provision of some other vacant buoy.

There are three floating pontoons off the Burnham waterfront at which boats may lie for short periods while seeking supplies or services ashore. The pontoons belong to the Royal Corinthian YC, the Royal Burnahm YC, and Prior's boatyard.

It is possible that before long the RCYC will have a number of pontoon berths extending downstream from their clubhouse. Already great changes are afoot behind the clubhouse to allow flats to be built while the long-established boatyard has moved several hundred yards to the E.

Facilities at Burnham-on-Crouch	
Water	From stand-pipes near most landing places.
Stores	Shops in main street. EC Wed.
Petrol and oil	From garage in town.
Repairs	Several shipwrights along waterfront. Also marine engineers.
Chandler	On quay and at yacht harbour.
Sailmakers	In town and at yacht harbour.
Transport	Train service to London via Wickford except on Sundays in winter months. (Station fifteen minutes' walk.)
Clubs	Royal Corinthian Yacht Club. Royal Burnham Yacht Club. Crouch Yacht Club. Burnham Sailing Club.
Telephone	Near *White Hart*.

There are facilities for the yachtsman close at hand. The little town is a pleasant place, and many of its people are in some way connected with sailing.

Burnham Yacht Harbour

The opening of the Burnham Yacht Harbour at the end of 1988 brought about a considerable change in the river; most of the yachts that were lying to swinging

A safewater buoy marks the outer end of the channel leading into Burnham Yacht Harbour

moorings belonging to Tucker Brown moved into the harbour, leaving that stretch of river virtually free of moorings that had been used by generations of yachtsmen. The new harbour, which can be entered at all states of the tide, has berths for some 350 craft, alongside floating pontoons equipped with all the services now expected in a modern marina. Facilities in the harbour include a 100-ton slipway as well as a crane and a 30-ton travel hoist and a harbour master or security officer will be on duty at all times.

The entrance to the harbour is marked by a Safewater buoy (Fl R 10s) and a couple of posts with red and green flashing lights.

Wallasea Bay

On the opposite shore and about a mile up-river from Burnham is Wallasea Bay. Here again the moorings are numerous, but this time located along the S as well as the N side of the river. Many of the yachts at Wallasea Bay remain afloat along the outside of pontoons of a floating harbour in plenty of water at all states of the tide.

The Essex Marina suffered extreme damage during the October 1987 hurricane, but new finger-berth pontoons and some pile berths have been established along with improved toilet, shower and laundry facilities.

Facilities at Wallasea Bay	
Water	From pontoon.
Stores	Shop near boatyard.
Fuel	Petrol and diesel from fuel barge.
Chandler	Near yard.
Repairs	Yard with slipway and crane.
Meals	At restaurant nearby.
Transport	Buses to Southend-on-Sea.
Club	Wallasea Bay Yacht Club.
Telephone	W end of sea wall.

The western end of Burnham fairway is marked by the No 13 buoy off the timber wharf at which a Russian ship will often be berthed. There is shallow water on the north side of the river just below Creeksea.

The river now turns north-westerly through Cliff Reach; so called because of the modest (40-50ft) cliff just above Creeksea. Cliff Reach is important to the yachtsman inasmuch as it provides shelter from south-westerly winds, when most of the other reaches in the Crouch are made uncomfortable. Towards low tide a good look-out should be kept for a line of concrete sinkers that can be found along the low water line below the cliff. At the top of Cliff Reach the main stream turns

south-westerly round Black Point, where the shore is steep-to, into Easter Reach. But a minor branch continues north-westerly behind Bridgemarsh Island — becoming Althorne Creek.

Althorne Creek

A yellow racing buoy marked 'Cliff Reach' is usually located off Black Point, and it provides a mark for entering Althorne Creek.

The entrance to the creek is now marked by a port-hand beacon (with a red light) and a series of three red can buoys. The course when entering is roughly N (Mag), leaving the beacon and the first red can close to port.

At Bridgemarsh Marina there are more than a hundred boats moored to pontoons between piles along the centre of the creek both above and below the point where there was once a ford leading on to Bridgemarsh Island. On the N bank there is a yard with two docks, a slipway and a crane. There is water, and will be power, to the pontoons, and toilet and showers are provided. Althorne station is only about a quarter of a mile away whence it is no more than an hour to Liverpool Street station in London.

It is possible in a small craft, with a rising tide and a commanding wind, to sail through Althorne Creek and Bridgemarsh Creek to join the Crouch again some two miles further up-stream; but the channel is extremely narrow and tortuous.

From the Cliff reach buoy the river flows south-westerly through Easter Reach, where during the summer the last of the racing buoys — 'Canewdon' — is located in mid-stream in about 5 metres at LW. Then, from abreast the point where Bridgemarsh Creek emerges from behind the western end of the island, the river flows westerly for two or three miles straight through Shortpole and Longpole Reaches up to and beyond North and South Fambridge. There is no less than 4 metres of water in mid-channel up as far as North Fambridge.

North Fambridge

Francis B Cooke, whose many books on small boat cruising have become collectors' items, on the occasion of his hundredth birthday, contributed an autobiographical note entitled : 'Birth of a Great Yacht Station' to *Yachting Monthly* and in it he wrote: *'Anyone seeing Fambridge today for the first time could hardly imagine what a delightful waterside hamlet it was when I first discovered it (in 1893). The only buildings near the water were Fambridge Hall, the old Ferry Boat Inn, a tiny school, a row of four or five small timber built cottages, an old barn and the little church nestling among the trees. The road leading down to the Ferry hard was just a narrow country lane, with wild roses blooming in the summer. My friends the Viner brothers had decided to spend the summer there and asked me to join them. I readily agreed and we arranged with the landlady of the Ferry Boat Inn to board there. She agreed to take us for twelve shillings a week and hoped she was not charging too much, but of course that would include our laundry.'*

There are four lines of moored boats off Fambridge a fairway between them, so the only possible places to anchor are above or below these moorings. But there is plenty of water (2.5m) even at LWS.

Landing is possible on the hard, or at the floating pontoon near the clubhouse on the N Fambridge side. Landing on the S bank is not easy.

Facilities at North Fambridge	
Water	Near boatshed.
Stores	Shop and PO at N Fambridge (½ mile).
Fuel	T V O and diesel from yard.
Repairs	Yard with slipway and crane.
Transport	Trains to London from Fambridge station (1 mile) except on Sundays in winter months.
Club	North Fambridge YC.
Meals	At *Ferry Boat Inn*.

Stow Creek

Rather less than a mile above Fambridge, Stow Creek enters the river from the N side.

The entrance is now marked with a pile, and this should be left close to starboard when entering. The creek is then marked (occasionally) with starboard hand withies up to the entrance to Westwick Marina, just over half a mile from the entrance. Here, boats lie to pontoons, in about 1m at LWS.

Facilities at Westwick Marina	
Water	On pontoons.
Stores	From village (½ mile).
Fuel	Diesel from pontoon.
Repairs	Shipwright at marina with slipway.
Transport	Trains to London from Fambridge (1 mile) except Sundays in winter.
Club	Westwick YC.

Above Stow Creek the river narrows and shallows fairly rapidly. Clementsgreen Creek is navigable only

around HW, and since it is dammed it is of little interest to yachtsmen. From abreast this creek the river turns south-westerly through Brandy Hole Reach into Brandy Hole Bay, which is a water-skiing area and very busy at weekends. Moorings begin again off Brandy Hole YC and continue for a mile or more up to the entrance to Fenn Creek, just above the ford at Hullbridge. Anywhere along here, a boat will take the ground for an hour or two either side of LW. Except near HW, watch out for a spit extending from the N bank just above Brandy Hole YC.

There are two other yacht clubs on the S shore and one on the N bank near the road down to the ford.

Facilities at Hullbridge (Brandy Hole)	
Water	At hard and clubhouses.
Stores	At Hullbridge village, or near Hullbridge YC.
Fuel	Garages (1 mile).
Repairs	Boatyard adjacent to club.
Transport	Buses from Hullbridge to Southend (from *The Anchor*).
Clubs	Brandy Hole YC. Up River YC. Hullbridge YC. Woodham Ferrers YC.

Above Hullbridge the river becomes very narrow and tortuous, and in places is no more than thirty yards wide between the retaining walls, although there are some moorings in Long Reach. At springs, a boat drawing 2m can take the tide right up to Battlesbridge, but unless the return trip is commenced almost immediately, it would be best to tie up alongside a small concrete landing quay. Elsewhere the drying mud steeply shelves into the gutway.

HW at Hullbridge is 25 minutes later than at Burnham.

Facilities at Battlesbridge	
Water	From *The Barge* (by request).
Stores	Shops nearby.
Petrol and oil	Garage nearby.
Transport	Trains to London from Battlesbridge station, except on Sundays in winter. Buses in Maldon and Southend.

The River Crouch is quite wide at Hullbridge near HW, but all the boats dry out at LWS

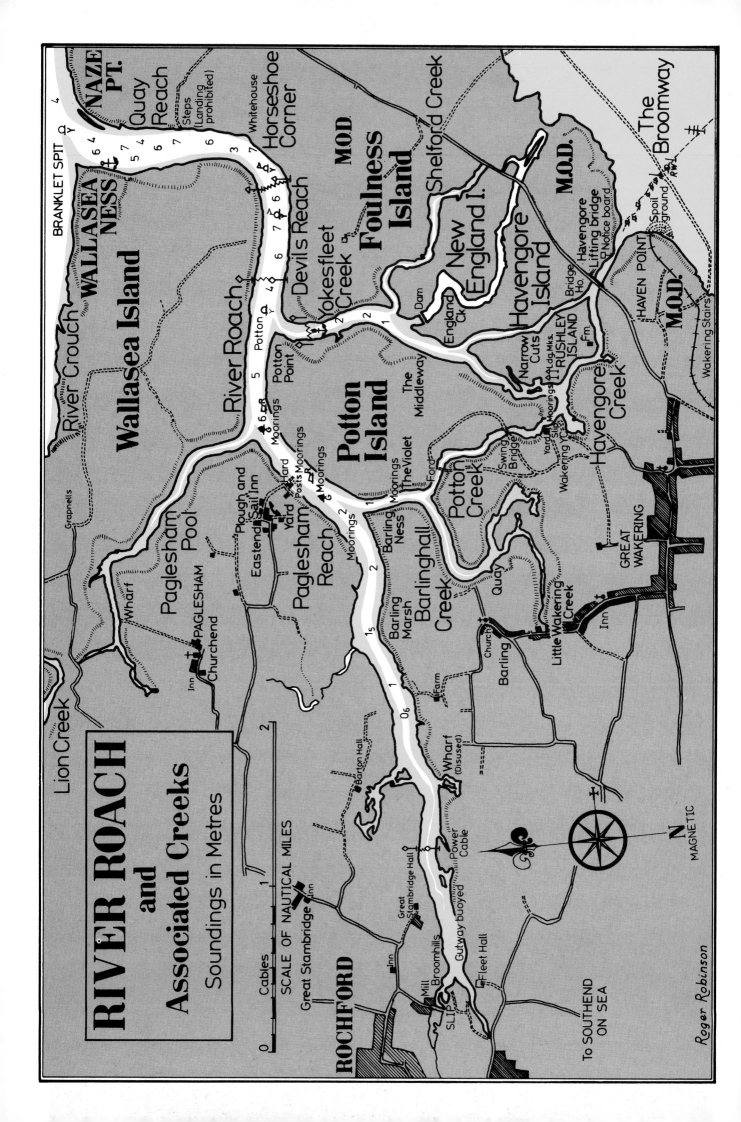

RIVER ROACH
and
Associated Creeks
Soundings in Metres

SCALE OF NAUTICAL MILES

Cables   0   1

0   1   2

NAZE PT.

BRANKLET SPIT

Quay Reach

Steps
(Landing prohibited)

Whitehouse

Horseshoe Corner

Devil's Reach

WALLASEA NESS

River Crouch

WALLASEA Island

Wallasea Island

River Roach

Potton

Potton Point

Yokesfleet Creek

MOD.

Foulness Island

Shelford Creek

New England I.

England Ck

Dam

M.O.D.

Lion Creek

Grapnels

Wharf

Paglesham Pool

Eastend Sail Inn

Plough and

Hard

Yard

Posts Moorings

Moorings

Moorings

Moorings

Inn PAGLESHAM
Churchend

Paglesham Reach

Potton Island

The Violet

The Middleway

Moorings

Barling Ness

Barlinghall Creek

Barling Marsh

Ford

Swing Bridge

Narrow Cuts

Ldg. Mks.
RUSHLEY ISLAND

Moorings

Yard

Havengore Island

Havengore Lifting bridge
Notice board

Bridge Ho.

Fm

M.O.D.

HAVEN POINT

Havengore Creek

M.O.D.

The Broomway

RW

Wakering Stairs

Wakering Yc
Slip

Little Wakering Creek

GREAT WAKERING

Quay

Barling

Church

Inn

Barton Hall

Farm

Wharf
(Disused)

Gutway buoyed

Power Cable

Great Stambridge Hall

Great Stambridge

ROCHFORD

Inn

Mill

SLIP

Broomhills

Fleet Hall

To SOUTHEND ON SEA

N
MAGNETIC

Roger Robinson

The River Roach and Havengore

Tides (Paglesham)	**Waypoint**
HW Dover +1.10 Range: Springs 5.2m Neaps 4.2m	East Shoebury Beacon 51.30.52.N 0.53.99.E

Charts	
Admiralty 3750	
Stanford No 4	**Hazard**
Imray Y17	Havengore route — except on rising tide.

THOSE of us who are based on the Roach consider it to be a better river than the Crouch because its several changes of direction offer a wider variety of sailing and also because its upper reaches have remained quite unspoilt. Another advantage is that Havengore is nearby to provide us with a 'back-door' to the Thames and Medway or even across the Estuary to the Foreland.

From its junction with the River Crouch, about three miles inside Shore Ends, the Roach winds for some six miles in a mainly south-westerly direction up to its tidal limit at Stambridge Mill. Apart from the lower reaches below Paglesham, the Roach is very narrow at low water and not many craft use the river above Barling Ness.

What does make the Roach interesting to many yachtsmen is the network of subsidiary creeks which link the river with the sea over the Maplin Sands. The best-known and most important of these small channels is Havengore Creek, passing Havengore and Rushley Islands and through a lifting bridge at its eastern end. By using this creek after crossing the Maplins near HW, it is possible for small and shallow craft to reach the Roach without having to sail down the W Swin and up the Whitaker Channel.

At its mouth at HW the Roach is more than a quarter of a mile wide, but mud extends from both banks to reduce the LW channel to half that width. The mud extending from Wallasea Ness is marked by the Branklet Spit buoy (Spher Y). On the eastern side of the entrance much mud extends from Naze Point and many boats have been tripped up here.

Quay Reach

There is not much less than 6m at LW in the middle of the river right along Quay Reach. The direction of this lowest reach of the Roach is roughly N-S, and because of this it often provides a more comfortable berth than any anchorage in the Crouch below Creeksea. Not only is there good protection from westerly and easterly winds, but there is also plenty of room and good holding ground in stiff mud towards either shore. The E shore used to be the more popular — because there are some landing steps built into the sea wall nearby, but landing is now prohibited by the Ministry of Defence and yachtsmen can no longer walk to Church End for a drink at the pub.

From the entrance to Horseshoe Corner at the southern end of Quay Reach is just over a mile, and then the river turns through more than a right angle to continue westerly into Devil's Reach. The deep water round this bend, known as Whitehouse Hole, is marked by a yellow buoy ('Roach') in about 6m at LW.

The next buoy is the 'Whitehouse' located about a mile farther up-river, after which the channel divides abreast the Potton buoy. The principal arm, Paglesham Reach, continues westerly along the northern side of Potton Island, while the other branch turns S along the eastern side.

Paglesham Reach

Just before the moorings are reached in Paglesham Reach the main channel turns to the SW abreast the entrance to Paglesham Pool (or Creek). This narrow creek carries so little water at low tide as to be of little interest for navigation. At one time it was possible at HW to pass round the western side of Wallasea Island via Paglesham Pool and Lion Creek into the Crouch opposite Creeksea, but the roadway on to the island now separates the two creeks.

Just above the junction of Paglesham Pool with the Roach are the first of the Paglesham moorings, which extend both below and above Shuttlewood's isolated building shed. The moorings are laid on both sides of the channel, and the Crouch Harbour Board has laid

There is regular freighter traffic up the River Roach to mills and wharf at Stambridge

The Hard has been widened at Paglesham, but the posts marking its end may have been replaced by two oil drums

Janet Harber

port and starboard hand buoys to mark the extent of a fairway within which anchoring is now prohibited because of the commercial traffic that is trading at the quay near Stambridge Mill. Visiting yachtsmen are now advised to anchor just below the moorings off Paglesham Pool, whence a landing can be made near a 'pill box' on the sea wall. Alternatively craft with little draught or those that can take the ground, might sometimes be able to find an anchorage just outside the northern limit of the fairway. The hard has been widened, but boots of some kind are very desirable when landing.

A riding light is essential when anchored in the Roach overnight — the river is now quite frequently used by small (200-300 ton) freighters working the tide by day or night.

The hamlet of East End, which yachtsmen usually think of as Paglesham, is about half a mile from the landing beside Shuttlewood's shed. Sadly, there is no longer a shop at East End, but there is food at the *Plough and Sail*.

Facilities at Paglesham	
Diesel fuel and water	From yard.
Stores	None.
Repairs	Shipwright at top of hard
Transport	Buses from East End to Rochford, whence trains to London.
Telephone	Near *Plough and Sail*.

Above the Paglesham moorings the river forks again at Barling Ness, the main stream continuing westerly towards Rochford and the other arm turning S between Barling Marsh and Potton Island. The continuation of the main channel west of Barling Ness is sometimes referred to as the Broomhill river. There is 1 to 1.5m of water at LWS up as far as disused Barling Quay on the S bank, after which the channel narrows rapidly into a gutway that can be navigated only towards HW, and then only with much sounding or local knowledge. At

HW boats drawing 1 to 1.5m can continue as far upriver as the mill at Stambridge — a mile short of the town of Rochford. On the whole, best water will be found roughly midway between the banks in these upper reaches, but the broad entrance to Bartonhall Creek must be avoided on the N bank. A power cable crosses the river hereabouts and is marked by a green conical and a red can buoy.

Just below Stambridge Mill the river divides for the last time, the southern arm becoming Fleethall Creek where there is a wharf that is regularly used by small freighters and a slipway capable of handling craft up to 60 tons and 70ft LOA. However, this yard (Sutton Wharf) is not interested in taking boats smaller than 30ft LOA. Ships bringing grain to Stambridge Mill berth on the N side of the river just below the sluice gates, but yachts are not permitted to use the quay. There are no other landing places.

Yokesfleet Creek

Returning now to the S bank of the river, the branch of the Roach which turns S at Potton Point is variously known as Yokesfleet Creek and the Gore Channel. The entrance to this creek requires care as a spit of mud stretches out from Potton Point and there is also an extensive mud flat off the opposite point. Best water will be found close under the Potton or western shore for the first few cables inside. There are depths of about 2 metres at LW for the first quarter of a mile or so inside the creek, and the spot provides a quiet and comfortable anchorage during either W or E winds.

About a mile within Yokesfleet Creek two lesser creeks branch out on the eastern side. The first is Shelford Creek, which once reached the sea along the S side of Foulness Island; and the second, New England Creek, has been dammed just within its entrance. This barrier across New England Creek provides a useful reference point as it is at the next division of the main channel that Narrow Cuts leads off south-easterly towards Havengore Bridge.

Right: Walton Backwaters

Left: St Osyth. Above: Heybridge Basin

Mark Fishwick

Mark Fishwick

Below: Pyefleet Creek

Left: West Mersea. Above: Tollesbury Marina looking across to West Mersea

Above: Maldon. Below: Burnham on Crouch

Below: Smallgains Creek

Above: Great Wakering

Below: Kingsferry Bridge on the Swale

Shelford Creek is blocked by a fixed road bridge towards its seaward end and is therefore of little use to yachtsmen, but there is enough water for most small boats to lie afloat in Yokesfleet Creek or the Middleway, which it becomes above the junction of Shelford and New England creeks. About half a mile along the Middleway the channel again divides, this time around Rushley Island. Narrow Cuts, the more easterly arm, is used by craft passing to and from Havengore Bridge. Although it all but dries out at LW, there is enough water in the gutway through Narrow Cuts to allow boats drawing up to 1.5m to get through towards HW. But the narrow channel is tortuous and must be followed, even at HW, to avoid grounding. After leaving Yokesfleet Creek at the junction of the Middleway, keep close to the port hand sea wall up to a sluice, then begin to alter course towards the starboard bank, using the low roof of a distant barn as a mark. There may be a stake marking a hump on the starboard hand and then an even more important red topped stake to be left to port, after which there may be no more marks. Because of this, it is certainly preferable for a stranger — if he can — to make his first acquaintance with Narrow Cuts early on a tide, while the mud is still largely uncovered.

Just before reaching the bridge the channel emerging from Narrow Cuts is joined by Havengore Creek which winds round the western side of Rushley Island to join the Middleway. Unless bound for Wakering or Paglesham, there is little point in taking the longer route to the Crouch via Havengore Creek.

There is an extensive shoal extending from the S end of Potton Island opposite the YC and the best water is outside a black and white perch marking the southern tip of the mud. However, when leaving the yard or club at Wakering, bound for the Roach or Crouch around HW, the shoal can be crossed close to the sea wall of Potton Island, although careful sounding will be necessary as the leading marks on Rushley Island have gone.

When bound seaward through Havengore Bridge, keep close to the Rushley Island side for about half a mile because best water will not be found on the outside of the bend as might be expected.

Potton Creek

Potton Creek joins the Roach between Potton Island and Barling Ness and runs in a southerly direction to join up with Havengore Creek.

A very long spit extends NW'ly from Barling Ness and it is safest to hold the E shore when entering Barling Creek from the Roach. The first reach in the creek, known locally as 'The Violet', is largely occupied these days by local fishing boats and so it may be difficult to find a space in which to use an anchor.

Barlinghall Creek, leading to Little Wakering Creek, leaves Potton Creek about half a mile south of Barling Ness, and leads up to the villages of Barling and Little Wakering. Although barges used to visit the quays dotted about the upper reaches of these creeks, the landings are mostly disused, and of course no water remains at low tide.

About a quarter of a mile above the junction of Barlinghall Creek, beware of a concrete ford between Potton Island and the mainland. It is not safe to try to pass this way before half-flood. From here, the bridge over Potton Creek will be seen about half a mile ahead. This swing-bridge, which is used only by the Ministry of Defence, will be opened on request (three toots on a horn, Dutch fashion) at any time during daylight hours. Keep well over to the E side of the creek when approaching the bridge.

There is a boatyard with a slipway just S of the bridge.

Facilities at Wakering	
Water	At yard.
Stores	None nearer than Gt Wakering (about 1¼ miles).
Repairs	At yard. Slip and cranes.
Transport	Buses from Wakering to Southend.
Telephone	At yard.
Club	Wakering Yacht Club, nearby.

The boat yard at Wakering has a slipway, located about a quarter of a mile south of the swing bridge on to Potton Island

The Havengore Route

This passage to the River Roach across the Maplin Sands and via the Havengore bridge, Narrow Cuts, Middleway and Yokesfleet Creeks should only be made during spring tides, and then only by craft drawing no more than 1.5m.

The approach to Havengore Creek over the Maplins crosses the Shoeburyness Gunnery Range, and as firing is more or less continuous on weekdays, it is as well for yachtsmen to understand their rights and responsibilities when intending to use the Havengore route. The complete bye-laws governing firing practice over the Maplin and Foulness sands are to be found in Statutory Rules and Orders No 714 of 1936, obtainable from HMSO. But the section of these bye-laws which is of greatest importance to yachtsmen reads: 'Any vessel wishing to enter Havengore Creek during such time or times as the whole of the target area is not closed in accordance with Bye-law No 3 must enter the target area not later than half an hour before high water and proceed by the shortest possible course to the Creek.'

Red flags are hoisted from a number of points along the sea wall; among them at Wakering Stairs and at Havengore Bridge, an hour before firing commences and throughout the period of firing. It is, however, difficult if not impossible to see these signals before setting course across the Maplins from the West Swin.

As firings are almost continuous in daylight hours on weekdays, it is dangerous to make the passage without first obtaining permission. Yachtsmen should telephone the Range Planning Officer at Shoeburyness (see page 67 for details) when, if possible, the bridge will be lifted and firing suspended. Every consideration is given to yachtsmen in this respect.

Night firing is normally confined to periods when the Maplins are uncovered, and in any case, as the swing bridge is no longer manned between sunset and sunrise, the passage cannot be made after dark.

The Maplin sands cannot be crossed from the Swin much earlier than three-quarters flood, and it is impossible for any other than light draught boats to get over the Broomway much before high water. The Broomway is sometimes described as a raised military road, but it is really the highest point of a large expanse of sand along which traffic passes.

There is probably about 1.5m of water over the Broomway at HWOS, but often no more than 0.75m at HW neaps.

Havengore Creek cannot be distinguished from the West Swin, as any marks off the entrance are too small to be seen over the 2½ miles.

The survey platform close to the E Shoebury beacon offers a good departure point from which a course of 345° mag will lead towards the entrance to Havengore Creek. There have been several attempts in recent years to establish marks that would assist yachtsmen using the Havengore route but it is extremely difficult to erect structures strong enough to withstand wind and tide for more than a year or so.

Wakering YC takes responsibility for marking the last few cables into the creek with a line of red cans on the port hand side of the gutway. It also tries to maintain an offing buoy (Spher RWVS) out on the Broomway, but this is not always in position. Once between the sea walls best water will be found towards the N. bank up to the bridge.

It must be realised that depths over the Maplins and the Broomway will vary considerably with the direction

Best water through the swing bridge at Potton will be found on the eastern side of the creek

The bascule of the new Havengore bridge lifted for the first yacht to pass through in November 1988

and strength of wind as well as with barometric pressure. Northerly winds will raise and southerly winds will lower the tidal levels, while a decrease or increase in barometric pressure equivalent to one inch of mercury will respectively raise or lower the height of water by one foot. Therefore, the more settled the weather, the more likely is the pressure to be high and the tides lower than predicted.

Havengore Bridge

The new bridge over Havengore Creek was opened in November 1988, and its lifting bascule allows unrestricted passage for any yacht. The bridge will be opened as required for 2 hours each side of HW during daylight hours — *provided the firing range is not being used.* Fortunately, firing seldom takes place at weekends, but anyone planning to use the Havengore route is advised to check by telephoning the Range Operations Officer on Southend (0702) 292271 Ext 3211; or by VHF radio on Ch 16, using the call sign 'SHOE BASE'. The bridge keeper can be contacted during HW periods on (0702) 292271 Ext 3436.

The tidal streams hereabouts are somewhat complicated —largely because of the barrier formed by the Broomway. The flood tide from the Roach and the flood over the Maplins meet and cover the Maplins about two hours before HW, after which the tide runs back into Havengore Creek until HW. Then with virtually no period of slack, the ebb runs out of the creek with great strength until the Broomway is again uncovered. These facts should be remembered when using the Havengore route since, when coming from the Swin, it is important to reach the bridge before the ebb commences; and when bound out of the creek it is equally desirable to be at the bridge before the last hour or so of the flood which runs N into Narrow Cuts.

When bound through the bridge and out of the creek it helps the bridge keeper if some kind of signal can be made to indicate that the bridge should be raised. Traffic signals will indicate when it is safe to proceed.

In Conrad's novel *Chance,* the character Powell was in the habit of disappearing mysteriously from the Thames Estuary in his small cutter, but was eventually followed (probably into Havengore) by Marlow, who describes the chase: '*One afternoon, I made Powell's boat out, heading into the shore. By the time I got close to the mud flats his craft had disappeared inland. But I could see the mouth of the creek by then. The tide being on the turn I took the risk of getting stuck in the mud suddenly and headed in. Before I had gone half a mile, I was up with a building I had seen from the river . . . it looked like a small barn.*'

There would have been no bridge over the creek when Conrad wrote *Chance,* but the barn may still exist for a similar building (at Oxenham Farm) continues to serve as a mark to be seen over the sea walls in the Havengore area.

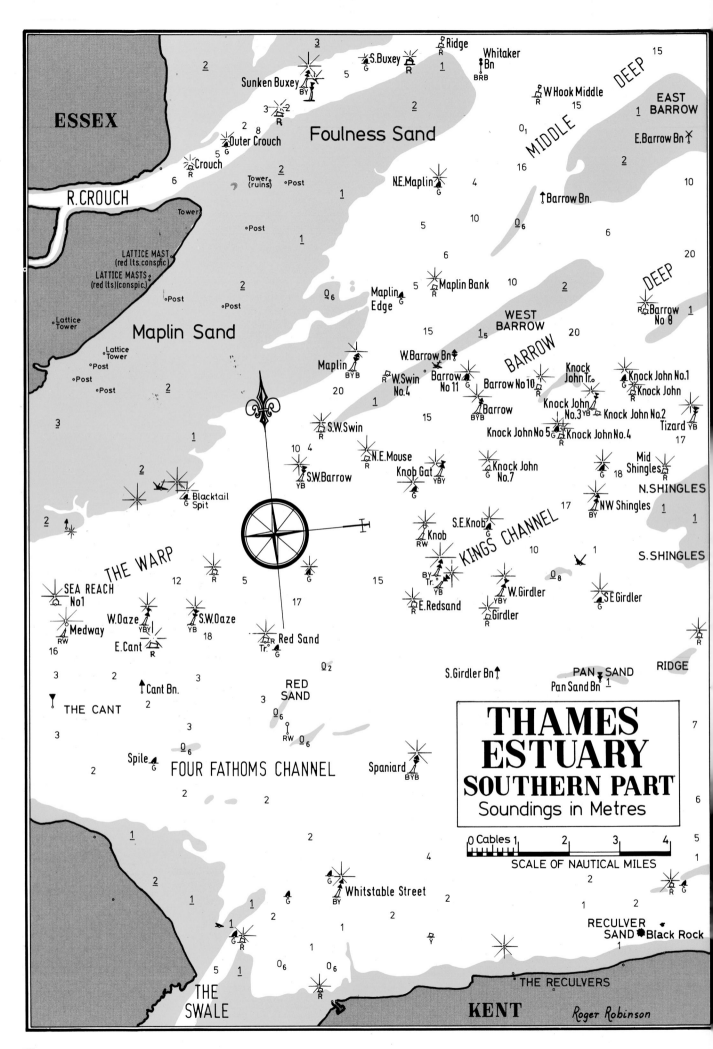

ESSEX

R.CROUCH

LATTICE MAST
(red lts.conspic)
LATTICE MASTS
(red lts)(conspic.)

Lattice
Tower

Lattice
Tower

Maplin Sand

°Post
°Post

3

2

2

Tower

3

6

5

2

8

2

2

3

°Post

°Post

Sunken Buxey

Outer Crouch
R

Crouch
R

Tower
(ruins)

Foulness Sand

S.Buxey
G

Ridge

Whitaker
Bn
BRB

W Hook Middle
R

MIDDLE

DEEP

15

15

EAST
BARROW

1

E.Barrow Bn

DEEP

20

Barrow
No 8
R

1

°Post

°Post

°Post

°Post

Maplin Sand

2

3

1

1

2

2

N.E.Maplin
G

Barrow Bn.

4

10

5

6

Maplin
Edge

5

Maplin Bank
R

10

6

10

15

15

1
5

WEST
BARROW

BARROW

20

Maplin
BYB

Q 6

2

Q 6

15

Q 6

16

0 1

Q 6

2

1

W.Swin
No.4
R

W.Barrow Bn

Barrow
No 11
G

Barrow No 10

Knock John Tr.

Barrow
BYB

Barrow

Knock John
No.3 YB

Knock John No.2

Knock John No 5
G

Knock John No.4

Knock John No.1

Knock John
YB

Tizard YB

17

18

3

2

1

20

15

1

S.W.Swin
R

N.E.Mouse
R

Knob Gat
G

Knock John
No.7

Mid
Shingles

N.SHINGLES

10 4

S.W.Barrow
YB

NW Shingles
BY

1

S.E.Knob

S.SHINGLES

1

THE WARP

2

2

3

12

5

15

Blacktail
Spit
G

17

Knob
RW

E.Redsand

KINGS CHANNEL

17

W.Girdler
YBY

SE Girdler
G

10

Q 8

1

SEA REACH
No1

W.Oaze
YBY

S.W.Oaze
YB

Red Sand
Tr.

Girdler
R

Medway
RW

E.Cant
R

18

Q 2

R

16

3

2

3

Cant Bn.

2

THE CANT

RED
SAND

Q 6

S.Girdler Bn

PAN SAND

Pan Sand Bn
1

RIDGE

7

3

3

Q 6
RW

Q 6

Spile
G

FOUR FATHOMS CHANNEL

2

Spaniard
BYB

THAMES
ESTUARY
SOUTHERN PART
Soundings in Metres

6

5

2

0 Cables 1   2   3   4

SCALE OF NAUTICAL MILES

R

G

1

2

2

4

2

1

2

Whitstable Street
BY

2

2

RECULVER
SAND ✹ Black Rock

1

2

1

1

1

2

1

2

1

1

2

THE
SWALE

5

1

Q 6

Q 6

THE RECULVERS

KENT

Roger Robinson

13
The River Thames

Tides (Southern Pier)

HW Dover +1.20 Range: Springs 5.7m Neaps 4.8m
(HW Tower Bridge approx 1.20 after HW Southend)

Charts

Admiralty 1185 (Sea Reach)
        2484 (London to Thames Haven)
Stanford No 5
Imray Y13

Waypoints

NE Maplin Buoy 51.37.43.N 1.04.90.E
Maplin Buoy 51.34.00.N 1.02.40.E
Blacktail Spit Buoy 51.31.45.N 0.56.85.E
Southend Pierhead 51.30.84.N 0.43.51.E
Sea Reach No 1 Buoy 51.29.41.N 0.52.76.E

Hazards

Large ships (Steer clear of dredged channel)
Floating debris in upper reaches.

JOHN EVELYN, whose diary is not so often quoted as that of Samuel Pepys, reported on a day on the Thames he had with Charles II in 1661: *'I sailed this morning with His Majesty in one of his pleasure-boats, vessels not known among us till the Dutch East India Company presented that curious piece to the King; being very excellent sailing vessels. It was a wager between his other new pleasure-boat frigate-like, and one of the Duke of York's — the wager 100-1: the race from Greenwich to Gravesend and back. The King lost in going, the wind being contrary, but saved stakes in returning.'*

Since then there has never been a time when yachts have not sailed on the Thames, and present signs are that an increasing number of people are visiting London in their boats now that the river is clean and free from commercial traffic. Unfortunately, there are still very few comfortable or attractive anchorages between Leigh or Hole Haven and St Katharine's Yacht Haven near Tower Bridge, so that a journey up or down the river is best done on one tide when possible.

Before embarking for the first time on a voyage up the London River to Tower Bridge, there are several things to be considered:

1 By using the tide wisely, the distance (some 40 miles) can usually be covered in seven hours, arriving in London just before high water.

2 Do not expect to find any easy or undisturbed anchorages en route.

3 In the upper reaches, keep a particularly keen look-out for floating rafts of debris. Besides drums, crates and bottles these will often include large, half-submerged baulks of timber which can stall an engine, damage a prop or bend a shaft. A particular danger nowadays are invisible plastic sheets.

4 Stow all loose gear. With a fresh wind some reaches of the Thames can be remarkably rough and the wash from fast moving tugs can sometimes come as a surprise.

5 Make sure you understand the procedure for passing through the Thames Barrier in Woolwich Reach.

When sailing in the Thames Estuary or farther up-river, it should always be remembered that the dredged channel for shipping is not wide enough to allow a deep-draught vessel to alter course, and in any case there is plenty of water either side of the channel for yachts.

Approaches

Coming into the Thames from the Channel or the North Sea, it is convenient to consider Sea Reach No 1 buoy as marking the seaward limit of the river. At this point the estuary is about eight miles wide, to the north Shoeburyness and the Maplin Sands, and to the south,

Warden Point and the Isle of Sheppey. The edge of the Maplins is steep-to, but the water shoals more gradually to the south, over an area known as the Cant.

Sea Reach

From Sea Reach No 1 Buoy to Lower Hope Point, some 15 miles up-river, the general direction of the channel is westerly and as there is no really high ground on the Kent shore west of the Medway, a fresh south-westerly wind blowing against the flood tide will quickly kick up a short steep sea.

Shipping bound up the Thames follows the well marked Yantlet dredged channel, which has a least depth of 10m and a width of about 2 cables up as far as Shell Haven. This channel is marked by a series of seven 'Special' buoys, either pillar or spherical, and coloured either yellow or with red and white vertical stripes. But small craft will normally prefer to steer clear of the main channel, and fortunately there is plenty of water on both sides.

When following an inward course to the north of the dredged channel, a watch must be kept for an obstruction to navigation extending off-shore to a point about 1 mile SE of Shoeburyness. This obstruction — part of a wartime barrier — has a light (Fl Y 2.5s) but does not reach as far as the drying edge of the Maplin Sands, although another post (Fl (3) G 10s) does mark the point where the barrier once reached deep water.

If visibility is reasonable, Southend Pier can be seen from abreast the Shoeburyness obstruction, although a direct course between the two is not advisable between half-ebb and half-flood because it leads over the edge of drying flats. Instead, the West Shoebury (Con G Fl G 2.5s) should be left to starboard or close to port.

There is a meteorological station at Shoeburyness, from which weather forecasts can be obtained by telephoning 03708-2271 Ext 476 or 475 on weekdays or Ext 476 at other times, and a Coastguard station.

Southend Pier

This mile-long pier dates from 1829 and seems never to be out of trouble for very long. A fire at the pierhead in 1978 destroyed the Coastguard and Lloyd's stations and a freighter cut clean through the structure and wrecked the RNLI station in 1986. Much of the damage has been repaired and the pier is up and running again. It is even possible for a yacht to tie up alongside for a while to take on water or collect stores from the town. The local RNLI station is at the head of the pier. Port of London (PLA) Navigation Services can be contacted at Gravesend on Channels 12, 14 or 16.

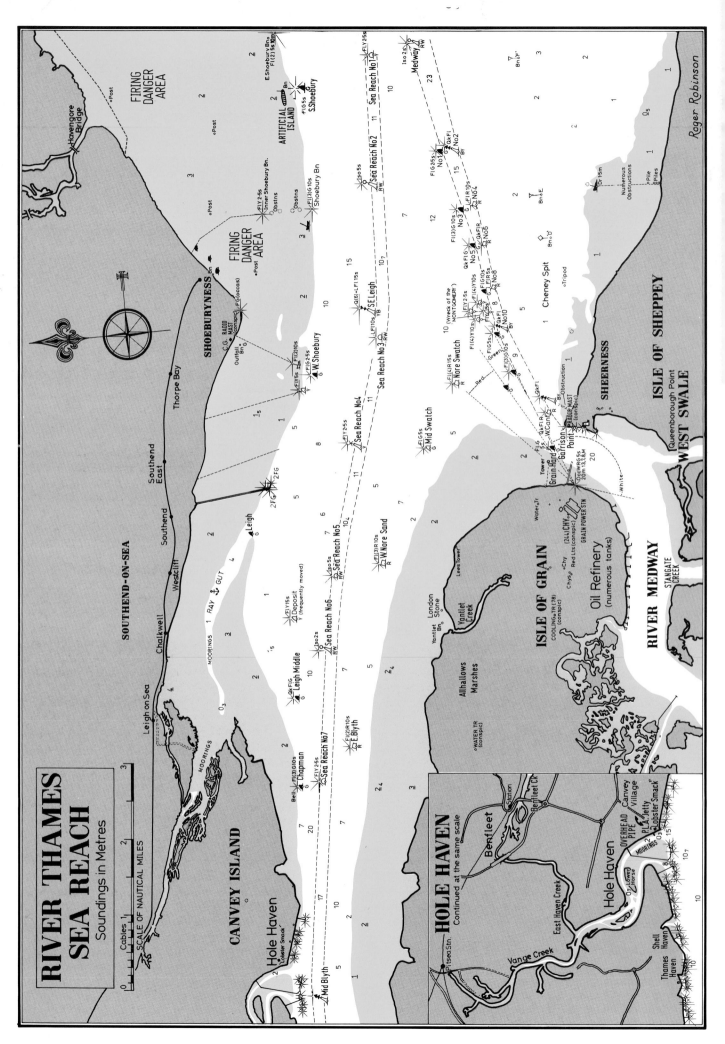

RIVER THAMES SEA REACH
Soundings in Metres

Cables
SCALE OF NAUTICAL MILES

SOUTHEND-ON-SEA

Leigh on Sea
Chalkwell
Westcliff
Southend
Southend East
Thorpe Bay

SHOEBURYNESS

CANVEY ISLAND

FIRING DANGER AREA

Havengore Bridge

E.Shoebury Bho FI(2)5s
Inner Shoebury Bn.
Shoebury Bn
ARTIFICIAL ISLAND
S.Shoebury

FIRING DANGER AREA

Outfall
C.G. RADIO MAST(conspic)
W. Shoebury
Leigh
Chapman
Bell
Leigh Middle
E.Blyth
Sea Reach No7
Sea Reach No6
Sea Reach No5
W.Nore Sand
Sea Reach No4
Sea Reach No3
SE Leigh
Sea Reach No4
Mid Swatch
Sea Reach No2
Sea Reach No1
Nore Swatch
Cheney Spit
(Wreck of the MONTGOMERY)

Medway

Roger Robinson

ISLE OF SHEPPEY

Queenborough Point
WEST SWALE

SHEERNESS

Garrison Point
Grain Hard
ISLE OF GRAIN
COOLING₅TR(TB) (conspic)
Chy
(244)CHY (conspic)
GRAIN POWER STN
Oil Refinery
(numerous tanks)

Lees Tower
London Stone
Yantlet Bn.
Yantlet Creek
Allhallows Marshes
WATER TR (conspic)

RIVER MEDWAY
STANGATE CREEK

Numerous Obstructions
Piles

HOLE HAVEN
Continued at the same scale

Benfleet
Station
Benfleet Ck.
Canvey Village
OVERHEAD PIPE
PLA Jetty
Lobster Smack
MOORINGS
Pitsea Stn.
East Haven Creek
Hole Haven
Vange Creek
Shell Haven
Thames Haven

CANVEY ISLAND
Hole Haven
Lobster Smack
Mid Blyth

70

It can be useful to land at the end of Southend Pier to take on water or to obtain stores from the town

For a mile or more on either side of the pier, there are some 3,000 small boat moorings — all of them drying out on to a more or less muddy bottom.

There is plenty of water off the end of the pier (10m or 12m) and an anchorage can usually be found on the edge of the flats on either side of the pier. There is little protection except from the north.

During the sailing season the PLA will lay spherical red racing buoys on the N side of Sea Reach Channel off Southend.

From the end of Southend Pier, a course due west (M) will lead to the West Leigh Middle buoy (Con G Q G). Leigh Middle is a shoal area that almost dries out along the S edge of the drying sands that extend eastward from Canvey Point.

A spoil ground buoy is usually located somewhere to the E of W Leigh Middle buoy, and is often in little more than 2m at LWS. The westerly course continued past the W Leigh Middle buoy will lead about a quarter of a mile south of the drying edge of the Chapman Sands half a mile off the Canvey Island shore. A green conical bell buoy (Fl (3) G 10s) is established close south of the old lighthouse position. The edge of the sand near here is extremely steep-to, there being depths of 20m within half a cable of the light.

A westerly (Mag) course held for another 1½ miles will pass close to Scars Elbow (no longer marked by a buoy) at the E end of a series of jetties with a background of oil containers on shore.

At certain states of tide — particularly during the ebb at springs, considerable overfalls occur about 300m S of Scars Elbow, where there is a patch of hard broken ground. Because of this, it will often pay to pass farther south, near the dredged channel, which hereabouts is only half a mile from the north shore.

About a mile west of Scars Elbow is the entrance to Holehaven Creek — a favourite anchorage with earlier generations of Thames' yachtsmen, but becoming less attractive as each year passes and our appetite for oil increases. At one time there was a half-mile gap between the tanker jetties, making the position of Holehaven obvious, but lately, another jetty has been erected directly opposite Holehaven Bay so that the opening is less easy to distinguish.

There are no further marks on the north side of Sea Reach, but there is deep water right up to the numerous jetties, dolphins and mooring buoys that serve the oil refineries and storage depots. All the jetties and dolphins show two vertical fixed green lights at night.

Powerful traffic lights are shown up and down the river from Hole Haven Point and Scars Elbow when tankers are berthing or unberthing.

Leigh-on-Sea

Almost the whole of the foreshore off the adjoining towns of Leigh, Westcliff and Southend dries out soon after half-ebb, so yachts drawing more than 1m should not expect to cross Canvey Point Shoals or Marsh End sands at less than three hours before or after high water.

Leigh Creek, however, does enable craft of moderate draught to reach the quays at Old Leigh, and the town is interesting and important to yachtsmen because of its several boat yards.

Except at or near to HW, an approach to Leigh should be made from a position close to the Leigh or 'Low-Way' buoy (Con G), located about half a mile W of Southend Pier. A recent amateur survey carried out by members of the Leigh SC showed that although the Leigh buoy is conical and green, it should be considered a port-hand mark when entering the Ray Gut, since there is practically no water to the W of it at LWS. The Gut is just over a cable wide between its steep-to banks, and it carries some 3 metres at LW for a distance of nearly a mile in a generally north-westerly direction. A little way in from the entrance, deep water in the Ray is marked by permanent moorings and fishing craft.

Leigh Creek, although marked by a series of mostly port hand buoys, is very difficult for a stranger to find, unless a local boat can be followed in. In fact it is usual even for local craft to await the latter part of the flood to take them up to Leigh.

The best general mark for Leigh is the distinctive long brick wall of Chalkwell Station, just to the east of Leigh itself. But unless a craft is able to take the ground

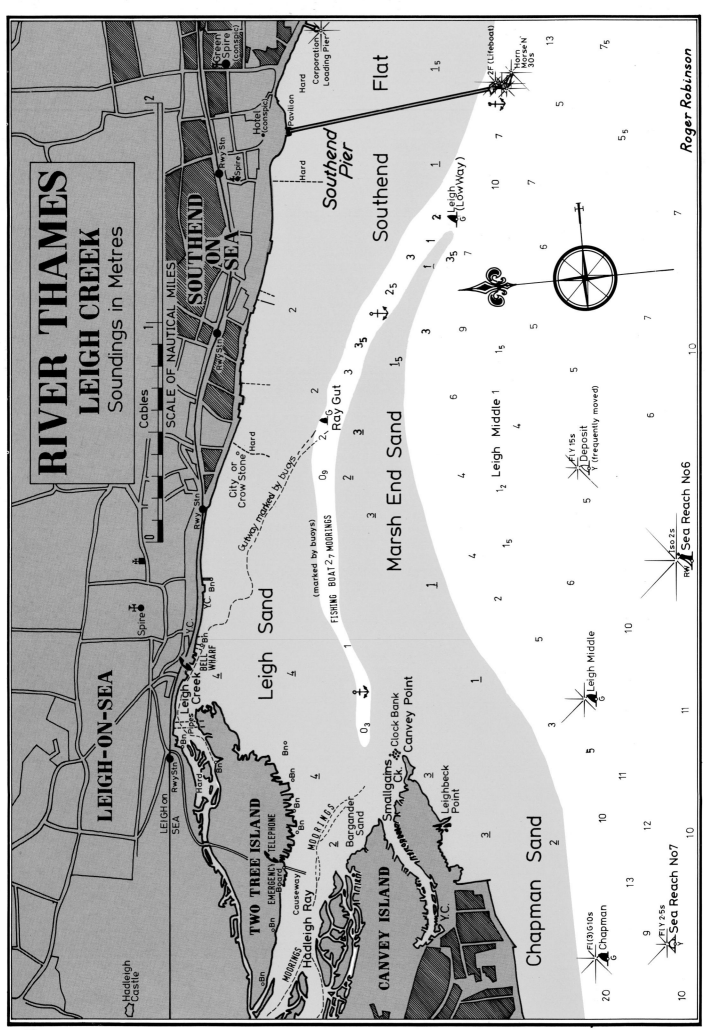

RIVER THAMES
LEIGH CREEK
Soundings in Metres

Cables

SCALE OF NAUTICAL MILES

LEIGH-ON-SEA

SOUTHEND ON SEA

Hadleigh Castle

Spire

Spire

Green Spire (conspic)

Hotel (conspic)

Pavilion

Hard

Corporation Loading Pier

Southend Pier

Flat

Southend

Hard

Hard

RwyStn

RwyStn

RwyStn

LEIGH on SEA RwyStn

City or Crow Stone

Hard

Gutway marked by buoys

2F (Lifeboat)

Horn Morse'N' 30s

13

2

Leigh G (LowWay)

5 5

5

5

7

1

10

7

7

7

6

9

3

5

3 5

3

2 5

2

2

Ray Gut

G

3

2

0 9

2

3

3

Marsh End Sand

Leigh Middle 1

4

Fl.Y 15s
Deposit
Y (frequently moved)

5

6

4

1 2

5

1 5

5

6

4

2

1

5

10

5

Leigh Middle
G

3

11

Sea Reach No7

10

12

9

13

10

Chapman Sand

2

3

Leighbeck Point

3

Smallgains Ck.

Clock Bank

Canvey Point

Y.C.

CANVEY ISLAND

TWO TREE ISLAND

Hadleigh Ray

MOORINGS

Causeway

EMERGENCY TELEPHONE Board

oBn

Bn

oBn

oBn

Bn

Bn

Bno

MOORINGS

Bargander Sand

2

4

Leigh Creek

BELL WHARF

Y.C. Bn

Y.C.

Bn

Bno

Pipes

Bn

4

4

4

Leigh Sand

1

FISHING BOAT MOORINGS
(marked by buoys)

2 7

3

0 3

1

Leigh Sand

1 5

1 5

9

3 5

3

Fl Y 2.5s
Sea Reach No6

Iso 2s

RW

10

Fl(3)G10s
Chapman
G

Fl.Y 2.5s
Y

20

10

Roger Robinson

72

Cocklers still work out of Leigh Creek, although no longer under sail   *Eric Stone*

without much inconvenience, it will be preferable to bring up in Hadleigh Ray, where several of the local bawleys are usually moored. There is enough water to stay afloat in Hadleigh Ray almost as far west as Canvey Point, but there is little protection except from the north.

At or near HW, a cross-sand route may be taken direct from West Leigh Middle Buoy to Bell Wharf on a bearing of 005°M.

It is sometimes possible for a deeper draught boat to find a berth alongside Bell Wharf, where Leigh Creek closely approaches the old town of Leigh. There is a landing place — a narrow strip of beach — just west of Bell Wharf, and it is also possible towards HW to land on the groynes farther E, close to the clubship *Bembridge* belonging to the Essex YC.

From Leigh it is about two miles to Hadleigh Castle from which there are striking views of the estuary just as there were in Constable's day.

Facilities at Leigh-on-Sea	
Water	From Bell Wharf or Yacht Club.
Stores	From shops in town nearby. EC Wed.
Chandler	Near Bell Wharf.
Repairs	Several boatyards with slips or cranes and travel hoist.
Fuel	Only from garages in Leigh.
Transport	Good train service to London (Fenchurch Street).
Telephone	Outside *The Smack*.
Clubs (In district)	Leigh-on-Sea Sailing Club. Essex Yacht Club. Alexandra Yacht Club (Southend). Thames Estuary Yacht Club (Westcliff). Thorpe Bay Yacht Club.

Hadleigh Ray and Benfleet Creek

The deep water moorings in Hadleigh Ray extend westward almost to Canvey Point, but thereafter only the shallowest of craft can remain afloat throughout even a neap tide. However, there are hundreds of small craft moored between Canvey Point and the causeway at Two-Tree Island and in Smallgains Creek, the

entrance to which is marked by an E cardinal buoy abreast Canvey Point. The landing and launching place on Two-Tree Island is approached from the Ray via a shoal patch, which may easily stop a yacht around low water. Otherwise, a course from one moored yacht to the next, following the larger craft, will lead to the causeway, which extends to the low water mark.

There is a car park and a road to Leigh Station. A hard-master is present during the day and there is water available while he is there, together with an emergency telephone.

Benfleet Bridge is about two miles from the causeway at Two-Tree Island, and the channel of the creek is best learned by sailing up early on the tide. The gutway is marked by a series of red port hand buoys numbered 2, 4, 6, 8 and 10, and two yellow starboard hand marks, numbered 3 and 5. There is a beacon with a conical topmark on the north shore near No 5 buoy, and at this point course must be changed to bring a pair of leading marks in line on the opposite (S) bank. The front one of these two beacons has a triangle topmark and the other a diamond shaped topmark. Moorings are then continuous up to Benfleet Bridge, and these indicate the channel.

In 1984, Benfleet YC opened its fine new land-based clubhouse, alongside one of the best slipways in the Thames Estuary. The club always welcomes visitors.

Facilities at Benfleet	
Water	From yacht club or yard.
Stores	Shops in Benfleet.
Repairs	Shipwright near bridge; slipway.
Fuel	Petrol and diesel.
Transport	Trains to London (Fenchurch Street).
Club	Benfleet Yacht Club.

Smallgains Creek

This little creek off the eastern tip of Canvey Island is hardly more than a mile long, but is packed with moorings and stagings belonging to the Island YC, whose clubhouse is near the head of the creek.

Many of the boats at Benfleet are moored to stagings and all of them dry out

Facilities at Canvey Island (eastern end)	
Water	At Club.
Stores	All kinds.
Repairs	Yards at the Point. Dry dock.
Transport	From Benfleet Station (2 miles).
Clubs	Island Yacht Club. Chapman Sands SC.

The Kent Shore

If the course in from the Estuary has been along the Kent coast, S of the dredged channel and N of the Medway channel, then a course keeping about half a mile S of the Yantlet dredged channel, will serve as far as the East Blyth buoy, some five miles away.

The Nore Sand (the first shoal ever to be marked with a light in the Thames Estuary in 1732) used to dry out, but now has nowhere less than a fathom (2m) over it.

When passing south of the Nore Sand, as from the Medway, an entrance to the swatchway should be shaped from a position close to the Nore Swatch buoy (Can R Fl(4)R 15s). From this mark, a course approximately 300°M will lead close to the Mid Swatch buoy (Con G Fl G 5s) guarding the south side of the shoal. Close south of the Mid Swatch buoy there is 8-9 metres, but there is little more than two cables between the buoy and the very steep edge of Grain sands to the S. The same course (300°M) continued from the Mid Swatch buoy will lead out of the swatchway and up to the W Nore Sand (Can R Fl(3)R 10s).

Yantlet Creek

There are not many landmarks along the south shore of Sea Reach, but the Yantlet Beacon (black with ball topmark) marking the west side of the entrance to Yantlet Creek can be seen from the W Nore Sand buoy. Small craft can reach this creek via a gutway running roughly north-easterly through the Yantlet Flats, and there is a 'hole' carrying about a metre, approximately a cable SW of the beacon.

The route is still used by yachtsmen in search of a remote and secluded anchorage although the whole area is overshadowed by the great oil refinery located just to the south on the Isle of Grain. However, a useful temporary anchorage can be found along the edge of Yantlet Flats in about 4m.

The next light buoy is the E Blyth (Can R Fl(2)R 10s), located about a quarter of a mile off the edge of the flats, which at this point extend for almost a mile from the Kent shore. The drying edge is particularly steep-to abreast the E Blyth buoy although it shelves more gradually farther west, and changes from sand to sand and mud and then mud alone at the western end of the Sea Reach. The next buoy is the Mid Blyth — particularly useful to yachtsmen coming down river, as it is a convenient mark from which to set a course to the entrance of Holehaven.

Holehaven

Holehaven beacon is not easy to distinguish on the east side of the entrance to the creek but it bears approximately 50°M from the Mid Blyth buoy, and is about half a mile distant. At HW, the entrance to Holehaven appears easy because of its apparent width, but in fact the only deep water runs about half a cable from the Canvey, or east side of the inlet. Drying mud with a steep-to edge stretches for nearly half a mile from Shellhaven Point. After entering, a useful leading line is usually provided by the craft already moored or anchored in the creek, all of which should be left close to port.

There is only about 1.5m of water in the entrance abreast the beacon at LWS, but once over this bar depths increase to more than 2m past the PLA pier while, about a quarter of a mile inside, soundings increase to more than 5m in a 'hole' which no doubt gave the creek its name. Although the best water in this first reach is well over towards the east bank, it is necessary to choose an anchorage carefully on the edge of the mud on the west side of the channel, because the Canvey Island shore is embanked with stone and has stone groynes extending well into the deeper water. Furthermore, towards HW, at night as well as in the daytime, there is regular lighter traffic through the creek, the lighters being towed in strings which swing wide behind their tug.

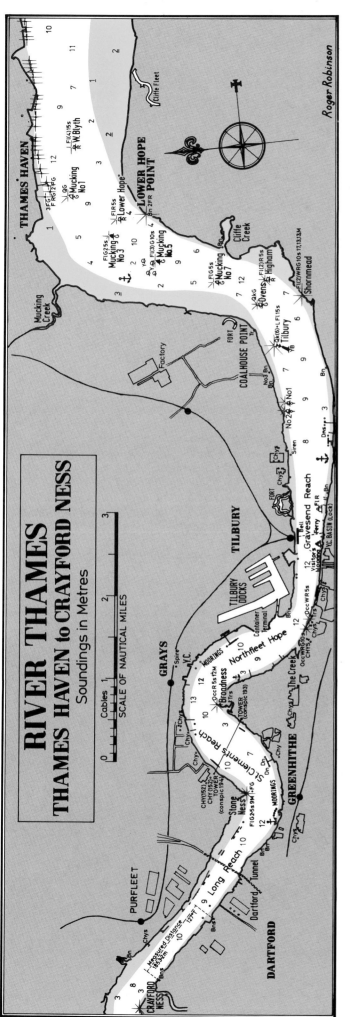

RIVER THAMES
THAMES HAVEN to CRAYFORD NESS
Soundings in Metres

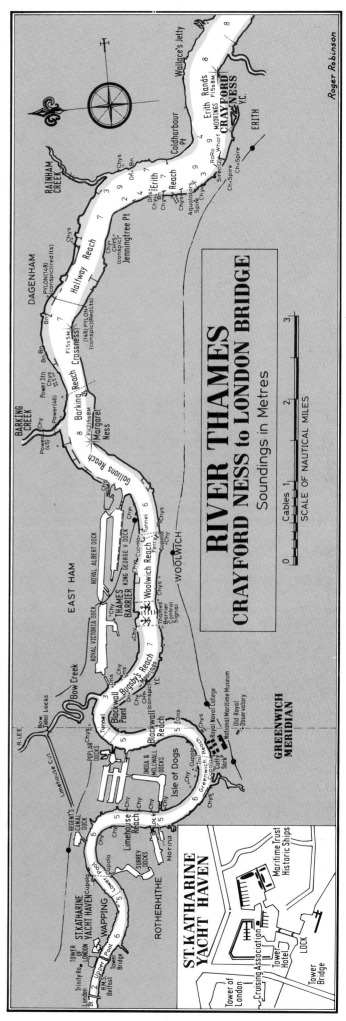

RIVER THAMES
CRAYFORD NESS to LONDON BRIDGE
Soundings in Metres

Roger Robinson

Fortunately the holding is good along the edge of the mud along the west side of the channel, but there is some risk of swinging on to the mud unless a kedge is used. Riding lights are essential at night. Both flood and ebb tides run at about 2½ knots at springs and are strongest near the Canvey shore.

Landing, to consult the piermaster, is permitted at the PLA jetty, but otherwise there is a wooden causeway just to the south of the pier. Once over the sea wall, the *Lobster Smack* will be there waiting for you as it has for generations of sailing men before.

About half a mile within the entrance an overhead pipe line crosses the creek from the new jetty to Canvey Island. This structure gives a clearance of 30ft (9.2m) at HWS so some boats can pass under and proceed with the tide towards Pitsea, Vange or Benfleet. At Benfleet there is a fixed bridge with only 6ft (2m) clearance at HWS.

Facilities at Holehaven

Facilities at Holehaven	
Water	From yard of *Lobster Smack* (by request), or at PLA jetty.
Stores, petrol, oil, etc.	From Canvey village (1 mile). EC Thurs.
Transport	Buses from Canvey village to South Benfleet. Trains from S Benfleet to London.
Pier Master	Phone: Canvey 0268 683041 or 0836 248472.

Vange Creek

There are many small boat moorings in this creek, which leads up to the Watt Tyler Country Park. There is a slipway, a chandler and telephone nearby. Pitsea station is about a mile away.

The London River
Lower Hope

Above Thames Haven, the river turns south round Lower Hope Point into Lower Hope Reach, the width of which diminishes quite quickly from about two miles down to less than a mile off Coalhouse Point. There is room to anchor on Mucking Flats well out of the channel and inside a line of large mooring buoys near to Mucking No 5 buoy (Con G GplFl(3)G 10s). This can be a useful place to be in a strong SW'ly. The 'Tilbury' buoy (S Car YB QkFl(6) LFl 15s) off Coalhouse Point is the last of the channel buoys and, for the rest of the way up-river, shore marks are used to navigate from reach to reach.

Gravesend

Gravesend Reach runs for about four miles in an EW direction, with Tilbury Docks to the north and Gravesend to the south of the river.

A convenient anchorage can usually be found to the east of the several piers and jetties, just below the entrance lock gates to the Gravesend Canal Basin.

At night piers and stagings of the north bank are marked by two fixed green lights (vert) and those on the south side by vertical pairs of red lights.

A temporary mooring can sometimes be found off the club, where there are two visitors' buoys, one of which can dry out at LWS, but the other, about a cable downstream and marked GSC, gives a clear depth of 2m at all times. There are steps for landing at the lockside near high water, but at other times, use the causeway about 200 metres up-river. Entry and departure are controlled by traffic lights.

The lock-keeper (Tel: 0474 52392) is normally on duty around the time of HW, and the gates can be opened from 1½ hrs before until just after HW.

Assistance is always available from members of the

A catamaran enters the Basin at Gravesend. Gravesend Y.C. fronts the Thames nearby

The aircraft carrier _Ark Royal_ passing through the Thames Barrier at Woolwich

James Stevenson of the National Maritime Museum

Gravesend SC at weekends. The club has scrubbing posts near the river wall and masts can be stepped or unstepped by prior arrangement. Craft should not be left unattended in the Gravesend anchorage, but arrangements can usually be made with the Lock Master to leave a boat in the Canal Basin.

Facilities at Gravesend	
Water	From standpipe near entrance to lock.
Stores	From shops in town. EC Wed.
Chandlers	Nearby.
Fuel	Petrol from garage in Milton Rd.
Derrick	At canal entrance. Can be used with permission from club.
Club	Gravesend SC (formed in 1884).

If bound up-river, it is not very useful to emerge from the lock at Gravesend just before HW so it will sometimes be preferable to lie to an anchor in the river throughout an ebb tide. This can be done by choosing a quiet spot about a mile down-river from the lock and just below the _Ship and Lobster_. The holding ground is good, and there is room to swing well out of the fairway. This is a time honoured anchorage but it is remote from Gravesend.

Grays Thurrock

Northfleet Hope adjoins Gravesend Reach and runs SE-NW for just over a mile to Broadness on the south bank and Grays Thurrock on the north bank.

Moorings belonging to members of the Thurrock YC are located just below the town causeway and abreast the old lightship that once served as the club's head-quarters. The club now has a new building nearby, where visiting yachtsmen are welcomed and sometimes a mooring can be arranged. All kinds of supplies from the town nearby.

Greenhithe

There are some small boat moorings and a useful causeway at Greenhithe, opposite Stone Ness (Fl 2.5s), and anchorage can usually be found in line with, and to the west, of the Paper Mills jetty.

Dartford — Thurrock Bridge

Construction began in September 1988 on the new bridge over the Thames between Dartford and Thurrock. During the course of the work, which will take three years, a waypoint will be established off West Thurrock Power Station and all vessels bound up river should report to Gravesend Radio before proceeding.

Two new light buoys will be established to indicate any deviation of the channel shown on Admiralty Chart No. 2151.

Erith Rands

This short reach between Crayford Ness and the town of Erith runs for about a mile in an E-W direction.

A useful anchorage can be found on the S shore in Anchor Bay, where the Erith YC has its headquarters in the old Norwegian car ferry _Folgefonn_. The club has moorings abreast the clubship and a buoy can usually be found for a visitor. If anchoring, a berth should be sought either above or below the line of club moorings.

A landing can be made at the club causeway, where there is a standpipe. A telephone at the club is useful for calling a taxi to save walking into Erith for supplies.

Woolwich Reach

When passing through Woolwich Reach, there are two hazards to contend with — the ferries which ply between north and south Woolwich, and the Thames Barrier about halfway along the reach.

Yachts leaving St Katharine Yacht Haven at high water

Nicholas Jones

The Thames Barrier

The tidal-surge barrier across the Thames in Woolwich Reach became operational in 1983.

A system of extremely powerful light signals is now used by day and night to indicate which spans are to be used and which are barred to traffic. Two green arrows pointing inwards will be displayed from each side of a span that is open to oncoming traffic, while red crosses shown from each side of a span will mean that no traffic must pass through the span in that direction. Anchoring is prohibited in the vicinity of the barrier.

Large illuminated notice boards are in position upstream near Blackwall Point and downstream near Cross Ness and amber lights shown at these boards warn ships to proceed with caution while red lights require them to stop. Audible warnings can also be issued from these stations.

The PLA are continuing to encourage yachtsmen to talk to traffic control on VHF Channel 14, call sign Woolwich Radio.

Barrier closures

From time to time the Barrier is closed for testing purposes, usually only one gate at any one time but occasionally all gates at the same time. Information regarding the dates and times of closures are given by Woolwich Radio on Ch 14 and in PLA's *Notice to Mariners*.

Drying moorings of the Greenwich YC are situated on the south side of the river in the bight between Woolwich and Bugsby's reaches. As part of the Tideway Sailing Centre the club now has extensive premises and many new moorings, including some for visitors who must be prepared to dry out if staying for a whole tide. There is a shingle patch near the causeway and this can be useful if a propeller has been fouled by debris in the river. Anchorage is possible on good holding ground on the same side of the river.

Greenwich Reach

This short E–W reach links Blackwall and Limehouse reaches round the Isle of Dogs. The Royal Naval College is prominent on the south bank and near it is the National Maritime Museum, the *Cutty Sark* and *Gipsy Moth IV,* while not far away at Deptford, the *Mary Rose* was built in the first year of the reign of Henry VIII.

Small craft can usually anchor just below and in line with Greenwich Pier, which is much used by water buses and pleasure steamers.

South Dock Marina

Part of the old Surrey Dock complex on the S bank of the river has now been converted into the South Dock Marina. The locked entrance, from Limehouse Reach, about three miles down river from Tower Bridge, will be operated for about two hours either side of HW. There are berths for some 350 craft, with all the usual marina facilities. VHF watch kept on Channels 37 or 80.

St Katharine Yacht Haven

St Katharine Yacht Haven is close to the Tower of London and immediately below Tower Bridge on the north bank of the river. This marina, with berthing facilities for more than 200 craft, must surely be one of the most superbly sited yacht harbours in the world.

Entry to the harbour is by way of a tidal lock (30ft × 100ft) which can be worked for about two hours either side of HW, between 0600 and 2100hr in summer and between 0800 and 1800hr in winter. There is a permanent harbourmaster, and the telephone number is 01-488 2400. The VHF Channels are: 14, 06 and 12.

A 200ft pontoon in the river near the entrance to the harbour may be used by craft arriving outside locking times.

For those who wonder whether they could pass under Tower Bridge without requesting that the bascules be raised, there is a gauge at Cherry Garden Pier, showing just what the clearance is at any state of the tide.

Cruising Association

The headquarters of the Cruising Association is in Ivory House at St Katharine by the Tower, adjoining the Yacht Haven.

14
The Medway

Tides (Queenborough)
HW Dover +1.35 Range: Springs 5.7m Neaps 4.8m

Charts

Admiralty 1834 (Grain Pt to Folly Pt)
      1835 (Folly Pt to Rochester)
Stanford No 5
Imray Y18

Waypoints

Medway No 1 Buoy 51.28.48.N 0.50.62.E
S Montgomery Buoy 51.27.88.N 0.47.17.E
Grain Hard Buoy 51.26.95.N 0.44.28.E
Queenborough Spit Buoy 51.25.78.N).44.04.E

Hazards

Wreck of *Montgomery*
Overfalls near Sheerness Fort on ebb.

FOR centuries, the Medway was the Navy's river, with bases at Sheerness and Chatham, but those days are history now and the only evidence of them are the dockyard buildings and the even older forts at Folly Point and Darnett Ness.

For the yachtsman, the Medway offers very good sailing in the lower reaches where on the south side there are some quiet anchorages in settings that can have changed little since the Romans established their potteries and even less since the prison-hulks were moored in the area during the Revolutionary and Napoleonic wars. Those who are not afraid of mud can still find relics of both these periods, even though they were separated by many thousands of years. By contrast, the north shore of the river as far west as Long Reach is now almost entirely given over to oil refineries and power stations.

The river is navigable by quite large vessels for some 13 miles from its mouth at Sheerness to Rochester, where the headroom under the bridge is 30ft at LWS. The tide flows for a further 12 miles to Allington Lock, one mile above the lower arched bridge at Aylsford. Then, for a further 17 miles, the river winds through pleasant country to Maidstone and Tonbridge, with eleven locks. Craft drawing 2m can reach Maidstone, while those drawing 1.2m can reach Tonbridge. Maximum length 18m, beam 4.5m.

Since 1968, the Medway Port Authority has been responsible for the ports at Sheerness, Isle of Grain, Faversham and Rochester and there is a considerable commercial traffic in both the Medway and the Swale.

VHF Channel 74 and 14 Medway Radio.

Landmarks

From the Thames Estuary the tree-covered cliffs of Warden Point on the Isle of Sheppey, some six miles east of the entrance, are conspicuous. On the west are the tall chimneys of the oil refinery and the new Grain Power Station, the chimney of the latter being 800ft high and therefore the most prominent daylight mark in the whole of the Thames Estuary, sometimes visible from as far north as the Wallet. The chimney displays four sets of four vertical red lights, the top ones of which are flashing.

On the east side of the entrance there is the fort at Garrison Point, Sheerness, from which a powerful flashing light is shown by day or night when large tankers are under way, while on the west side the massive buildings of the power station are very prominent.

Approaches

There are three main approaches to the Medway (see page 70):

(i) The main deep water route. From the Medway Pillar Lt Buoy (R W V S Iso 2s Sph topmark) some three-quarters of a mile south of Sea Reach No 1 Buoy, the channel runs in a W by S'ly direction between Sheerness Middle Sand and Grain Spit to the west, and the flats of the Cant to the east. It is wide and well lit, all the starboard hand buoys having white or green lights and the port having red. The stranded wreck of the ammunition ship *Richard Montgomery* lies on Sheerness Middle Sand, very near No 7 and No 9 buoys. It is dangerous but very well marked by special buoys (yellow) on all sides.

Garrison Point, at the entrance to the Medway. One of the Olau Line Ferries is at its berth, just inside the river

Judith Jones

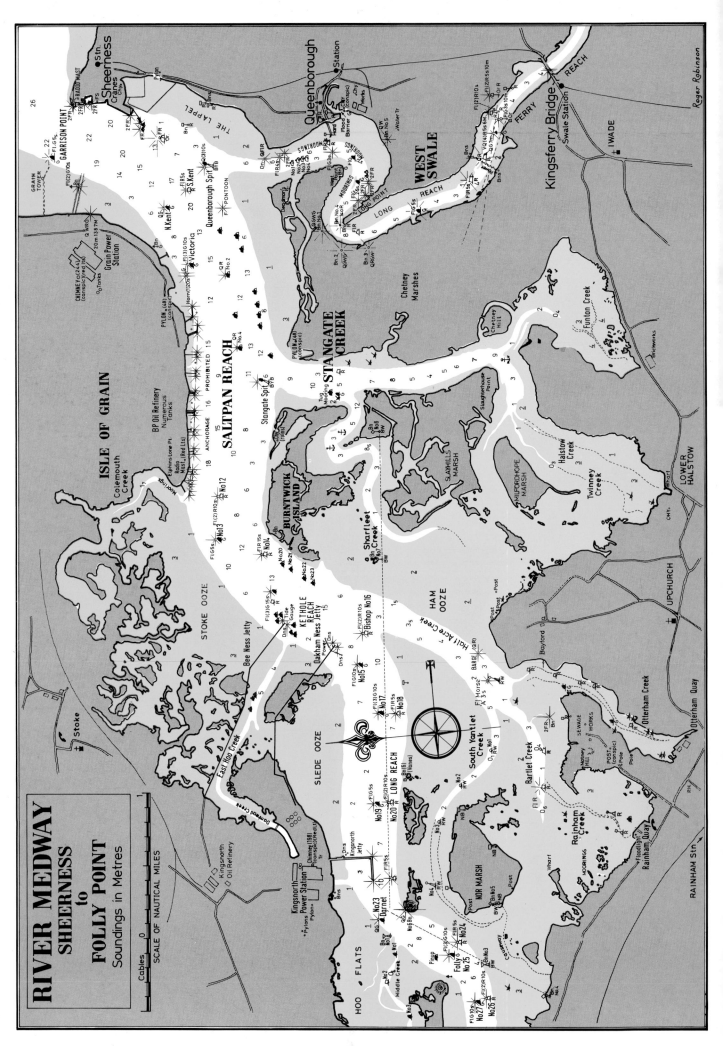

RIVER MEDWAY
SHEERNESS
to
FOLLY POINT
Soundings in Metres

SCALE OF NAUTICAL MILES

Cables

ISLE OF GRAIN

Colemouth Creek

BP Oil Refinery
Numerous Tanks

Elphinstone Pt.
Radio Mast (Red Lts)

Grain Power Station
CHIMNEY(244V/)(conspic)(red lts)
PYLON (48) (conspic)
Tanks
Q WRO 20m 13.87M

GRAIN TOWER

Stoke

Kingsnorth Oil Refinery
Kingsnorth Power Station
Pylons
Chimney(198)(conspic)(Red Lt) Tr
Pylon

Damhead Creek

East Hoo Creek

STOKE OOZE

Bee Ness Jetty

Oakham Ness Jetty

KETHOLE REACH

SLEDE OOZE

LONG REACH

HOO FLATS

Middle Creek

Folly Pt
No25

Garnet
No23

Kingsnorth Jetty

RAINHAM Stn

NOR MARSH

Rainham Creek

Rainham Quay

Bartlet Creek

South Yantlet Creek

Half Acre Creek

HAM OOZE

BURNTWICK ISLAND

Sharfleet Creek

STANGATE CREEK

Stangate Spit

SALTPAN REACH

ANCHORAGE
PROHIBITED

Bishop No16

Slaughterhouse Point

SLAYHILLS MARSH

MILFORDHOPE MARSH

Chetney Marshes

Chetney Hill

Bayford

UPCHURCH

Otterham Creek

Otterham Quay

SEWAGE WORKS

Motney Hill

Halstow Creek

Twinney Creek

LOWER HALSTOW

Funton Creek

Brickworks

IWADE

Kingsferry Bridge

Swale Station

FERRY

WEST SWALE

LONG REACH

LONG POINT

MOORINGS

Queenborough

Station

Works

QUEENBOROUGH SPIT

N.Kent

Victoria

S.Kent

THE LAPPEL

Sheerness
Cranes
GARRISON POINT
RADIO MAST
Stn.
Chy.
Pylon

Roger Robinson

80

There is regular commercial traffic past Queenborough and the fairway must always be kept clear.
The 800ft chimney in the distance is on the Isle of Grain

Judith Jones

The tidal stream off the approach sets W by N and E by S at a max rate of 2½ and 3 knots respectively, slightly across the channel, but as Garrison Point is neared they run fairly up and down the channel.

(ii)   The Nore Swatch, formerly known as the Jenkin Swatch, is not quite so important now that the Nore Sand has 2m or more over it at LWS. From the west the Swatch can be located by the West Nore Sand Lt Buoy (Can R Fl(3) R 10s) which lies on the south side of Sea Reach almost opposite Southend Pier. A course of 120°M leads to pass the Mid Swatch light buoy (Con G Fl G 5s) close to port and, continued, reaches the Nore Swatch light buoy (Can R Fl(4)R 15s). From here a S'ly course leaving Grain Edge Buoy (Con G) to starboard leads into the main channel. It is important not to skirt the edge of Grain Spit hereabouts because building debris has been dumped in a position centred on 51° 27'.75N, 0° 44'.70E.

(iii)   Across the Cant. Vessels making from the eastward via the 'Four Fathom Channel' or out of the West Swale, can carry about 3m least water on a course 300°M from the Spile Buoy (Con G Fl G 2.5s), keeping about two miles from the Sheppey shore. Several unlit beacons and Cheney Spit, a shingle bank with about 1m least water, extend eastwards from Garrison Point. These hazards make it inadvisable to get much closer than a mile offshore. Cheney Rocks, an unmarked drying patch of stones, lies half a mile off the eastern end of Sheerness town. A N cardinal buoy (QFl) marks the seaward end of an obstruction extending from the shore just east of Garrison Point. Tides over the Cant are slacker than those in the channels. The Medway may also be entered through the Swale (see Chapter 15).

Entrance

The entrance to the Medway is between Garrison Point to port and Grain Hard buoy (Con G Fl G 5s).

Massive landmarks have been created on the west side of the entrance in the form of Grain Power Station with its enormous buildings and 800ft chimney, the latter showing four vertical red lights at night.

Garrison Point is steep-to, but small craft working close inshore from the east should be careful to avoid the sewer outfall just outside it, the end of which is marked by a N Cardinal Pillar buoy (BY Q). On the first of the ebb during spring tides, there are considerable overfalls on the east side of the entrance near the Garrison shore.

A powerful white light (Fl 7s) shown from Garrison Point means that a large tanker is under way, and small craft must keep clear.

On the Grain shore the flats run out for half a mile almost to the Grain Hard buoy. No attempt should be made to pass to the west of this buoy as there are the remains of an obstruction running out from the Martello Tower.

Once inside, the river broadens out, and the former Sheerness Naval Dockyard, now a busy commercial harbour, will be seen to port. The flood runs at 2½ knots at springs, setting sharply on to Garrison Point, and causing a pronounced north-going eddy along the Sheppey shore.

The ebb runs hard, 3 knots or more at springs on the Sheerness side causing overfalls, but is much weaker on the Grain side of the river, so a yacht entering against the stream should seek this shore, remembering that the edge of the mud is quite steep.

Anchoring is prohibited on the NW side of the river because of the tanker traffic. On the east shore a berth can be found off The Lappel, east of a line between Sheerness Quay and Queenborough Spit.

Queenborough

A much better and more sheltered berth will be found at Queenborough, a mile and a half further south and just inside the West Swale. The entrance is narrow and is marked by Queenborough Spit Pillar buoy (E Car BYB Q(3) (10s) which should be left close to starboard. After this, two dolphins with flashing red lights, marking the

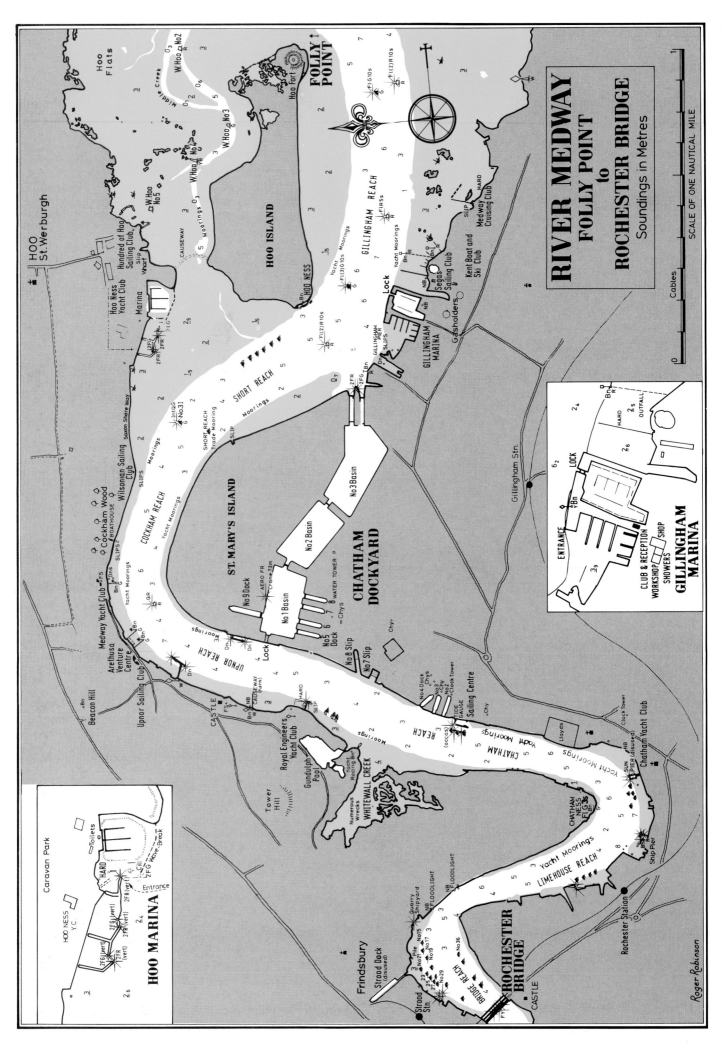

RIVER MEDWAY
FOLLY POINT
to
ROCHESTER BRIDGE
Soundings in Metres

SCALE OF ONE NAUTICAL MILE

Cables

HOO MARINA

HOO NESS Y.C.

Caravan Park

Toilets

HARD

Wave-Break

Entrance

2FG (vert)
2FR (vert)
2FG (vert)
2FR (vert)
2FR (vert)
2FR

3
2·6
2·4

GILLINGHAM MARINA

CLUB & RECEPTION
WORKSHOP
SHOWERS
SHOP

ENTRANCE
LOCK

HARD
OUTFALL

Bn R
Bn R

2·4
2·5
2·6
6·2
3·9

Gillingham Stn.

HOO
St.Werburgh

Hoo Flats

Middle Creek

O·3
3
O·6
2
O·2
5
5

W.Hoo No2 R
W.Hoo No3 G
W.Hoo No4 R
W.Hoo No5 G

Moorings

Hundred of Hoo Sailing Club

Slip Wharf

CAUSEWAY

Hoo Ness Yacht Club

Marina

2FG
2FR
2FR

Cockham Wood
BOATHOUSE

Medway Yacht Club

Bn Bns

Arethusa Venture Centre

Beacon Hill

Bn

Wilsonian Sailing Club

Saxon Shore Way

SLIPS

Yacht Moorings

Upnor Sailing Club

Bn G

FS

COCKHAM REACH

5

Yacht Moorings

Bn G
Bn R

6

UPNOR REACH

7

CASTLE

FS
Bn W CAUSEWAY (runs)
Bn NB

Dn
Dn

HARD
SLIP

3

Royal Engineers Yacht Club

Gundulph Pool

Tower Hill

Numerous Wrecks

WHITEWALL CREEK

Yacht Racing Bn

Moorings

HOO ISLAND

HOO NESS

Bn

Fl(3)G10s
G

Yacht Moorings

SHORT REACH

Moorings

IntG No31

SHORT REACH Trade Mooring

SLIP

Fl(2)R10s
R

3

Fl(2)R10s
R

2FR
Bn
2FR
2FG

ST.MARY'S ISLAND

No3 Basin

No2 Basin

No1 Basin

No9 Dock

AERO FR
Crane 73m

WATER TOWER

Chys

No5 Dock
6 7 8
Lock

No8 Slip

No7 Slip

Chy

CHATHAM DOCKYARD

No4 Dock
No3 Chy
Clock Tower
Chy No2

Sailing Centre

TIDE GAUGE

CHATHAM REACH

(occas)

Chy

Lloyds

Clock Tower

Chatham Yacht Club

SUN NB
PIER (disused)

CHATHAM NESS
Fl.G.3s
Bn

Yacht Moorings

LIMEHOUSE REACH

Yacht Moorings

Ship Pier

Rochester Station

Frindsbury

Strood Dock (disused)

Strood Stn.

Quarry
Shipyard
NB
FLOODLIGHT
FLOODLIGHT

Pile No5
No7
No9 No17
No29
No36

23
3
2

BRIDGE REACH

ROCHESTER BRIDGE

CASTLE

FY

FOLLY POINT

Hoo Fort

Hoo Flats

Fl.G10s
G

F(2)R10s
R

Fl.G10s
G

GILLINGHAM REACH

FIRS
R

Yacht Moorings

Lock

NB
NB

Segas Sailing Club

Gasholders

GILLINGHAM PIER
SLIPS

GILLINGHAM MARINA

Medway Cruising Club

HARD
SLIP

Kent Boat and Ski Club

Bn R

Roger Robinson

remains of the old packet pier, should be left strictly to port because of the extremely foul ground inside them. It is interesting that the Queenborough pier was in regular use by the Flushing ferry a hundred years ago, and now there is a Sheerness-Flushing service once again.

For the next mile or more the river is lined on both sides by more than a hundred moorings that are controlled by the Swale Borough Council. Two of the buoys near the causeway are intended for visitors, who should note that the causeway extends a long way and care must be taken to avoid its submerged end.

A concrete barge moored on the west side of the river, opposite the causeway, can sometimes be used for alongside mooring of large craft and arrangements to do this should be made with the Harbour Controller, (Tel: Sheerness 662051). The barge shows a flashing green light, while the east side of the channel is marked by a red can (Fl R 3s). Anchorage is forbidden in the fairway because of the large commercial ships that come by, but a berth can usually be found close to the mud on the east side of the river just south of the causeway, although the holding ground is not too good.

Keep clear of the entrance to Queenborough Creek, a narrow gut that leads in behind the town, the course of which is marked by half a dozen red can and green conical buoys. Queenborough Quay can be reached via the creek around HW.

The tide runs south past Queenborough for the first hour after HW.

Facilities at Queenborough	
Water	From tap near top of causeway.
Stores	Shops in town. EC Wed.
Repairs	Yard with slip in Queenborough Creek.
Fuel	From yard at head of creek or garages in town.
Chandlers	Near top of causeway.
Transport	Train service to London via Chatham. Station, ½ mile.
Moorings Supevisor	Tel: Sheerness 2051.
Club	Sheppey YC (Cruiser Section). Queenborough YC (Near top of hard).

Sheerness to Rochester

Standing on up the Medway through Saltpan Reach the river widens and tidal streams are less strong. Almost the whole of the north shore is occupied by tanker berths for the oil refinery on the Isle of Grain and these are marked by vertical pairs of fixed green lights. At the western end of all these jetties is Colemouth Creek, which formerly joined the Yantlet Creek in the Thames to form the Isle of Grain. This carries 2m at low water for half a mile, but is of little interest because of its environment.

A line of large, unlit buoys extends along the south side of Saltpan Reach about ½ mile east of the entrance to Stangate Creek. Three other mooring buoys (Nos 2, 3 and 4) are located in mid-channel, the first and last of which are lit (Q R).

Stangate Creek

This creek, running south of Saltpan Reach, provides perhaps the most useful anchorage in the Medway. A spit extends from the western side of Stangate Creek and this is marked by an E Cardinal pillar buoy (BYB VQ (3) 5s). The eastern side of the entrance is fairly steep-to.

Half a mile into the creek wreckage on the starboard hand is marked by a green conical buoy and just beyond, opposite a red can buoy, is the entrance to Sharfleet Creek.

For a further mile to the south, the depths in Stangate Creek decrease gradually from some 10m to about 4m LWS at Slaughterhouse Point, where the creek divides. Funton Creek to port holds water for only a little way, but can provide a quiet berth. To starboard, the main channel carries 2m for a quarter of a mile or so and then divides again into Halstow, Twinney and Milford Hope Creeks, all of which dry out. At tide time it is possible for shoal draught craft to reach the wharf at the head of Halstow Creek, where there is an inn and the Lower Halstow SC. If staying, one must take the ground.

Sharfleet Creek

There is a sheltered anchorage in relatively deep 'pools' within Sharfleet Creek, where at weekends there is often not very much room. From about 4 hours flood it is possible to wriggle right through the creek and out into Half Acre, passing just south of Beacon No 7 (BW triangle topmark). The whole area is a maze of creeks and saltings and for the first time, passages over drying areas should only be attempted on a flood with frequent soundings.

Middle Reaches

Leaving Stangate for the main river it is desirable to stand well out before turning west in order to pass round the pillar buoy marking the spit at the entrance. Once clear of this all is plain sailing until the river takes its SW'ly turn at Sharp Ness. The passage is well marked with fairway buoys, which are all lit, but a good look-out must be kept, especially at night, for any unlit mooring buoys on the east side of the channel opposite Bee Ness Jetty.

There are two conspicuous jetties in Kethole Reach, Bee Ness and Oakham Ness, both of them used for unloading oil from tankers. Close to the west of the first one — Bee Ness Jetty — is East Hoo Creek which, although uniformly narrow, carries a useful depth of water for about half a mile within its entrance and therefore offers a quiet anchorage except in E'ly or SE'ly winds. No more than two cables north-east of the end of this jetty lies the wreck of *Bulwark,* marked with one green conical buoy (Fl(3) 15s) and one unlit red can.

Towards the south end of the Kethole Reach opposite Oakham Ness Jetty is the entrance to Half Acre Creek. This broad creek carries 4 to 6 metres at low water for about a mile, where it splits into Otterham, Rainham and South Yantlet Creeks, the junction being marked by a red and white Otterham Fairway light buoy flashing the Morse 'A' (· −) every 3 seconds. Otterham and Rainham creeks both lead south towards the shore before drying out, but South Yantlet Creek, marked by three spherical buoys (RWVS) joins the main river just south of Darnett Fort, where it dries 0.7m at LWS, although at half tide there will be some 2m over the bar. The best water will be found on a W'ly (mag) course from No 4 pillar buoy (R W V S) with a spherical topmark.

All the craft using the new basin at Gillingham Marina, lock in and remain afloat alongside the clubhouse

Eric Stone

Otterham Creek

The four buoys marking the gutway of Otterham Creek are unlit because this narrow channel is little used by commercial traffic nowadays. The quay at the head of the creek was once used by sailing barges to load cement. Now there is a yard and two small shops nearby.

Rainham Creek

Small freighters occasionally use Rainham Creek at H W to reach Bloors Wharf. There is also a little quay near the ruins of Goldsmith's old cement works, the mud for which was dug from the neighbouring marshes and brought to the dock in spritsailed 'muddies'.

The entrance to the creek is marked by a red can light buoy (Fl R (2) 5s), while a couple of unlit red nun buoys with topmarks mark the gutway farther in.

The main river from the entrance to Half Acre Creek tends westward along Long Reach, where the deep water is hardly more than a quarter of a mile wide. Long Reach is dominated by the buildings and chimneys of Kingsnorth Power Station on the north shore. Three port hand buoys (Nos. 18, 20, & 22) mark the south side of the channel along this reach.

Hoo Marsh Passage

Middle Creek which near its entrance provides a useful anchorage, leads through Hoo Flats towards the old wharves near the village of Hoo. The creek is tortuous, but quite well buoyed. The entrance to the creek is marked with a conical green buoy to be left close to starboard, after which a red can must be left to port and then; turning SW with Gillingham gas holder ahead, another conical green buoy is left to starboard. After turning sharply to the north with Hoo Church ahead, the fourth mark, a yellow and black South Cardinal pillar buoy, is passed on its S side, after which the remaining buoy, a red can, is left to port before reaching either the quays or the marina at Hoo. This passage should only be attempted on the last hour or so of the flood, until it is known, as the gutways are narrow and very tortuous.

The lock leading into Gillingham Marina, with the conspicuous gasholder in line

Middle Creek to Gillingham

At the western end of Long Reach, opposite the entrance to Middle Creek, the main river bends to port round Darnett Ness into Pinup Reach. Darnett Ness, on which stands a fort, is marked by a red and white lattice beacon (QR) and is steep on its northern face, but should not be approached too closely on its western side because of a causeway projecting from it. South of this causeway there is anchorage with shelter from easterly winds, near the entrance to South Yantlet Creek.

In Pinup Reach the flood sets sharply towards Folly Point on the starboard hand, on which stands another fort. A rocky spit projecting some 200m from this point is marked by Folly Beacon (B W Con topmark) and no attempt should be made to pass between it and the shore — in fact this corner should be given a wide berth because a spit of mud seems to be extending from it.

Rounding Folly Point into Gillingham Reach, the mud extends some 300 yards from the north shore and the course should be set for the left hand side of the

Hoo Yacht Marina is entered over a sill after leaving a withie close to port and a spherical yellow buoy to starboard

large gas holder at Gillingham until out in mid-stream.

The south side of this reach is lined with the moorings of the Medway Cruising Club, which stands on Gillingham Strand, just east of the gasworks. Landing is possible at the causeway at all states of the tide, or at the pier to the west of the gasworks. At the western end of this reach is the entrance to Chatham Dockyard.

There is a small marina off the end of Gillingham Pier with pontoon berths for some 35 boats with fuel, power and water.

Facilities at Gillingham

Water	On eastern arm of pier.
Stores	Several shops in vicinity. EC Wednesday.
Fuel	Diesel on pier. Petrol from garage near gasworks.
Transport	Trains to London, Dover, Ramsgate.
Telephone	On pier.
Club	Medway Cruising Club. (Can usually supply a mooring for visiting yachtsmen.)

Gillingham Marina

The new, eastern section of Gillingham Marina can accommodate 250 craft and it is accessible through a

lock for about four hours each side of HW, but tides run hard across the entrance. The yachts in the older section of the marina can arrive or leave for about two hours before or after each high tide. There are deep water moorings available for arrival or departure at other times. Facilities include repairs, slipway and grid, fuel from floating station, chandlery, boat hoist, water and electricity to all pontoons, telephone, showers and 24 hours gate security. (Tel: Medway 54386.)

The river now turns NW round Hoo Ness into Short Reach, with the high wooded bank of Cockham Reach ahead. Hoo Ness, with a small jetty (two pairs vertical fixed green lights), is steep-to, but to the NW of it a large expanse of mud, covered at half-tide, must be crossed to reach the marina at Hoo.

Hoo

Changes have taken place at and near the site of the original floating yacht harbour at Hoo. The pontoons and barges of the old marina — the first to be established on the East Coast — are being rearranged to extend and improve access to the berths, all of which dry out.

A new marina, Hoo Yacht Harbour, has been

Yachts lie afloat behind a sill at Hoo Yacht Marina

The waterfront at Upnor is always busy at weekend hightides. The Dragon fleet of the Medway Yacht Club are on the starting line in the distance

constructed adjacent to the old one, but the new basin is protected by a sill so that there is about 1.5m inside. Usual services are supplied to the finger berths and there are toilets and showers ashore.

Both marinas can be approached across the mud flats near HW, but can be reached sooner via a creek or gully known locally as the *Orinoco*. Entrance to this gully is almost a mile from the yacht harbours and about half a mile NW of Hoo Ness. The creek mouth is usually marked by a small conical green buoy, but will be found just inside a line of large Medway Port Authority mooring buoys and two orange coloured yacht moorings, one of which can be used while waiting for the tide to make.

The *Orinoco* is marked by withies to be left to port and the last which is quite near the entrance to Hoo Yacht Harbour and should also be left close to port. The final mark, a small yellow buoy, must be left close to starboard immediately before crossing the sill.

Facilities at Hoo

Water	At Hundred of Hoo SC.
Stores	Shops at Hoo village. EC Tues.
Fuel	From marina.
Repairs	Slip and crane in W Hoo Creek.
Transport	Buses to Rochester.
Telephone	Nearby.
Clubs	Hoo Ness YC. Hundred of Hoo YC. (Mooring sometimes available for visitors.)

Cockham Reach

The Medway YC at Lower Upnor is situated in Cockham Reach, the prettiest reach on the tidal Medway. The river here is thick with yacht moorings on both sides, three lines on the north shore and a single trot round the bend on the south side. Because it is risky to anchor anywhere near the YC a walk along the foreshore under the woods or a trip in the dinghy will be necessary if a mooring cannot be found. A brief stay (10 min) can be made at the pontoon off the Medway YC. Unfortunately the four master *Arethusa* no longer graces the scene. She was sold to the US and can now be seen (as the *Peking*) at the South Street Seaport Museum, Fulton Street, New York, the Billingsgate of that city.

Facilities at Upnor

Water	From clubhouse or Cabin Yacht Stores.
Stores	Shop in village nearby (open Sundays).
Fuel	From club.
Chandler	Nearby.
Transport	Buses to Rochester and Chatham.
Clubs	Medway YC. Wilsonian SC.

Above the clubs is Upnor Castle which once guarded the river against the marauding Dutch fleet. About 2 miles on, round Chatham Ness into Limehouse Reach and Bridge Reach, the river reaches into the busy port of Rochester.

Chatham

Ambitious plans (not yet fulfilled) have been made to convert the historic site of Chatham Dockyard into a modern housing, business and leisure complex that will include a marina (comprising two of the original naval basins) with 900 berths. The history of the Dockyard can be recalled by visiting St Mary's Church to see the Medway Heritage Centre, which is open daily (except Mondays).

There is a landing stage at Sun Pier with a telephone and a large chandler nearby. Diesel fuel can be obtained from a barge moored just downstream of the pier.

Many yacht moorings line both sides of the river at Chatham, some belonging to Chatham YC but an increasing number to the Medway Ports Authority. There is a group of clubs based near to Rochester Bridge. The Strood YC can sometimes arrange for a visitor to moor below the bridge, while the Pelican and Rochester Cruising Clubs are on the north and south banks respectively, both above the bridge.

The clearance under Rochester road and rail bridge is approximately 20ft (6m) at HWS. There is not much depth of water at LWS, but the best arch to use is on the starboard side going up river.

Facilities at Rochester

Stores	Shops nearby.
Repairs	Boatyard and marine engineer close to pier.
Transport	Trains to London, Maidstone, Chatham.
Clubs	Rochester Cruising Club. Strood YC.

15
The Swale

Tides (Harty Ferry)
HW Dover +1.25 Range: Springs 5.7m Neaps 5.1m

Charts

Admiralty 2571 (East Swale)
2572 (West Swale)
Stanford No 5
Imray Y14

Waypoints

Whitstable Street Buoy 51.23.84.N   1.01.20.E
Pollard Spit Buoy 51.22.84.N   0.58.68.E

FOR ten consecutive editions this section had been been headed 'The River Swale', but Don Goodsell, who lives at Oare, then pointed out to me that the Swale is not a river and could more correctly be described as a 'ria' — meaning a submerged valley.

Whatever we do call it, it divides the Isle of Sheppey from the mainland of Kent, is seventeen miles in length and follows a tortuous course in a general east-west direction. In ancient days it was the usual route for craft bound for London from the Channel, and it still provides an inside passage between the Medway and the North Kent shore off Whitstable.

The opposing tidal streams meet somewhere near the mouth of Milton Creek. A good time to start through the Swale from W to E, is an hour or so after low water at Sheerness.

The West Swale is entered from the Medway between the drying flats south of Sheerness known as The Lappel, and the extensive Queenborough Spit, the end of which is marked by an E cardinal Pillar buoy (BYB Q(3)10s).

The facilities at Queenborough have already been described in Chapter 14 since this anchorage is often thought of as being part of the Medway rather than the Swale.

Loden Hope

Above Queenborough the river turns SW through Loden Hope. Drying mud flats fill the whole of the SE bight from Queenborough hard to the jetty on the NE face of Long Point. A drying horse in mid-stream almost opposite the jetty is marked by a green conical buoy but if the north side is taken, Long Point should be rounded in mid-channel with due regard to mud flats off the north shore.

As the river turns south along Long Reach the best water is towards the west side of mid-channel.

About a mile after Long Point (in Horse Reach) two prominent cable notice boards will be seen on NE bank. Abreast of these, there is a small horse practically in mid-channel. This is marked by two red can buoys and should be passed on its SW side about one-third of river width off the Kent shore.

There are two sets of leading marks, with lights to assist boats through Horse Reach. The first pair of marks and lights (flashing green) are on the south bank and provide a leading line of 120°M while the second pair, bearing 105°M are located on the west bank and flash red.

From Horse Reach, Kingsferry Bridge spanning the river is seen ahead. Although here the river is narrow, and carries quite large ships, small craft can usually find temporary anchorage on the SW shore just by the

bridge. This is also the best spot for landing from a dinghy as the surface is hard.

Kingsferry Bridge will open to permit vessels with fixed masts to pass on request, provided always that railway traffic permits. If a train is on the line between Sittingbourne and Sheerness, the bridge may not be opened and do not be surprised if this sometimes results in a wait of half an hour or so.

Two more lights, on the W bank near Ridham Dock, serve to lead ships through the bridge, the front is 2 F G and the rear 2 F W on a line of 155° mag. Sets of six 'traffic lights' are displayed on the south buttress of the bridge, near the bridge-keeper's cabin. The lights are grouped in two vertical lines of three, the top pair being white, the middle pair orange, and the lowest pair green.

The accepted signals for a yacht to give when wishing

The traditional signal to indicate that a yacht wishes to pass through the bridge at Kingsferry, is to hoist a bucket in the rigging

Judith Jones

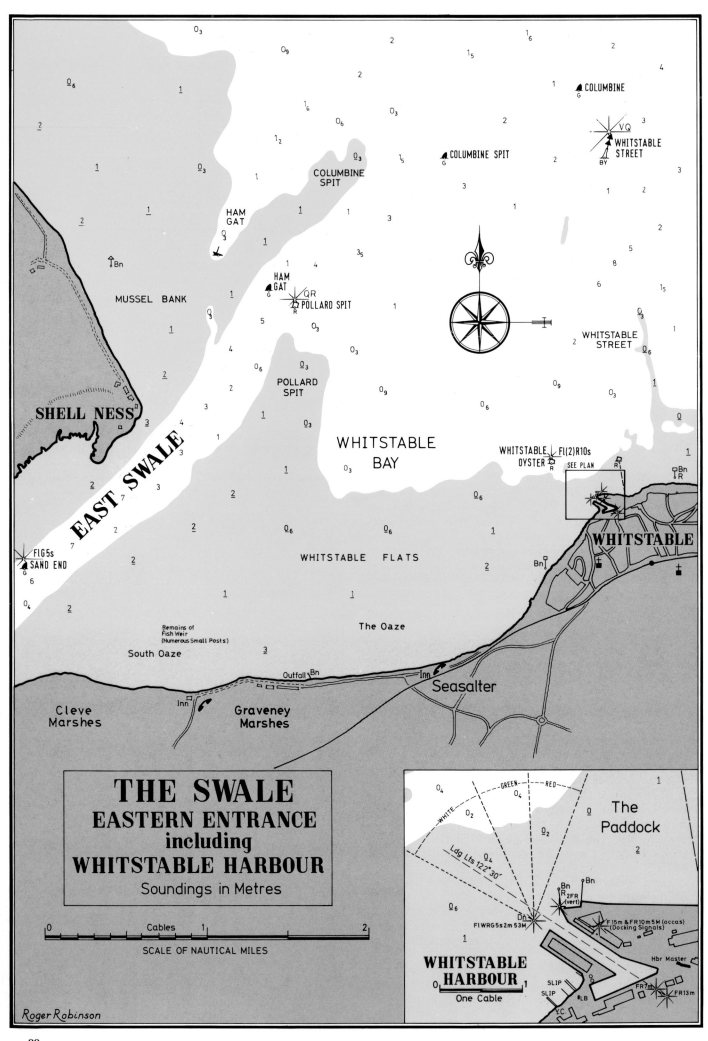

THE SWALE
EASTERN ENTRANCE
including
WHITSTABLE HARBOUR
Soundings in Metres

Cables

SCALE OF NAUTICAL MILES

WHITSTABLE
HARBOUR
One Cable

Roger Robinson

to pass through the bridge is to hoist a bucket in the rigging, or one long and four short 'toots'.

When both green and orange lights are flashing, the bridge is about to be lifted. When fixed green lights are shown it has been fully raised. Flashing red lights indicate that the span is being lowered, while if no lights at all are shown, then nothing will happen because the bridge is shut down.

VHF Channel 10 Kingsferry Bridge.

The height clearance with the span raised is 27m at LWOS. The width between the bascules is also 27m. Tidal streams run strongly; from 3 to 4kn on the first flood and first of ebb.

Just beyond the bridge on the SW shore is Ridham Dock, used by large coasting vessels for which look-out should be kept around high water when they may leave via the bridge.

Two port- and two starboard-hand light buoys have been established in Ferry and Clay Reaches between Ridham Dock and Grovehurst Jetty, where the channel is no more than half a cable wide at LW.

A little over half a mile farther east is the nominal point at which the two tidal streams meet (see later). The river then turns to the east past a modern jetty on the west shore, the entrance to Milton Creek, which may be considered the end of the western half of the Swale.

Ridham dock is purely commercial serving the large paper mills nearby and usually occupied by sizeable freighters.

Milton Creek

The creek is marked by a sequence of three poles topped by green cones and four poles with red can topmarks. This rather depressing area is likely to be of greatest interest to industrial archaeologists who may wish to visit the barge museum at Sittingbourne; but even they may be well advised to get there by road rather that via the creek. (The museum is open on Sundays and Bank Holidays from Easter to mid October.)

East Swale

The approach from seaward commences at the Columbine buoy (Con G) about 2½ miles north of Whitstable Town, but from this distance the precise entrance to the Swale is not easily recognised. A course of 235°M passing along the SE edge of the Columbine Shoal, leaving the Columbine Spit buoy (Con G) to starboard will lead to the next visible marks in about a mile. The Pollard Spit light buoy (Can R QR) should be left to port and the Ham Gat buoy (Con G) to starboard. The Pollard Spit extends north from Whitstable Flats, an area of sand and mud to the east of Whitstable.

From a point midway between Ham Gat and Pollard Spit buoys a course 220°M leads into the river, passing Shell Ness to starboard about a quarter of a mile off. Cottages and coastguard buildings are conspicuous above its light-coloured shell shingle beach, and in conditions of poor visibility Shell Ness is a useful check on distance from the next mark — the Sand End buoy (Con G Fl G 5s) about a mile away on the same course.

Whitstable Flats and the Swale entrance are an oyster fishery area, and care should be taken not to anchor or ground on the oyster beds.

Once inside the river entrance the tides set fairly but at the entrance they are affected to some extent by the main Thames Estuary streams, and there is a tendency for vessels entering on the flood to be set over towards the Columbine; while leaving on the ebb, the set is towards Pollard Spit.

Throughout this long entrance the width of the channel is between two and three cables up to the Sand End buoy, after which the channel narrows.

Next there is a pair of unlit buoys off the entrance to Faversham Creek. The one to the starboard marks the south side of the Horse Shoal while the other (N Card BY) is on the end of the spit extending from the north bank of the creek.

Immediately to the west is Harty Ferry, the most popular anchorage in the Swale. The ferry no longer operates but the hard on the north shore provides access to the *Ferry House Inn*. A favourite berth (except during strong easterlies) is under the north shore near the hard, but beware the fierce current on the early ebb, particularly at night. This can be a dangerous anchorage with strong winds from the east.

Facilities at Harty Ferry

There are few facilities available to the boats moored at Harty Ferry, although water can be obtained from a spring on the south shore near the hard, or from the Inn on the north shore, where yachtsmen are welcomed. There is an emergency telephone near the top of the ferry hard on the south bank. For other services and stores the nearest places are Oare (1 mile) or Faversham (2 miles).

West from Harty a green conical buoy half a mile ahead should not be approached too closely, as in SW winds it wanders well up over the mud.

From here onwards the channel shoals and becomes narrower. Ahead to port will be seen the higher parts of Fowley Island, a long shoal parallel to the Kent shore, marked by an E Cardinal buoy, behind (S of) which lies South Deep and the entrance to Conyer Creek.

The N Cardinal buoy is small and not too easy to pick out, but the eastern spit is long and shoals steeply to the south, so a careful watch must be kept on the depth.

The main channel, which soon narrows to little more than half a cable, leaves Fowley to port, and lies approximately midway between the north edge of Fowley and the Sheppey shore. Passing Fowley Island the only guides are four buoys which indicate the best water if kept *close* to port. The channel is, however, so narrow that a fair wind is essential anywhere near low water.

Farther west, two posts mark the hards of Elmley Ferry. The hards extend well off-shore beyond the posts and that off the south shore has some stakes embedded in it. The best water lies a trifle to north of a line midway between the posts. The ferry no longer functions but the remains of the Ferry House can be seen on the south bank.

Anchorage

Just west of Elmley Ferry, on the mainland side, there is space to anchor, out of the fairway, in about 1½ fathoms.

From here, the river swings round a green conical buoy towards the north, passing the patch of saltings, the Lillies, that largely masks the entrance to Milton Creek. The best water will be found more or less in a direct line towards Grovehurst jetty, which shows 2 FG lights at night.

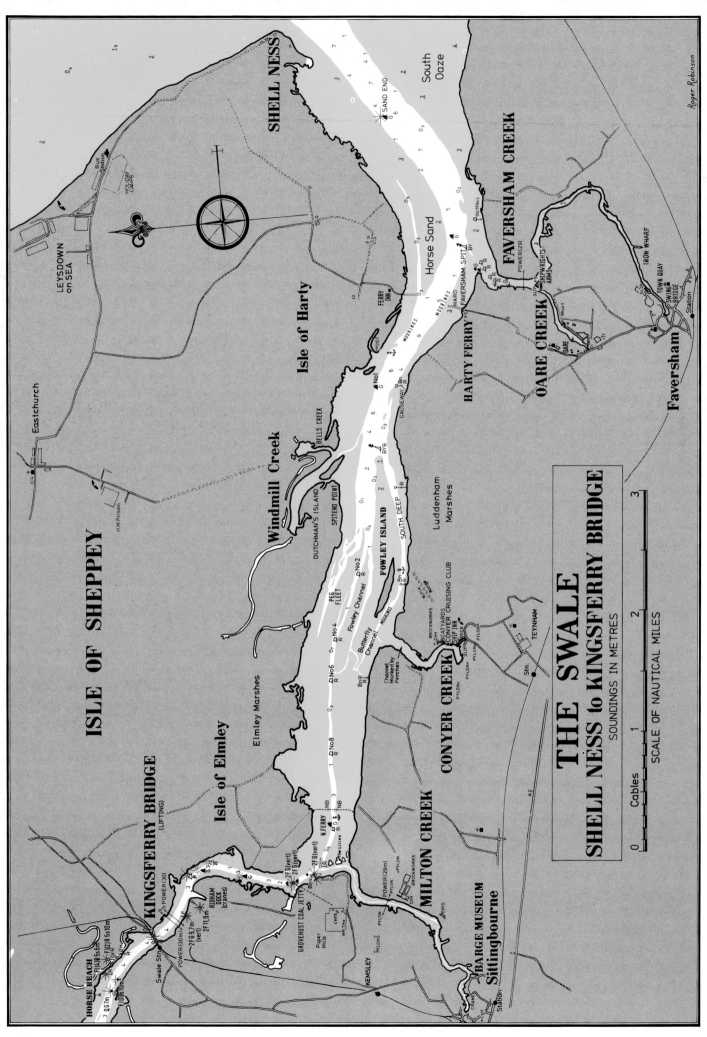

THE SWALE
SHELL NESS to KINGSFERRY BRIDGE
SOUNDINGS IN METRES

SCALE OF NAUTICAL MILES

Cables   0   1   2   3

Roger Robinson

ISLE OF SHEPPEY

KINGSFERRY BRIDGE
(LIFTING)

Isle of Elmley

Isle of Harty

SHELL NESS

Leysdown on Sea

Eastchurch

H.M.Prison

Windmill Creek

BELLS CREEK

DUTCHMAN'S ISLAND

SPITEND POINT

PEG FLEET

Fowley Channel

Butterfly Channel

FOWLEY ISLAND

Elmley Marshes

Luddenham Marshes

Horse Sand

South Oaze

SAND END

FAVERSHAM CREEK

OARE CREEK

HARTY FERRY

SOUTH DEEP

CONYER CREEK

MILTON CREEK

BARGE MUSEUM
Sittingbourne

HORSE REACH

RIDHAM DOCK (cranes)

GROVEHURST COAL JETTY

KEMSLEY

Paper Mills

BRICKWORKS

N.FERRY

The Lilies

TEYNHAM

CONYER CRUISING CLUB

SHIP INN

BOATYARDS

Faversham

IRON WHARF

TOWN QUAY

SWING BRIDGE

Station

OARE

SHIPWRIGHTS ARMS

FERRY INN

FAVERSHAM SPIT

90

For a short while around high-water springs, the Creek at Faversham can look like this. At low water it dries out to a gulley

Past Milton Creek, the banks of the river are closer together, and the good water now occupies about a third of the available river width. Although there are few marks to assist, it is fairly easy to negotiate this part of the river as there is appreciably more water than in the eastern end.

Remember that the direction of buoyage and marking changes here, off Milton Creek.

The East Swale Creeks
Faversham

Faversham Creek branches off to the south of the Swale just east of Harty Ferry and is marked at its entrance with a N Cardinal (B Y) buoy, to be left to starboard when entering. Sometimes there is also a port hand buoy or beacon at the entrance to keep boats off the mud on the east side of the channel.

The creek itself pursues a winding course for about 3½ miles up to the town of Faversham.

For the first half mile up to the junction with Oare Creek (to starboard) the channel is fairly wide and marked by four red can buoys with red can topmarks, a green buoy with a conical topmark and a green post with a triangular topmark marking a wreck. Above the junction the channel is marked by nine unlit buoys — five green conical and four red cans. It carries about 1m at LWOS. In behind the seawall at Hollow Shore is the *Shipwright's Arms,* a pub with character but without mains electricity, gas or water. The yard nearby is always interesting because of the traditional craft that congregate there. The services at the yard are those that relate to repairs and maintenance: a slip, a crane and a dock.

Landing is possible at steps near the inn from about four hours before to four hours after HW. Shallow draught boats can lie afloat throughout a neap tide off the inn, but remember that Faversham Creek is often used by commercial craft and a few sailing barges.

Oare Creek

It is about a mile to the village of Oare which can be reached around HW by boats requiring up to 2m of water by way of a creek marked by withies. There are

The pontoon berths at the head of Oare Creek all dry out, but they have the advantage of being quite close to the village.

Although they dry out for much of the time, yachts at Conyer can be reached by pontoons

stages with boats moored to them practically all the way along the SE bank of Oare Creek, while at the head of the creek drying pontoons have been constructed to form a small marina within a few yards of the road to Faversham.

Above the junction Faversham Creek narrows and dries right out. Barges and oil tankers work up to Faversham on the tide; so shoal-draught craft with power can make the trip, starting at about four hours flood.

The first yard to be reached will be at Standard Quay, on the south shore. There are extensive alongside moorings here and, just as at Hollow Shore, there are always interesting craft to be seen. The services are largely aimed at DIY enthusiasts but include water, power and diesel fuel as well as a dry dock large enough to take a Thames barge. Further up the creek and on the opposite bank there is a yard re-occupying the site of the original Faversham shipyard. Finally, there is a third yard with pontoon moorings just below the bridge and almost in the town itself.

Facilities at Oare and Hollow Shore	
Water	From yards at Oare and Hollow Shore.
Stores	From shop at Oare.
Chandler	At Oare.
Fuel	Diesel from yards.
Repairs	Yards at Oare and Hollow Shore. Slipways. Crane up to 5 tons at Hollow Shore and 15 tons at Oare.
Transport	Bus from Oare to Faversham.
Club	Hollow Shore Cruising Club.

Facilities at Faversham	
Water	From yards.
Stores	Shops in town, EC Thurs.
Repairs	Yards at Faversham. Dry dock to 55ft.
Fuel	Petrol and diesel from garages.
Transport	Trains to London, Dover and Ramsgate.

Conyer Creek

When entering Conyer Creek for the first time it is advisable whenever possible, to follow local craft of at least equal draught, as the position of the perches is not always reliable.

Craft entering the creeks from the east should keep to mid channel until level with the first perch, which should be left close to starboard. Two or three more perches, also left to starboard, lead into Conyer Creek, which is marked by posts. Those with white disc marks should be left to port and those with white triangles to starboard.

Although very narrow, the Butterfly Channel is deeper and offers an alternative when a craft is early or late on the tide, or during neaps. The entrance to the Butterfly is marked by a perch and is about 50m to the W of the main or E entrance. The channel carries a considerable depth of water and runs close to the west shore, joining the main channel after an abrupt turn east at a tall perch topped with two triangles, which must be left to starboard when entering. Like Conyer Creek, the Butterfly is marked with disc-topped perches to port and triangle-topped marks to starboard.

Shoal draught craft approaching Conyer from the west or leaving Conyer bound for Queenborough can, just before HW, save considerable distance by entering at the west of South Deep, about a cable to the west of Little Fowley and abreast No 4 buoy, sounding across the spit into South Deep and then turning in a generally easterly direction to leave the perch marking the

Facilities at Conyer	
Water	Laid on at boatyards.
Stores	From chandler.
Repairs	Two yards, with slipways, boat lift and cranes. Sailmaker.
Sailmaker	At quayside.
Fuel	Diesel at yards.
Transport	Bus service to Teynham and Sittingbourne. Trains to London, Dover and Ramsgate from Teynham or Sittingbourne.

entrance to the Butterfly to the starboard. There are two yards at Conyer, both offering complete services to yachtsmen, most of the berths are alongside drying pontoons.

Conyer Marine will keep a VHF watch if requested (Tel: 0795 521276) and will guide boats into the creek from South Deep.

Windmill Creek

Runs off to the north about one mile west of Harty Ferry. The spit off its western side is marked with a post. It formerly ran some miles inland, but it has now been blocked and is of little interest except to wildfowlers.

Whitstable Harbour

This small harbour lies two or three miles east of the entrance to the East Swale. It is controlled by Canterbury Council and is used regularly by small freighters and by local fishing boats and barges, but it offers shelter to yachtsmen who are prevented from making the Thames or Medway during a westerly or south-westerly blow. Berthing for yachts is, however, temporary and at the discretion of the harbourmaster.

> **VHF** Channels 16, 12, or 9 between 0800 and 1700 (Mon-Fri) but also on any day from 3hrs before and 2hrs after HW. (Tel: Whitstable 274086).

The narrow entrance to the harbour can be reached only over the shoal water that extends for more than a mile off-shore. Best approach is from a position about a mile W of the Whitstable Street buoy (N Card VQ) on a course of 170°M held until within half a mile of the harbour entrance by which time, if it is dark, the Whitstable 'Oyster' buoy (Can R Fl(2)R 10s) will be seen on the starboard bow while continuing on the same course within the green sector of a flashing light on the W Quay dolphin just off the harbour entrance. This dolphin and a conspicuous tall granary building provide useful daylight marks. the light on the dolphin has WR and G sectors and flashes every 5 seconds. The white sector serves shoal draught boats approaching from the west, while the red sector is to keep craft off a shoal

called Whitstable Street. There are leading lights (FR) into the harbour on a bearing of 130°M.

Facilities at Whitstable	
Water	Alongside at Harbour.
Stores	Shops in town, EC Wed.
Chandler	Nearby.
Petrol and oil	Garages nearby.
Repairs	Several yards with slipways, and sailmaker.
Transport	Train service to London (Victoria).
Harbour Dues	Check with HM (Tel: Whitstable 4086).
Customs Office	At Harbour.
Club	At Whitstable Yacht Club. (Tel: 272345). (Can sometimes offer a mooring).

Swale Tides

Tidal streams are peculiar because of the two outlets to the sea. At LW Sheerness it is slack water almost throughout the Swale. As the flood commences, it naturally enters from both ends, the streams meeting at about Fowley, or even as far west as Elmley on very high tides. At HW Sheerness it is slack throughout the Swale, and for the first hour after H W *the whole body of water moves eastward,* when at about Long Point the westerly stream turns right round and ebbs back into the Medway; while the remainder of the water continues to move to the east. As the ebb continues, the point of separation of the stream also moves eastwards, until ultimately the separation occurs near Fowley.

As the result of this there is an east-going stream for about nine hours every tide at Elmley; while at Kingsferry Bridge the tide sets to the east for eight hours. By the time Harty is reached the duration of east and west-going streams is about six hours each, but it is sometimes useful to know that on the north side of the West Swale there is a west-going eddy for as much as an hour before the ebb stops flowing eastward on the south side of the river.

The early ebb is strong, until the banks are uncovered, approaching 3 to 4 knots at Kingsferry.

In the East Swale, tides are considerably affected by prevailing winds, easterlies causing the higher levels.

The Whitstable Yacht Club has its clubhouse on the seafront, near the RNLI boathouse.

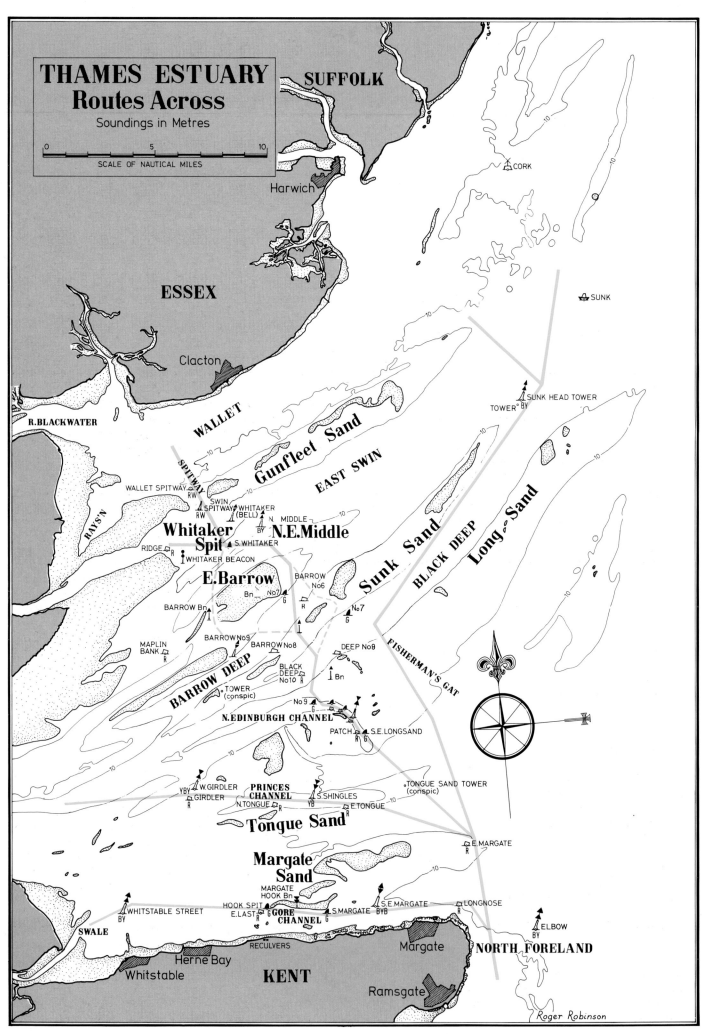

THAMES ESTUARY
Routes Across
Soundings in Metres

0   5   10
SCALE OF NAUTICAL MILES

SUFFOLK

Harwich

ESSEX

Clacton

R.BLACKWATER

WALLET

Gunfleet Sand

EAST SWIN

SPITWAY

WALLET SPITWAY
RW

SWIN
SPITWAY WHITAKER
RW (BELL)

N. MIDDLE
BY

N.E.Middle

RAYS'N

Whitaker
Spit

S.WHITAKER

RIDGE R

WHITAKER BEACON

E.Barrow

BARROW
No6

BARROW Bn

Bn No7

G

R

No.7

G

Sunk Sand

BLACK DEEP

Long Sand

CORK

SUNK

SUNK HEAD TOWER
TOWER BY

10

10

10

10

10

10

MAPLIN
BANK
R

BARROW No9

BARROW No8

BARROW DEEP

BLACK
DEEP
No10
R

Bn

DEEP No9

FISHERMAN'S GAT

TOWER
(conspic)

No.9 G

N.EDINBURGH CHANNEL

PATCH R G S.E.LONGSAND

10

10

W.GIRDLER
YBY

GIRDLER
R

PRINCES
CHANNEL
N.TONGUE R

S.SHINGLES
YB

E.TONGUE

TONGUE SAND TOWER
(conspic)

10

Tongue Sand

Margate
Sand

MARGATE
HOOK Bn

E.MARGATE
R

10

HOOK SPIT

E.LAST G GORE
R   CHANNEL

S.MARGATE BYB

G

S.E.MARGATE

LONGNOSE
R

WHITSTABLE STREET
BY

SWALE

RECULVERS

Herne Bay

Whitstable

KENT

Margate

Ramsgate

ELBOW
BY

NORTH FORELAND

Roger Robinson

94

Cross-Estuary Routes

THERE is a story by Archie White in which an old West Mersea barge skipper tells a young fellow with his first command how he can sneak through the Rays'n, past the Ridge Buoy (where it used to be) over the top of the Whitaker Spit and out into the Swin off Shoebury; thereby reaching the London River well ahead of all the other barges that had been storm-bound with him in the Blackwater.

It is a good story and probably true, because it certainly is possible to cut many corners by using the swatchways in the Thames Estuary.

Precautions

Before any yachtsmen sets out to cross the shoal infested mouth of the Thames, he must give careful consideration to a number of things that may not have seemed important to him during short distance cruising between adjacent rivers within sight of land. They are:

1. **Corrected Compass** If visibility should close in when half way across, a reliable compass will be essential.
2. **Corrected Charts** A copy of *East Coast Rivers*, even if it is the latest edition, is not adequate for crossing the Thames Estuary. Admiralty chart No 1183 will be necessary and must be corrected up to date. Even then it must always be remembered that during the several years that often elapse between surveys carried out by the PLA Hydrographic Department of a particular area, significant changes often take place, particularly in the very swatchways that are of special interest to yachtsmen.
3. **Tidal Information** Work out and understand what the tide will be doing at all important points along the route — not only at the time you hope to be there, but also for later times in case you are delayed. For this purpose the tidal diagrams included will be useful, although the larger scale Tidal Stream Atlas (No 249) published by the Admiralty will be even better.
4. If equipped with a Decca Navigator receiver, prepare a list of all waypoints that might prove useful.

Weather Forecast

The latest possible weather forecast for the area must be obtained for a period at least twice as long as the time the passage is expected to take.

Some useful numbers are:

London Weather Centre 01-836 4311
Coastal Weather Stations:
    Walton on Naze Coastguard ...:............... 02556 5518
    Shoeburyness .... 03708 2271 Ext 476
Thames VHF (Channel 12)
    Forecast times: 0803 and 2003.
Telecom Marineline Forecasts:
    Southend (0702) 333444 or Medway (0634) 44544.

Emergency Equipment

Ensure the adequacy of emergency equipment, including: VHF, flares/smoke signals, life-jackets, liferaft/dinghy.

Conditions in the Estuary

Since the passage across the Estuary will generally be made during the SW going flood tide, it must be realised that when the wind is from the SW, as it so often is, then a short and very steep sea gets up in anything more than a moderate breeze.

For many of us, the first time we find ourselves in command of a yacht out of sight of land is when we set out from one or other of the Essex or Suffolk rivers and proceed seaward beyond the Spitway and the Whitaker Bell buoy or round the NE Gunfleet. The distance across the Thames Estuary between say Clacton and the North Foreland is about 25 miles, so we should not be surprised that it feels different out there amidst the shoals when the buoys don't come up as soon as we would like.

Waypoints
Whitaker buoy to North Foreland
BARROW No 7 buoy   51.38.19.N   1.14.20.E
SW Sunk Beacon   51.36.32.N   1.14.90.E
N EDINBURGH No 9 buoy   51.33.42.N   1.16.70.E
N EDINBURGH No 1 buoy   51.31.49.N   1.21.34.E
TONGUE SAND TOWER (N)   51.29.60.N   1.22.12.E
E MARGATE buoy   51.27.00.N   1.26.50.E

Swin Spitway or Whitaker Buoy to North Foreland

There was a time when almost anyone crossing the Estuary passed from the East Swin into the Barrow Deep through a swatchway opposite Barrow No 9 buoy; but now No 9 buoy has been moved a mile or so SW and no longer marks the entrance to the swatch. This route can still be taken provided it is realised that there is very little water just north of the Barrow Beacon. A narrow shoal has extended for about two miles in a SW'ly direction from the NW side of the East Barrow Sand and the way through into the Middle Deep passes close north of the beacon and over a ridge with less than 1m at LWS.

Alternative route

Another possible route passes north of the E Barrow Sand and into the Barrow Deep that way. From close north of the Ridge (CanR) or the S Whitaker (ConG) buoy, shape an E'ly course (°M) to pass about a mile south of the N Middle (N Cardinal) buoy until Barrow No 7 buoy (Con G FlG 2.5s) bears S (°M). Then, with the sounder going, skirt round the NE edge of the East Barrow Sand to leave Barrow No 7 close to starboard. Another mile on a S'ly course will bring the SW Sunk Beacon in view, and this should be passed close to, on a course of 135°M (with the NW Longsand Bn ahead about three miles away), until deep water is found in the Black Deep. When safely through the swatch, change course to leave Black Deep No 10 buoy (Can R Fl(2)R 5s) a quarter of a mile to starboard.

A recent survey (1989) has shown there is a swatchway with 4 metres least water about 2 cables NE of the SW Sunk beacon. Unfortunately, it is not safe to pass on a direct line between No 6 buoy in the Barrow Deep and No 7 buoy in the Black Deep. Admiralty charts Nos 1975 or 1183 will show current configurations of these shoals.

From abreast Black Deep No 10 it should be possible to see No 9 and then No 7 green conical buoys in the western entrance to the North Edinburgh Channel.

The North Edinburgh Channel is marked on both sides with buoys at intervals of a mile or less and, apart from keeping out of the way of any big ships which sometimes come up astern surprisingly quickly, it should present no problem. However, because the buoyage in the North Edinburgh Channel is changed quite frequently, it is essential to have Chart No 1183 fully corrected and up to date and to keep to the north of No 4 red can buoy, because the shoal it guards is extremely steep-to.

After emerging from the North Edinburgh Channel, the Tongue Sand Tower will provide a useful mark from which to shape a course (about 140°M) to the East Margate buoy (Can R FlR 2.5s) and then on to the North Foreland.

The Tide

In order to make the most of the passage on a rising tide it will be necessary to be near the Whitaker Bell buoy just before low water — which is rather convenient for those leaving the Crouch but does mean that those coming through the Spitway will have to be careful. The aim is to get into the Barrow Deep just as the flood starts running SW'ly and then, by making an average of 4 or 5 knots over the ground, reach the North Edinburgh Channel while there is some E going tide to help and a chance to reach the Foreland before the N going stream starts, about an hour before HW Dover.

When crossing the Estuary for the first time from Dover or Ramsgate, it will be best to stem the last of the south going tide up the North Foreland so as to get the benefit of the flood through the North Edinburgh Channel and across the Estuary. Unfortunately this usually means arriving at the entrance to the Crouch or the Spitway at about HW, with the prospect of the whole of the ebb to run out of the Essex rivers. The only way this can be avoided is to take the risks involved in crossing the Estuary on a falling tide — *which certainly cannot be recommended for the inexperienced.*

Waypoints
Harwich to North Foreland
SUNK HEAD TOWERS   51.46.60.N   1.30.60.E
BLACK DEEP No 8 buoy   51.37.25.N   1.22.20.E
OUTER TONGUE buoy   51.30.78.N   1.26.47.E

Harwich to North Foreland
Those wishing to cross the Estuary from the Suffolk rivers need not use the Wallet and the Spitway, but can enter the Black Deep past the ruined Sunk Head Tower, marked by its N Cardinal buoy (N Card Q), and then, after proceeding about 10 miles to the SW, leave the Black Deep via the Fisherman's Gat and then proceed to the Tongue Sand Tower. There is 5 or 6 metres of water in the Fisherman's Gat at LWS and the swatch is entered about a mile and a half of the Black Deep E No 7 buoy (Con G QG) and an equal distance SW of Black Deep No 6 buoy (West Cardinal Q (a) 15s). Unfortunately, since the *Navaid's Review,* there is no nearer buoy from which to locate the swatchway.

Margate
A new yacht harbour is planned for Margate. Given enough water over its entrance sill, this could provide a useful haven for any yachtsman in difficulty off the North Kent coast.

Waypoints
Medway to North Foreland
W GIRDLER buoy   51.29.58.N   1.06.82.E
S SHINGLES buoy   51.29.20.N   1.16.11.E
N TONGUE SAND TOWER   51.29.60.N   1.22.12.E

Thames, Medway or Swale to North Foreland
There are two routes that can be taken in a W-E direction along the north coast of Kent, but in general craft from the Thames or the Medway will tend to use the Princes Channel, about five miles offshore, while those coming from the Swale or Whitstable are more likely to go through the Gore Channel, much closer inshore.

Waypoints
The Prince's Channel
GIRDLER buoy   51.29.15.N   1.06.50.E
SE GIRDLER buoy   51.29.46.N   1.10.00.E
S SHINGLES Bell buoy   51.29.20.N   1.16.11.E

Prince's Channel
The Prince's Channel can be said to commence between the Girdler (Can R Fl(4)R 15s) and the W Girdler (W Card Q(9) 15s Bell) buoys and to continue in an easterly direction past the SE Girdler (Con G Fl(3) G 10s) for about five miles between the South Shingles shoal to the north and the Ridge and the Tongue Sands to the south. At its narrowest point, abreast the North Tongue buoy (Can R Fl(3) R 10s), the deep water is almost a mile wide. From this position, an E'ly (mag) course will lead past the South Shingles (S Card Q(6) & LFl 15s) and the East Tongue (Can R Fl(2) R 5s) buoys, by which time the Tongue Sand Tower should be in sight pretty well straight ahead. When the Tower is close abeam a course can be laid, (about 150°M), to clear the Foreland after leaving the East Margate (Can R Fl (2) R 2.5s) about half a mile to port.

Waypoints
The Gore Channel
WHITSTABLE STREET buoy   51.23.84.N   1.01.70.E
HOOK SPIT buoy   51.24.10.N   1.12.65.E
S MARGATE buoy   51.23.88.N   1.16.75.E
SE MARGATE buoy   51.24.10.N   1.20.50.E
LONGNOSE SPIT buoy   51.23.90.N   1.25.83.E

Gore Channel
This route is closer inshore and rather more difficult because of the many drying shoals off the Kent coast between Herne Bay and Margate.

Starting from the Whitstable Street buoy (N Card VQ) a course of 95°M will lead (after about 6 miles) to the East Last (Can R QR) and Hook Spit (Can G) buoys marking the narrow swatch over the western end of the Margate Hook Sand. Because of rocky patches off the Reculvers, do not approach the shore closer than two miles or proceed eastwards until these two marks have been found. The twin rectangular towers of the Reculvers will help in locating the buoys.

Once through the swatch, shape a course of 110° mag to leave the Margate Hook Beacon (S Card Topmark) and the South Margate buoy (Can G FlG 2.5s) at least a quarter of a mile to the North. From the South Margate buoy an E'ly mag course will lead to the SE Margate buoy (E Card Q(3) 10s) a little more than two miles away. The passage can then be continued to round the Longnose buoy (Can R) about a mile offshore.

TIDAL CONSTANTS

Place		Add (+) to or Subtract (−) from times of HW at:		Height relative to Chart Datum (metres)			
				SPRINGS		NEAPS	
		Dover	Harwich	MHW	MLW	MHW	MLW
1 Southwold		−1.05	−1.45	2.6	0.7	2.1	1.0
2 Orford River	Orford Haven (Entrance)	+0.10	−0.30	3.0	0.3	2.2	0.9
	Orford Quay	+1.00	+0.20	2.4	0.4	2.1	1.3
3 River Alde	Slaughden Quay (Aldeburgh)	+1.55	+1.15	2.6	—	2.3	—
	Snape Bridge	+2.25	+1.45	2.0	—	1.6	—
4 River Deben	Woodbridge Haven (Entrance)	+0.25	−0.15	3.5	0.5	2.9	1.0
	Waldringfield	+1.00	+0.20	3.6	0.4	3.0	0.9
	Woodbridge	+1.25	+0.45	3.8	0.4	3.1	0.9
5 Harwich Harbour	Harwich	+0.40	0.00	4.0	0.4	3.4	1.1
6 River Orwell	Pin Mill	+0.50	+0.10	4.1	0.3	3.4	1.1
	Ipswich	+1.15	+0.35	4.2	0.3	3.4	1.0
7 River Stour	Wrabness	+1.05	+0.25	4.1	0.3	3.4	1.1
	Mistley	+1.15	+0.35	4.2	0.3	3.4	1.0
8 Walton Backwaters	Walton-on-Naze (Pier)	+0.35	−0.05	4.2	0.4	3.4	1.1
	Stone Point	+0.40	0.00	4.1	0.5	3.3	1.2
9 River Colne	Colne Point	+0.40	0.00	5.1	0.4	3.8	1.2
	Brightlingsea	+0.55	+0.15	5.0	0.4	3.8	1.2
	Wivenhoe	+1.05	+0.25	4.9	0.3	3.6	—
	Colchester (The Hythe)	+1.15	+0.35	4.2	—	3.1	—
10 River Blackwater	Bench Head Buoy	+1.20	+0.40	5.1	0.5	3.8	1.2
	West Mersea (Nass Beacon)	+1.10	+0.30	5.1	0.5	3.8	1.2
	Tollesbury Mill Creek	+1.00	+0.20	4.9	—	3.6	—
	Bradwell Quay	+1.10	+0.30	5.3	0.5	4.2	1.3
	Osea Island	+1.25	+0.45	5.3	0.4	4.3	1.2
	Heybridge Basin	+1.30	+0.50	5.0	—	4.1	—
	Maldon	+1.35	+0.55	2.9	—	2.3	—
11 River Crouch	Whitaker Beacon	+0.50	+0.10	4.8	0.5	3.9	1.3
	Burnham-on-Crouch	+1.10	+0.30	5.2	0.2	4.2	1.0
	Fambridge	+1.20	+0.40	5.3	0.3	4.2	1.1
	Hullbridge	+1.25	+0.45	5.3	0.3	4.2	1.1
12 River Roach	Paglesham	+1.10	+0.30	5.2	0.2	4.2	1.0
	Havengore Creek	+1.05	+0.25	5.0	0.3	4.1	1.1
13 River Thames	Southend Pier	+1.20	+0.40	5.7	0.5	4.8	1.4
	Holehaven	+1.30	+0.50	5.9	0.4	4.7	1.4
	Gravesend	+1.45	+1.05	6.3	0.3	4.7	1.4
	Erith	+2.00	+1.20	6.6	0.1	4.9	1.2
	Tower Bridge	+2.40	0.00	6.8	—	5.5	—
14 The Medway	Queenborough	+1.35	+0.55	5.7	0.6	4.8	1.5
	Rochester	+1.40	+1.00	5.9	0.3	5.0	1.3
15 The Swale	Whitstable	+1.20	+0.40	5.4	0.9	4.8	1.5
	Harty Ferry	+1.25	+0.45	5.7	0.6	5.1	1.2
	Mitton Creek	+1.35	+0.55	5.7	0.6	4.8	1.5

Thames Estuary

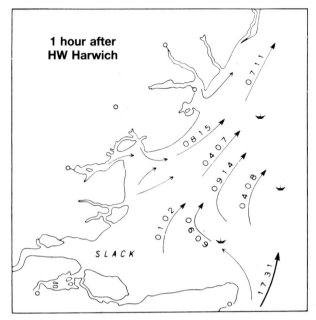

1 hour after
HW Harwich

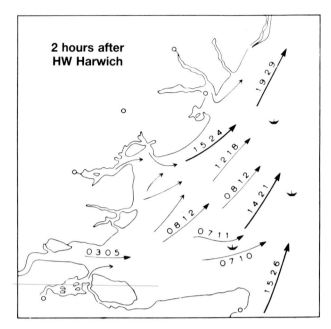

2 hours after
HW Harwich

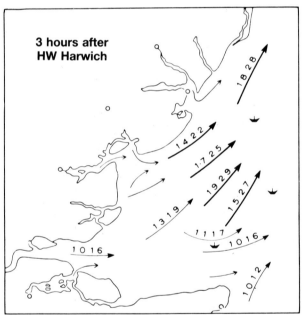

3 hours after
HW Harwich

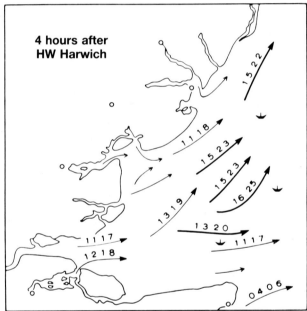

4 hours after
HW Harwich

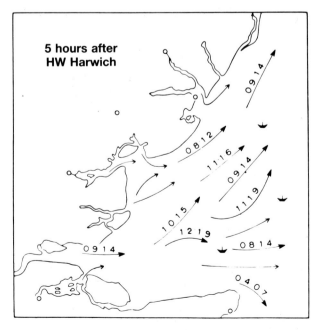

5 hours after
HW Harwich

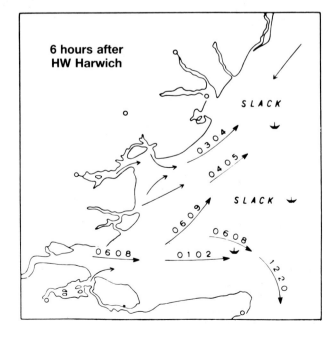

6 hours after
HW Harwich

THAMES ESTUARY: TIDAL STREAMS

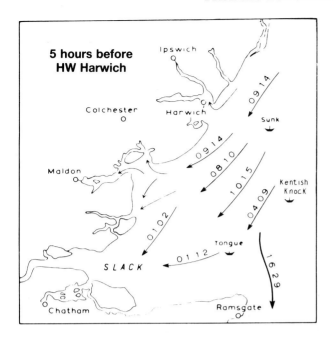

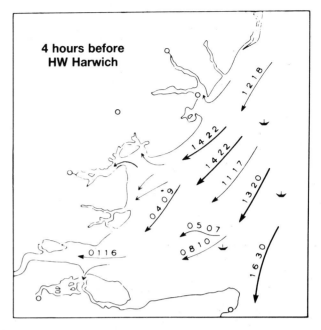

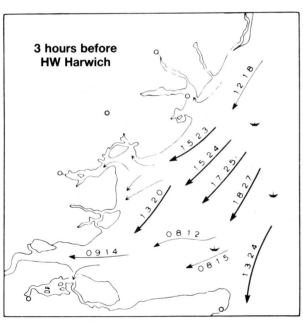

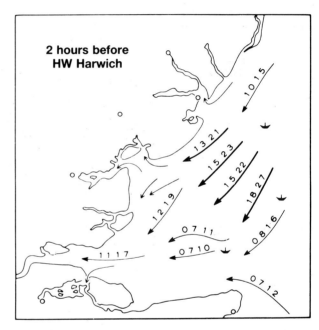

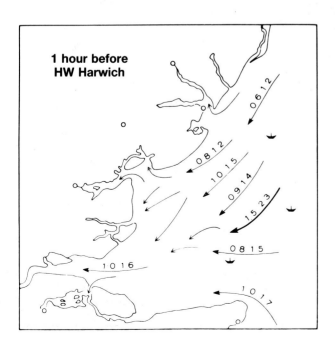

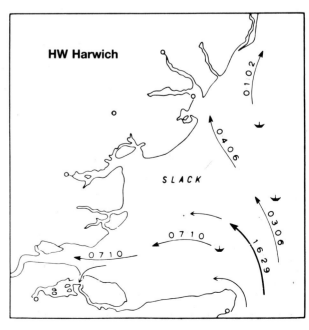

Glossary

ENGLISH	DUTCH	FRENCH	GERMAN
Abeam	Dwars	Par le travers	Querab
Ahead	Vooruit	En avant	Voraus
Anchorage	Ankerplaats	Mouillage	Ankerplatz
Astern	Achteruit	En arrière	Ruckwarts, achtern
Athwart	Dwars over	Par le travers	Aufwaschen
Bank	Bank	Banc	Bank
Bar	Drempel	Barre	Drempel
Bay	Baai	Baie	Bucht
Beach	Strand	Plage	Strand
Beacon	Baken	Balise	Bake
Bight	Bocht	Anse	Bay
Binoculars	Kijker	Jumelles	Fernglas
Board	Slag	Bordée	Schlag
Black	Zwart	Noir	Schwarz
Boatyard	Jachtwerf	Chantier	Yachtwerft
Breakwater	Golfbreker	Brise-lames	Wellenbrecher
Bridge	Brug	Pont	Brucke
(fixed)	(Vaste brug)	(Pont fixe)	(Feste brucke)
(lifting)	(Beweegbare brug)	(Pont basculant)	(Hubbrucke)
(swing)	(Draaibare brug)	(Pont tournant)	(Drehbrucke)
Buoy	Ton, boei	Bouée	Tonne, Boje
Cable (distance of approx 183m)	Kabellengte	Encablure	Kebellange
Causeway	Straatweg (door het water)	Chaussée	Damm
Castle	Kasteel, slot	Château	Schloss
Channel	Vaarwater	Chenal	Fahrwasser
Chart	Zeekaart	Carte marine	Seekarte
Chart Datum	Reductievlak: kaartpeil	Zero des cartes	Kartennull
Church	Kerk	Eglise	Kirche
Cliff	Steile rots	Falaise	Felsen am Seeufer
Conspicuous	Opvallend	Visible, en evidence	Aufflallig
Course	Koers	Cap, route	Kurs
Coastguard	Kustwacht	Garde, Côtière	Kustenwache
Creek	Kreek	Crique	Kleine Bucht
Customs	Douane	Douane	Zoll
Depth	Diepte	Profondeur	Tiefe
Degree	Graad	Degre	Grad
Diesel oil	Dieselolie	Gas-oil, mazout	Diesel-Kraftstoff
Dolphin	Dukdalf, meerpaal	Duc d'Albe	Dalben, Dukdalben
Draught	Diepgang	Profondeur	Wassertiefe
Dredged	Gebaggerd vaarwater	Chenal dragué	Gebaggerte fahrrinne
Dries	Droogvalland	Assèche	Trockengallend
East	Oost	Est	Ost
Ebb	Eb	Marée descendante	Ebbe
Echo Sounder	Echolood	Echo sondeur	Echolot
Eddy	Draaikolk	Tourbillon	Stromwirbel
Entrance	Ingang, zeegat	Entrée	Einfahrt

ENGLISH	DUTCH	FRENCH	GERMAN
Estuary	Mond	Estuair	Flussmundung
Fair tide	Stroom mee	Courant favorable **or** portant	Mitlaufender Strom
Fairway	Vaargeul	Chenal	Talweg
Ferry	Veer	Bac, ferry	Fahre
Flagstaff	Vlaggestok	Mât	Flaggenmast
Flashing light	Schitterlicht	Feu a éclats	Blinkfeuer
Flood	Vloed	Marée montante	Flut
Ford	Waadbare plaats	Gué	Durchwaten
Foreshore	Droogvallend strand	Côte découvrant à marée basse	Küstenvorland
Foul tide	Tegenstroom	Courant contraire **or** debout	Gegenstrom
Fuel	Brandstof	Carburant	Kraftstoffe
Green	Groen	Vert	Grun
Groyne	Golfbreker	Brise-lames	Wellenbrecher
Gully	Goot	Goulet	Graben
Gunnery Range	Ballistiek	Artillerie	Artilleriewissenschaft
Gutway	Goot	Goulet	Graben
Handbearing compass	Handpeilkompas	Compas de relevement	Handpeilkompass
Harbourmaster	Havenmeester	Chef **or** Capitaine de port	Hafenkapitan
Hard	Hard	Débarquement	Landung
Headland	Voorgebergte	Promontoire	Vorgebirge
Height, headroom	Doorvaarthoogte	Tirant d'air	Durchfahrtshöhe
High Water	Hoogwater	Pleine mer	Hochwasser
Hill	Heuvel	Colline	Hügel
Horizontal stripes	Horizontaal gestreept	à bandes horizontales	Waagerecht gestreift
Horse	Droogte	Basse	Untief
Island	Eiland	Île	Insel
Jetty	Pier	Jetée	Anlegesteg
Knot	Knoop	Noeud	Knoten
Landing	Ontscheping	Débarquement	Landung
Launderette	Wasserette	Laverie	Waschsalon
Leading Line	Geleidelijn	Alignement	Leitlinie
Lead	Lood	Plomb de sonde	Lot
Lifeboat	Reddingboot	Bateau de sauvetage	Rettungboots
Lighthouse	Lichttoren, vuurtoren	Phare	Leuchtfurm
Light Vessel	Lichtschip	Bateau-phare	Feuerschiff
Lobster	Zeekreeft	Homard	Hummer
Lock	Sluis	Écluse, sas	Schleuse
Low Water	Laagwater	Basse mer	Niedrigwasser
Magnetic	Magnetisch	Magnetique	Mißweisend
Marks	Merkteken	Parcours	Bahnmarke
Marsh	Moeras	Marais	Sumpf
Metes	Geleidelijn	Alignement	Leitlinie
Middleground	Middelgronden	Bancs médians	Scheidingstonnen
Mooring	Meerboei	Bouée de corps-mort	Ankerboje
Mud	Modder	Vase/Boue	Schlick, Schlamm
Narrow	Nauw	Etroit	Eng(e)

ENGLISH	DUTCH	FRENCH	GERMAN
Navigable	Bevaarbaar	Navigable	Befahrbare
Neaps	Doodtij	Morte eau	Nippitide
Occulting	Onderbroken	Occultations	Unterbrochenes
Offing	Open zee	Le large	Legerwall
Oil	Olie	Huile	Schimierol
Orange	Oranje	Orange	Orange
Oyster	Oester	Huître	Auster
Paraffin	Petroleum	Pétrole	Petroleum
Petrol	Benzine	Essence	Benzin
Perch	Steekbaken	Perches, pieu	Pricken
Piles	Palen, remmingwerk	Poteaux	Pfahl
Pilot	Loods	Pilot	Lotsen
Pier	Pier	Jetée	Pier
Pontoon	Ponton	Ponton	Ponton
Port	Bakboord	Babord	Backbord
Post Office	Postkantoor	La Poste	Postamt
Quay	Kaai	Quai	Kai
Railway	Spoorweg	Chemin de fer	Eisenbahn
Radio Beacon	Radiobaken	Pylone de TSF	Funkmast
Range (of tide)	Verval	Amplitude	Tidenhub
Red	Rood	Rouge	Rot
Repairs	Reparaties	Réparation	Ausbesserung
Riding Light	Ankerlicht	Feu de mouillage	Ankerlampe
Rocks	Rotsen	Rochers	Klippen, Felsen
Sailmaker	Zeilmaker	Voilier	Segelmacherei
Sand	Zand	Sable	Sand
Saltings	Zouttuin	Marais	Sumpf
Shelving	Hellen	Incliné	Neigung
Shingle (shingly)	Grind, Keisteen	Galets	Grober Kies
Shops	Winkels	Magasins	Kaufladen
Shoal	Droogte	Haut fond	Untiefe
Showers	Douche	Douche	Dusche
Slipway	Sleephelling	Cale de halage	Slipp, Helling
South	Zuid	Sud	Süd
Spit	Landtong	Pointe de terre	Landzunge
Springs (tides)	Springtij	Vive eau, grande marée	Springtide
Staithe	Kade	Quai	Kai
Starboard	Stuurboord	Tribord	Steuerbord
Steep-to	Steil	Côte accore	Steil
Stores	Voorraad	Provisions	Vorrate
Swatchway	Doorgang	Couloir/passage	Passage
Take the ground	Aan de grond	Echoué	Auf grund sitzen
Tanker	Tanker, Tankschip	Bateau citerne	Tanker, Tankschiff
Topmark	Topteken	Voyant	Toppzeichen
Town	Stad	Ville	Stadt
Tortuous	Bochtig	Tortueux	Gewunden
Vertical stripes	Verticaal gestreept	à bandes verticales	Senkrecht gestreift
Village	Dorp	Village	Dorf

ENGLISH	DUTCH	FRENCH	GERMAN
Visitor's berth	Aanlegplaats (Bezoekers)	Visiteur	Festmacheplatz
Water	Water	l'eau	Wasser
Weather	Weer	du temps	Wetter
West	West	Ouest	West
Wharf	Aanlegplaats	Débarcadère	Werft
Withy	Buigzaam en sterk	Perches, pieux	Pricken
Wreck	Wrak	Épave	Wrack
Yacht Club	Jacht Club, Zeilvereniging	Yacht Club, Club Nautique	Yacht Klub
Yellow	Geel	Jaune	Gelb

Notes

Navigable Distances (Approximate)

River Thames

		Sea Miles
Sea Reach No 1 Buoy	to Southend Pier .	6
	Sheerness . . .	5
	Holehaven . .	11
	Gravesend . .	19
	Erith . . .	25
	Greenwich . .	35
	London Bridge .	41
Southend Pier	to Sheerness . .	6
	Havengore entrance	9½
	Leigh (Bell Wharf)	3
	Benfleet . . .	6½

River Medway

Sheerness (Garrison Pt)	to Queenborough .	1½
	Gillingham . .	8
	Upnor	10½
	Rochester Bridge	12½

River Swale

Queenborough	to Kingsferry Bridge	2
	Harty Ferry . .	9
	Columbine Buoy	15

River Crouch

Whitaker Beacon	to Foulness . . .	7
	Roach Entrance .	9½
	Burnham . . .	12
Burnham	to Fambridge . .	5
	Hullbridge . .	7
	Battlesbridge . .	9
Foulness	to Bench Head Buoy (via Ray Sand)	8
	Bench Head Buoy (via Spitway)	18

River Roach

Entrance	to Paglesham . .	4
	Havengore Bridge	5

River Blackwater

Bench Head Buoy	to Sale's Point . .	4
	Nass Beacon (W Mersea)	5
	Bradwell Quay .	6
	Osea Island . .	10
	Heybridge Basin	13
	Maldon (Hythe) .	14½

River Colne

Colne Bar Buoy	to Brightlingsea . .	4½
	Wivenhoe . . .	8
	Colchester (Hythe)	11

The Wallet

Knoll Lightbuoy	to Clacton Pier . .	4
	Walton-on-the-Naze (Pier)	9
	Stone Banks Buoy .	12½
	Harwich Entrance .	15

Harwich

Harbour Entrance	to Burnham (via Wallet and Spitway)	30
	West Mersea (via Wallet)	23
	Brightlingsea (via Wallet)	22
	Woodbridge Haven (Deben Entrance)	6
	Orford Haven (Ore Entrance)	10

River Stour

Harwich Harbour (Entrance)	to Wrabness . . .	6½
	Mistley	9½
	Manningtree . .	11

River Orwell

Harwich Harbour (Entrance)	to Pin Mill . . .	6½
	Ipswich	11

River Deben

Entrance (Felixstowe Ferry)	to Ramsholt . . .	3
	Waldringfield . .	5½
	Woodbridge . .	9

River Ore

Entrance (Shingle Street)	to Havergate I . .	3
	Orford Quay . .	5

River Alde

Orford Quay	to Slaughden Quay (Aldeburgh)	
	Iken Cliff . . .	8½
	Snape Bridge . .	11